"The best leaders are those who recognize that they're not self-sufficient. The bigger the decision, the more we must rely on God for wisdom. Dwight Eisenhower learned that as a general and applied it as a president, quietly seeking insight through prayer, Bible reading, and godly counsel. That's a recipe for success at any level."

Jim Daly, president of Focus on the Family

"Historians have increasingly come to appreciate the outstanding performance of duty by Dwight D. Eisenhower as President of the United States. But little research and writing has been done about the religious background that sustained this exceptional leader through a life of distinguished service to his country. In *The Soul of an American President*, Alan Sears and Craig Osten reveal the fascinating spiritual history of a man who had to overcome daunting challenges, tragedy, and personal crises to ultimately become one of the nation's most admired presidents. This inspiring and compelling book provides a new and more complete understanding of the inspiration and fundamental beliefs that led Eisenhower from a humble beginning to true greatness."

Edwin Meese III, former attorney general of the United States

"Dwight Eisenhower is remembered as a man skilled in the arts of both war and peace, a leader whose instinctive civility is sorely missed in an age of bitter political acrimony. Biographers have captured many of Ike's finest qualities, but they often overlook one of the cornerstones of his character: his guiding faith in a provident God. Alan Sears and Craig Osten have added that final, essential element to our understanding of the man in their superb and engaging book."

Charles J. Chaput, OFMCap, archbishop of Philadelphia

"There are several fine biographies of Dwight D. Eisenhower. But until now, we lacked a biography zeroing in on the president and great war leader's spiritual life. Kudos to Alan Sears, Craig Osten, and Ryan Cole for filling that gap. In *The Soul of an American President*, they provide a window into Ike's life as a man of faith and explore the manifold ways his Christian convictions shaped the conduct of his presidency."

Robert P. George, McCormick Professor of Jurisprudence and director of the James Madison Program in American Ideals and Institutions, Princeton University

★ THE SOUL OF AN ★
AMERICAN PRESIDENT

★ THE SOUL OF AN ★ AMERICAN PRESIDENT

The Untold Story of Dwight D. Eisenhower's Faith

ALAN SEARS and **CRAIG OSTEN** with **RYAN COLE**

BakerBooks

a division of Baker Publishing Group
Grand Rapids, Michigan

Published by Baker Books
a division of Baker Publishing Group
PO Box 6287, Grand Rapids, MI 49516-6287
www.bakerbooks.com

Printed in the United States of America

Library of Congress Cataloging-in-Publication Data
Names: Sears, Alan, author. | Osten, Craig, author.
Title: The soul of an American president : the untold story of Dwight D. Eisenhower's faith / Alan Sears and Craig Osten.
Description: Grand Rapids, MI : Baker Books, a division of Baker Publishing Group, [2019] | Includes bibliographical references.
Identifiers: LCCN 2018038006 | ISBN 9780801093869 (cloth)
Subjects: LCSH: Eisenhower, Dwight D. (Dwight David), 1890–1969—Religion. | Presidents—United States—Biography. | Generals—United States—Biography.
Classification: LCC E836 .S43 2019 | DDC 973.921092 [B] —dc23
LC record available at https://lccn.loc.gov/2018038006

ITPE 978-0-8010-9387-6

19 20 21 22 23 24 25   7 6 5 4 3 2 1

In keeping with biblical principles of creation stewardship, Baker Publishing Group advocates the responsible use of our natural resources. As a member of the Green Press Initiative, our company uses recycled paper when possible. The text paper of this book is composed in part of post-consumer waste.

Faith is the mightiest force that man has at his command. It impels human beings to greatness in thought and word and deed.

Dwight D. Eisenhower, Address at the Second
Assembly of the World Council of Churches,
Evanston, Illinois, August 19, 1954

Contents

Acknowledgments

The authors wish to acknowledge and thank the following individuals, without whose contributions this book would not have been possible:

Tim Goeglein, for his encouragement, enthusiasm, and vision for this project.

Ryan Cole, for his work on this project, including visiting the Eisenhower presidential library to secure key source documents, and providing editorial assistance on several chapters.

Rev. John Boyles, for his tireless research that uncovered new insights into Ike's spiritual journey. This included the twenty-five items of unpublished, private correspondence between Dwight and Mamie Eisenhower and Rev. Robert A. MacAskill DD, their Gettysburg pastor and friend between 1958 and 1979, provided by Mrs. Linda MacAskill, as well as the correspondence between Dwight Eisenhower and Rev. Edward L. R. Elson DD.

John Harding, for his administrative support in the early days of this project.

Elise Gillson, for her administrative support as this project neared completion and her proofing of the final manuscript.

The Eisenhower Presidential Library in Abilene, Kansas, for the incredible treasure trove of materials made available to document Dwight Eisenhower's faith journey.

The Eisenhower National Historic Site in Gettysburg, Pennsylvania, and the National Park Service, for their welcome assistance with private and public tours to view the site and materials.

Introduction

I t seemed like just another day in Washington, DC. The nation's capital was buzzing with activity as people from across the nation and around the world visited the monuments honoring the heroes of America's past: Washington, Jefferson, and Lincoln.

Yet at the White House things were quiet as Fred Seaton, the current Secretary of the Interior, arrived for another day's work.

As he entered the White House, where every president except Washington had resided, Seaton, like so many others, might have reflected on the history that had taken place in the building.

It was here that Lincoln paced the halls, often late at night, during the bloodiest days of the Civil War. It was here that other presidents—Madison, Polk, McKinley, Wilson, and Franklin Roosevelt—made the difficult decisions to put young Americans in harm's way. For each of these leaders, these decisions were never easy, were always costly, and often had worldwide impact.

On this particular morning, Seaton stepped briefly into the Oval Office. Here he encountered something at once extraordinary and commonplace, something that shocked him—but at the same time made perfect sense. He found a man kneeling in prayer beside a desk. However, this was no ordinary man. This was arguably the most powerful man in the world: the President of the United States.

The secretary, embarrassed by his intrusion, quickly pardoned himself and left the room. However, as he went about his work that day, and each day following, Seaton was heartened by knowing that the president, facing a difficult and complex decision about sending troops to the Far East to deal with another potential international crisis, was on his knees.

Was the secretary's discovery the stuff of fiction, as some historians like to say? Apparently not. According to Seaton's account, this episode unfolded one morning in 1957 during the presidency of Dwight David Eisenhower—or "Ike."[1]

In January 1953, just days after his inauguration as the thirty-fourth President of the United States, Ike stepped out of the White House to make his way to the historic National Presbyterian Church on Connecticut Avenue.

The temperature was in the high 50s.[2] Despite the springlike air, Ike's wife, Mamie, had come down with a nasty cold and reluctantly agreed to stay home. So Ike walked the few blocks by himself to do something many men are reluctant to do without their spouse: attend church.[3]

Designed by famed architect Henry Hobson Richardson and constructed in the 1880s, the decade before Ike's birth, the magnificent church possessed a long spiritual heritage. The history of the congregation went back much further, nearly to America's founding. In fact, the congregation's first worshipers—a group of Scottish stonemasons building the White House—met in a much humbler location: a work shed on the grounds of the Executive Mansion.[4]

The church membership had grown well beyond those five artisans and their work shed. When he stepped through the doors that morning, Ike knew he was joining a congregation with a long heritage that had seen most previous United States presidents attend worship services and much American history unfold. Several other presidents, including James K. Polk, Andrew Johnson, Ulysses S. Grant, and Benjamin Harrison, had been part of the congregation.[5] In the church's previous building, parishioners had heard Frederick Douglass preach passionately from its pulpit on the need for all men to be free.[6] The church's pastor at the time, Reverend Byron Sunderland, was an abolitionist who also served as Chaplain of the US Senate during the Civil War and was a friend of Abraham Lincoln.

The pastor of National Presbyterian Church in 1953 represented a different period in American history: Dr. Edward L. R. Elson was a former US Army chaplain who had served under Ike during World War II.

On this Sunday morning in late January, as he sat directly behind former President Benjamin Harrison's old pew, Pew 41, Ike listened to the words of Dr. Elson as he talked about Saul of Tarsus, better known as the apostle Paul, whom Dr. Elson said, "encountered the living Christ and was transformed into a crusading evangelist of the gospel."[7] It is impossible to know exactly what Ike was thinking. Perhaps he was struck, as he listened to Dr. Elson speak, by the similarities between his own life path and that of the apostle.

Ike's had been a winding path, starting in abject poverty first in rural Denison, Texas, and then in Abilene, Kansas. The path had not always made sense, at least in human terms. Ike had left the dusty plains of Abilene for the US Military Academy at West Point, where he found the classes repetitive and sometimes dull but where he also discovered his life dream: to lead troops defending liberty into combat to fight for freedom.

However, after graduating from West Point, he found himself shuttled from one seemingly meaningless Army assignment to another, kept from fulfilling that dream. In the midst of these ongoing professional disappointments, a deeply personal and tragic family loss would strike and leave a deep mark on Ike's life—a mark that never fully healed.

Just when it seemed that Ike's life was on a fixed course of trivial assignments and relentless disappointments, historical events intervened. The explosion of World War II transformed his life.

And with its outbreak, it became immediately clear that through that string of disconnected military assignments, foreign exiles, and bypassed promotions, Ike had been uniquely prepared to lead the greatest military endeavor of all time. Unbeknownst to him, during the years when he felt he was being ignored and passed over, many influential leaders were taking note of his competence and faithfulness. When he finally began receiving meaningful assignments, such as playing a leading role in the Louisiana Maneuvers in preparation for entering the war, his exceptional leadership resulted in Ike becoming Supreme Commander of the Allied Forces in World War II. Ike would soon command the respect of the nation, starting him on a journey of service that would eventually land him in the White House.

When Ike received news of his fifth star, at the beginning of the Battle of the Bulge, he remarked to his colleague and friend General George S. Patton, "Every time I get a star, I get attacked."[8] Ike was probably referring to the thundering of German guns in front of him, to the rattle of the American media behind him, and to the attacks from Allied generals working alongside him. But Ike remained a man faithful to his conscience and to the core principles of duty, faith, and perseverance that he learned growing up on the streets of Abilene.

Ike's image, manipulated and oversimplified to fit a preconceived narrative, has met the same fate as so many other great leaders. Nowhere is this more evident than in scholarly and popular portrayals of Ike's presidency and his personal Christian faith.

In the decades immediately after his time in the White House, many historians and commentators painted a picture of Ike as a great general during the war but a lethargic, doddering grandfather during his years in the White House. The perception was he would rather play golf and paint with watercolors than deal with the social up-heaval occurring in the southern United States and the international turmoil of the Cold War 1950s.

Only a year after Ike left office, Arthur Schlesinger Sr.'s poll of American presidents ranked Ike twentieth among his peers—near the bottom third of the men who preceded him, among such lesser lights as Millard Fillmore, Chester A. Arthur, and the impeached and barely acquitted Andrew Johnson.[9]

As time went by, however, the historical events that unfolded cast a new light on Ike's decisions and leadership. His reputation began to improve among historians, while the image of the lethargic grand-father receded. By 1996, when Schlesinger Jr. issued his new rankings, he described Ike as "an astute, crafty, confident, and purposeful leader" and ranked him number ten, just on the cusp of joining the greatest presidents.[10] A 2017 poll saw Ike's standing rise to fifth, citing his "moral authority" as his top asset, landing fourth in that particular category. The only presidents who received higher rankings were Lincoln, Washington, and the two Roosevelts.[11]

The first major scholarly reexamination of Ike's legacy was *The Hidden-Hand Presidency*, written by Princeton University professor Fred Greenstein in 1982. Examining the long-term effects of Ike's presidency, Greenstein refuted the perception of Ike as a disengaged and reluctant president and instead revealed him as a perceptive political strategist and effective leader.

Other biographers followed suit, including the late Stephen Ambrose, scholarly writer Jean Edward Smith, acclaimed British journalist Paul Johnson, and former *Newsweek* editor Evan Thomas. These authors unanimously described Ike as a wise, cagey, and successful president. While Ike may not be on Mt. Rushmore, those who know history now recognize him as one of America's most revered and untouchable figures.

Both the left and right have used Ike as a political football to advance their respective agendas. But people on both sides of the partisan aisle now remember Ike as a president who successfully navigated the challenges of a booming postwar America, wisely assisted the emerging Civil Rights movement, and, perhaps most significantly, provided balance during the ever-looming nuclear threat of the Cold War.

It may have been that threat of global destruction that caused many Americans to look toward God for comfort and support during the 1950s. That decade was the high-water mark of American religious engagement during the twentieth century. According to a 1957 Gallup poll, 69 percent of Americans believed that religion was increasing its influence on the country's culture.[12] In contrast, sixty years later only 22 percent feel the same.[13] During the 1950s, almost half of all Americans, like their president, regularly attended a church or synagogue.[14] By 2017, that number dropped to 36 percent.[15] A survey conducted in 1954 found that nine out of ten Americans believed in the divinity of Christ.[16] In 2017, only 43 percent believed in Christ's divinity.[17]

Alan Sears's mother told him the story about the night of Ike's election on November 4, 1952, when Alan was just one year old. Television was still new, and the Sears family had yet to purchase one for their home, so they had to listen to the returns on the radio in their bedroom. As the evening wore on, Alan's parents lay awake, with Alan between them, until two o'clock in the morning to make sure the results were certain. When it became official that Ike had won, Alan's father was "really glad," as he had been in the Army during World War II and was confident that America would have solid leadership. Three hours later, with victory assured, Alan's nine months' pregnant mother went into labor and gave birth to his baby sister four hours later.

Throughout the 1950s, Alan's father spent his days keenly aware of the threat of nuclear war. In 1959, he left his job teaching science in public schools and joined the faculty of the Office of Civil Defense Mobilization Staff College, which was then under the Executive Office of the President (its successor is now part of FEMA). The agency, created by President Eisenhower's Reorganization Plan of 1958, was responsible for the preparedness activities of the federal government and for assisting other governmental units. Mr. Sears would remain in this job until his retirement, and the Secretary of Defense would recognize him for his service to the nation.

His job was to teach people all over the world how to prepare for, and survive, a nuclear attack. He worked with governments, armies, and ordinary citizens, teaching them how to "duck and cover," how to build shelters, what to place inside them, and how to live together in the event of a catastrophe, when a group of people would crowd into one of those cramped shelters and seek survival in a nuclear holocaust.

In one of the official US government manuals his father helped write, Alan found the following statement: "During the period following nuclear attack, religious worship and prayer would be useful to people in a fallout shelter." That statement matched the tenor of Ike's presidency: religious faith was a critical element of American society and something that should be encouraged rather than discouraged.

Though there is disagreement among scholars on this subject, there is a strong argument that Ike played a central role in nurturing a nationwide spiritual awakening. Throughout his presidency, Ike was a professed man of faith, perhaps rivaled only by Ronald Reagan with regard to public proclamations of that faith.

Ike was also the only president to open his inaugural service with a prayer he wrote on his own. He talked openly and frequently about his reliance on prayer. He regularly expressed his belief that religion calmed the terrors and uncertainty of the Atomic Age, and he said that divine providence guided the nation's very founding. He was never shy about sharing his convictions about the key role played by faith in the growth and development of society.

On the other hand, Ike's faith was personal and very private. He was not evangelistic in the modern sense of the word and not thought of as someone who actively proselytized. He did not promote any particular denomination, despite his choice to worship in a Presbyterian church. Instead, his statements often seemed to reflect less of a *proclamation* than an *assumption* of faith.

Several statements made by Ike during his presidency reflect this assumption, as well as the lack of his endorsement of any particular form of belief. In 1952, shortly before he took office, Ike declared, "Our government has no sense unless it is founded in a deeply felt religious faith, and I don't care what it is."[18] According to Ike's grandson, David Eisenhower, he was referring to our nation's Judeo-Christian heritage.[19] This was also in line with Ike's other religious pronouncements, which he kept neutral and ecumenical. As one historian noted, Ike's faith was seemingly "moderate, tolerant, simple, and firm."[20]

One of the ways that Ike helped reestablish this civic faith was to encourage and approve Congress's action to insert the words "under God" into the nation's pledge of allegiance. After Congress passed the resolution in 1954, Ike explained why he felt this was so important:

> In this way, we are reaffirming the transcendence of religious faith in America's heritage and future; in this way, we shall constantly strengthen those spiritual weapons which forever will be our country's most powerful resource, in peace or in war.[21]

Ike also used faith as a rhetorical weapon against communism and the aggression of the Soviet Union after World War II. He laced his speeches with language positioning religious faith as America's true advantage over the atheistic Soviet Union.

Just one week after assuming the US presidency, Ike, addressing the students in his farewell speech as president of Columbia University, described the Cold War as "a war of light against darkness, freedom against slavery, godliness versus atheism."[22]

Ike's faith was more than mere platitudes or vague beliefs that religion was good for society. His faith compelled him to stand against injustice to change people's hearts while also seeking to secure peace.

During his presidency, Ike saw the rise of the Civil Rights movement as African Americans in the South, unjustly denied the freedom they were promised after the Civil War, joined together to push for desegregation and receive the freedom to which all persons are entitled. He chose to take a measured approach that he hoped would change hearts and minds and minimize civil unrest, but he agreed with those calling for change that the ultimate objective was a society in which all experienced equality under the law, no matter the color of their skin. And when forced to it, Ike showed himself to be a man of action. When the governor of Arkansas tried to use the state National Guard to deny African Americans their civil rights, Ike cast aside his quiet approach and took decisive military action.[23]

Further evidence that Ike's faith was not just for show came from his choice to defer his baptism until *after* his inauguration. One week after his first Sunday attendance, on February 1, 1953, he would be baptized and formally join the National Presbyterian Church as a member—a step he had deliberately postponed until after the election, as he did not want to give any sense that he was using his religious life, an intensely personal thing for him, for political gain. He had seen others whose public piety seemed to increase as election day grew closer, a phenomenon that continues today.

Instead, on that February morning, Ike knelt on a prie-dieu, a prayer desk, in a small, private room, acknowledged his faith in Jesus Christ, and received baptism through the Presbyterian tradition of sprinkling. On that day, Ike became the first head of state known to be baptized in office since Clovis I, the first king of the Franks, who converted to Christianity in AD 496.[24]

21

From that day on, Ike attended church regularly, whether in Washington, DC; Augusta, Georgia; Denver, Colorado; Palm Desert, California; or Gettysburg, Pennsylvania. He also opened all of his cabinet meetings in prayer and developed strong relationships with religious leaders such as Billy Graham and Cardinal Spellman.[25]

Despite Ike's very public expression and practice of faith, some have doubted his authenticity. Senator Matthew Neely of West Virginia was perhaps the most vociferous, arguing that it was cynical and disingenuous for a president who had not belonged to a church before his election to attend every Sunday after his inauguration.[26]

William Lee Miller, a journalist and speechwriter who later served as head of the University of Virginia's religious studies department, took issue with the total lack of what he called "social philosophy" in Ike's "vague" view of religion.[27]

In 2012, historian Jean Edward Smith, author of *Eisenhower: In War and Peace*, cynically asserted that Ike "allowed himself to be convinced that the United States was a Christian country."[28] For these critics and others, Ike understood the political value of public religious pronouncements and grasped that the American people likely would not nominate or elect a man with no formalized religious faith. In their view, Ike cannily rode the prevailing religious mood of the nation for his own political gain. Others point to Ike's well-known use of "salty" language in times of frustration and his legendary temper as evidence that his faith was only skin-deep.[29] But Ike, like every human person, had a sinful nature he would wrestle with until the day he died, and that nature would sometimes rear its head in times of great stress.

All of this leads to the question that prompted us to write this book. For years, as students of history, it has nagged us: Was Dwight Eisenhower an imperfect man (like us all) of genuine faith, or was he a skilled politician who used religion, like so many others before and since, to further his agenda and popularity?

As we have read the multitudes of Ike's professions of faith, it is difficult not to be impressed with his eloquence and feeling as well as the consistency and regularity of his statements. But several of his biographers consistently remind us that Ike was also a shrewd man and a very skilled politician. Thus, the question lingered. Was Ike's public faith a cynical put-on?

In the following pages, we will briefly share some Ike's life journey—from Abilene, Kansas, to his farm in Gettysburg—and what we, along with some associates, have learned from years of detective work attempting to understand the contradictions and confirmations of Ike's faith.

There are already numerous biographies about Ike the person, the general, and the president. However, few biographers have discussed his faith. Beyond select quotes from some of his speeches and a few of his public proclamations, this is largely unexplored territory. It is clear from his own words and from the accounts of those closest to him that his faith became an essential part of how he viewed his own life, America, and America's need to respond to the evil, atheistic regimes of the Soviet Union, Mao Zedong's communist China, and later Castro's Cuba.

We invite you on our journey to view one of the most consequential, admired, and complex Americans of the twentieth century—the one whom *Time* magazine, in the height of its prime, dubbed on its cover, "The Man Who Beat Hitler"[30]—and whose steady hand and faith guided our nation during the frostiest days of the Cold War and beyond.

1

The Plain People

To understand Ike's spiritual journey and what would ultimately shape his core values and beliefs, we need to trace his faith heritage, the context of his family's faith, and the religious atmosphere of his childhood home. Like that of so many Americans, the story begins several centuries earlier, in Europe, and travels through a long and complicated series of churches and religious communities.

Let's begin our journey in the sixteenth century as the Protestant Reformation caused great upheaval across Europe. For the Eisenhauer family (only later would the name change to Eisenhower), the pivotal moment was the beginning of the Anabaptist movement, which became the roots of the Mennonite church. This religious community would go on to shape the family's faith and eventually result in their immigration to America.

The Anabaptists originated in Switzerland in 1525 as a group of radical Reformers, not happy with what they perceived to be the slow pace of others calling for reformation. They launched a movement to bring about what they believed were more quickly needed changes. They desired a "purer church," which in their view meant a church separated from both Catholics and other Reformers such as

Luther and Calvin. They also wanted to do away with tithing, usury, and military service, and sought to eliminate the role of the church in civil government while protecting freedom of conscience.[1] The Anabaptists rejected infant baptism and taught that only those who had accepted Jesus Christ as Lord and Savior by their own volition were eligible for baptism. "Ana" meant "again," as many of those baptized as infants who left other churches to become Anabaptists were rebaptized.

About this same time, a Dutch Roman Catholic priest named Menno Simons had a crisis of faith. Part of his crisis was rooted in his doubts on infant baptism, differing from Martin Luther, who as late as 1527–28 called infant baptism "the most certain form of baptism," and John Calvin, who affirmed infant baptism in his 1536 work, *Institutes of the Christian Religion*.[2] Simons left the Roman Catholic Church and joined the Anabaptist movement.

In 1536, Simons, in accordance with Anabaptist teaching, was rebaptized and became an official member of the religious community.[3] In less than a decade, after being ordained, he rose to a place of great prominence in the movement, just as divisions regarding pacifism began to appear in the group.

In the midst of the chaos, Simons aligned himself with the Anabaptists who remained pacifists. According to Simons, the Christian's duty was to suffer, not to fight. He asked, "If [Christ] had to suffer such torture, anguish, misery, and pain, how shall his servants, children, and members expect peace and freedom as to their flesh?"[4] They eventually split from the greater Anabaptist movement, and Simons became the leader of a group that eventually took his name: the Mennonites.[5] Other direct descendants of the Anabaptists include the Amish and various different forms of Brethren churches.

Among those intrigued by Simons and his teachings were the Eisenhauer family—a Bavarian name that likely meant "iron hewer" or "iron striker." Although they were technically Lutherans, they started to embrace Simons and his teachings and found themselves caught up in the Thirty Years' War (1618–1648), a violent conflagration that began as a religious war but eventually became a conflict between what one could call the superpowers of that era.

These developments forced the Eisenhauers to migrate from their native Germany. Over generations, the family traveled first to Switzerland, then to Holland, and finally, like so many others fleeing religious persecution, to the New World, reaching Pennsylvania in the early decades of the eighteenth century.[6] Interestingly, another family that made a similar trek across the ocean was the Stover family, who would also play an important role in Ike's faith journey.

Records from 1741 document the arrival of two Eisenhauer brothers, Hans Peter and Hans Nicholas, in the Commonwealth of Pennsylvania, sailing on the vessel *Europa* out of Rotterdam. Upon their arrival, they quickly swore oaths of allegiance to the British crown and the Commonwealth of Pennsylvania.[7] Just a few decades later, despite the pacifist beliefs of Simons and many of the Anabaptists, two members of the Eisenhauer family enlisted to fight in the American war for independence.[8]

The Eisenhauer family settled in Bethel Township near Harrisburg and joined the Pennsylvania German society formed by William Penn, the founder of Pennsylvania. Somewhere around the turn of the century, Eisenhauer became Eisenhower. Records show a gradual transformation from "Eisenhauer" to "Isinhower" to "Eisenhower,"[9] and in 1794, Ike's great-grandfather was born and christened—though probably not baptized as an infant, per Anabaptist teachings—as Frederick Eisenhower.

Somewhere in the late 1700s—the exact date is lost—two brothers, Jacob and John Engle, founded the Church of Brethren in Christ, which became more commonly known as the River Brethren. The name probably came about because the church started along the Susquehanna River, and the congregation used the river for baptisms.

According to Ray I. Witter, a minister in the Church of the Brethren in Christ and a childhood friend of Ike's, the name developed as the church grew. The congregation spread out geographically, and it became common for members who lived farther from the Susquehanna to say to each other, "Let's go down by the river and see how our brethren are doing."[10]

The Engles grew up in a Mennonite family, and they incorporated many Mennonite traditions into their new church. Because of this, people perceived them as an offshoot of the Mennonites.

The River Brethren's lifestyle mirrored that of the Mennonites. Although internally they were highly communal and close-knit, to the outside world the community appeared stark and plain. The men wore black suits, grew long beards, and covered their heads with bowl-shaped hats. The women wore long black dresses. The River Brethren forbade dancing, drinking alcohol, and gathering too many worldly possessions. They called themselves, aptly, "The Plain People."[11]

In 1816, Ike's great-grandfather Frederick Eisenhower married Barbara (also called Barbary) Miller, a member of the Plain People community. Soon after, he embraced her River Brethren faith, and they raised their family accordingly. Frederick and Barbara's son (and Ike's grandfather) Jacob was born in 1826.

Though the church encouraged its members toward an austere lifestyle, the River Brethren had no prohibition against accumulating wealth in the form of land, and the Eisenhower family did just that. Jacob acquired one hundred acres of farmland in and around the town of Elizabethville, located in Dauphin County in South Central Pennsylvania, which, according to Ike, appraised at $13,000 by 1870.[12]

Jacob and his wife, Rebecca, built a nine-room house on Main Street, a house that quickly became the center of activity, not only for Jacob's growing family but also for the River Brethren. Eventually the Eisenhower house served as a place of worship for the congregation, and by the middle of the century, Jacob Eisenhower was an active, respected, and influential minister in the church.

Walking into the Eisenhower home in Elizabethville in the mid-1800s, visitors entered a large room on the first floor, where a cupboard stood near the door. Instead of holding cups or assorted knickknacks, it was full of hymnals and spiritual books, which received plenty of use from the dozens of people who regularly passed through the home for worship services, prayer, and community gatherings. Jacob led prayer meetings at the house, in both English and German to accommodate newcomers from the Old Country. The River Brethren in the area came to hear his sermons, which often stressed brotherly love and practical kindness toward each other. However, Jacob did not simply talk about these virtues; they permeated the Eisenhower family's whole way of life.

Another prominent feature of the River Brethren faith was the tradition of giant potluck dinners and church suppers, coupled with sermonizing and socializing. These meetings were much like the modern-day "camp meetings" still held by several church denominations, and the Eisenhower acreage was a natural site for many of these well-attended events.

Over a hundred years later, in his 1967 memoir *At Ease: Stories I Tell to Friends*, Ike wrote with obvious respect about his grandfather Jacob, "In my memory, he is a patriarchal figure, dressed in black, wearing an under beard with upper lip shaved clean."[13]

Years later, Ike's brother Milton dedicated a plaque that honored Jacob on the house's front lawn. Ike commented, "My name is in the center of the plaque. This is a compliment I appreciate, but I think Jacob Eisenhower's worth rests far more on his own deeds, on the family he raised, and the spiritual heritage he left them, than on one grandson."[14]

The River Brethren were staunchly antislavery, but because of their commitment to pacifism, it was difficult for them to give unmitigated support to the abolitionist movement as the tension and rhetoric surrounding the issue escalated in the 1850s. Although Jacob Eisenhower supported Abraham Lincoln and even named one of his sons after him, he struggled to balance his hatred of slavery with his distaste of violence, and as a pacifist he decided he could not participate in the war.[15]

When the Civil War came to Pennsylvania, Confederate General Richard Ewell's men came within miles of the home prior to the battle of Gettysburg, which occurred just months before the birth of Jacob's son David, Ike's father. Ike would eventually serve at Camp Colt, the training grounds of which were on the soil where Pickett charged, and later in life he purchased a farm in Gettysburg, where he and Mamie would enjoy their last days.

The Civil War also left its mark on the Stover family. Ida Stover, like her future husband, David Eisenhower, was born during the Civil War. But despite the families' shared German heritage, there was a stark cultural difference between them, as the Stovers had settled not in abolitionist Pennsylvania but in the slave state of Virginia, where they were successful farmers as well.

While the Eisenhowers were staunch Union supporters, General Stonewall Jackson and the Confederate Army frequently camped near the Stover family estate. Though the Battle of Gettysburg nearly touched Jacob Eisenhower's farm, the Stovers witnessed some of the worst devastation of the war unfolding outside their very windows. They lived in the Shenandoah Valley, through which Union General Philip Sheridan waged a savage and destructive campaign akin to General Sherman's march through Georgia.[16]

The years following the Civil War were hard ones for both families, as they were for many others. Ida's mother died in 1867 and her father in 1873, leaving the eleven-year-old an orphan.[17] As the only girl with seven brothers, she went to live with her mother's family, the Links.[18]

The Links did not believe that girls should receive a formal education but required Ida to study the Bible instead, which would result in her becoming a Bible memorization champion, memorizing 1,365 verses.[19] However, Ida possessed a strong will and eventually rebelled against her grandfather's refusal to allow her to further her education.[20]

Meanwhile, the international economy faltered. The US government had made a serious overinvestment in railroad construction, which coincided with the German Republic's decision to suspend the minting of coins made from silver, a major US export. These two events sparked the economic panic of 1873, which led to an extended depression that lasted until the end of the decade.

This depression had stark consequences for Eastern farmers like the Eisenhowers and their fellow River Brethren members. Wheat prices collapsed, forcing many of these farmers to look westward and strike out across the continent in search of new opportunities. While Jacob maintained his prosperity—his wealth would be approximately nine million dollars today[21]—many members of his community were not so fortunate. Jacob's ties to the River Brethren ran deep, and he decided to join his fellow members in their cross-country trek because he wanted to start a new River Brethren colony.[22] Ike said that his grandfather also based his decision to move on the perceived "richness" of the Kansas lands. He wanted to acquire more land so he could give some to his children to start their own farms, and land was cheap and plentiful in Kansas.[23]

Jacob, now in his fifties, was hardly a candidate for a cross-country move, especially with all the difficulties such an endeavor involved in nineteenth-century America. But he, along with the other members of the River Brethren, had heard about the success of other Pennsylvanians who had made the trek, and they joined the widespread westward migration, drawn by the dream of a River Brethren community on the Plains.[24]

In 1877, a River Brethren scouting group visited Dickinson County, on the eastern plains of Kansas. The group found that land there was affordable, the soil was fertile, and the railroad connected the region to the eastern coast. The River Brethren settled on Dickinson County as the site of their new colony. In 1878, Jacob sold the Elizabethtown farm for approximately $175 an acre and bought land in Kansas for as little as $7.50 an acre.[25]

On a cold day in March 1879, Jacob, his family, and the other River Brethren colonists packed all their earthly belongings and headed for the train depot at Harrisburg, the Pennsylvania capital. The group journeyed west in a fifteen-car train heading to Abilene, Kansas.[26] This was a well-organized venture; the River Brethren community brought about $500,000—or nearly $12 million in today's dollars—to serve as the basis of their new community.

Once they arrived in their new home, the colony split in half, with one part settling north of the Smoky Hill River, which snakes through the heart of Kansas, and the second part settling south of the river in Belle Springs, just south of Abilene. The Eisenhowers chose Belle Springs. Meanwhile, five years later, Ida Stover, now age twenty-one, received a thousand-dollar inheritance from her late father and, seeking an education that she would not receive if she remained in Virginia, departed her grandparents to join two of her brothers, who had settled in Kansas. Thus, the saga of Ike's family would begin.[27]

In the mid-nineteenth century, Abilene was a "cow town," a small, wild, and occasionally violent place where cattlemen stopped on their long, arduous cattle drives across Kansas. In Abilene, legendary figures of the Old West, such as Wild Bill Hickok, started gunfight after gunfight beyond the swinging doors of the local saloon. The rough-and-tumble town did not seem to be an ideal location for the peaceful, faithful, and community-oriented River Brethren.

However, in the 1870s, things began to change. The cattle trade had started to subside, sparking a small-scale war between farmers and cattlemen as the advancing agricultural frontier swallowed up land previously used to raise cattle. The farmers won, and Abilene, located twenty miles from the geographical center of the country and characterized by its fertile soils and clear streams, began to flourish as an agricultural community.[28] The River Brethren took part in that renaissance, immediately starting to work the land when they arrived on March 29, 1879.

Jacob Eisenhower quickly established a thriving farm and a creamery—the Belle Springs Creamery Company—and the Eisenhower home once again served as a communal place of worship until a new church was built in Belle Springs fifteen years later. It was in these surroundings that Ike's father, David Eisenhower, came of age.

From early on, it was clear that David was different from most of his family, who were all farmers or veterinarians. He had little or no interest in either occupation. He left Abilene to go to Lane University in Lecompton, which served as one of the early territorial Kansas capitols. Even with this decision, however, David did not go far from his roots, as the River Brethren owned and operated the university. David, the Pennsylvania Yankee, went to Lane for one year, hoping to begin a career as a civil engineer. His plans changed after he met Ida, the Southern lass from Virginia, who was also a student at the college.

David and Ida quickly fell in love and, feeling the need to support his prospective wife, he decided to drop out of school, but not before getting married in the Lane University chapel in September 1885. He and Ida then returned to Abilene to start their life there.[29]

Jacob had wanted to give his children their own farms, including his son David and his new bride, Ida, probably hoping that David would follow in his footsteps and become a successful farmer in the Abilene area.[30] However, David spurned his father's offer. Regrettably, as events unfolded, it would become evident that David did not have the same economic good fortune and judgment as Jacob.

David asked his father to mortgage the farm he wanted to give him so he could use the money to construct a general mercantile store on property Jacob owned in Hope, Kansas, approximately twenty miles south of Abilene. Though this likely disappointed Jacob, he agreed to honor his son's desires. David, along with his business partner, Milton Good, opened the store on Main Street in Hope on March 30, 1885.[31]

Unfortunately, it soon became clear that David and Milton did not work well together. In November 1886, David mortgaged the entire stock of the store to Jacob in exchange for $3,500 to buy out his partner.

Three days later, Jacob released David from his obligation to repay the money, turning the mortgage into an outright gift of the entire business.[32] David's younger brother, Abraham, a veterinarian, became his new partner. The store was renamed "Eisenhower Brothers," and it did better. However, David remained unhappy. His temper—which was always bad—became downright testy, and he got involved in disputes with other tenants in the building, eventually quitting the store altogether.[33] Ike inherited his hot temper and struggled with it his entire life.

Abraham Lincoln Eisenhower, or "Uncle Abraham," was a fiery evangelist and would become Ike's favorite relative. In his memoir, *At Ease*, Ike would reminisce fondly about his uncle, saying, "Uncle Abe was now more concerned with saving souls than saving animals."[34]

Uncle Abraham engaged in the soul-saving business with flare. According to Ike, Uncle Abraham designed a vehicle that was seven feet wide, fourteen feet long, and six-and-a-half feet high to the canvas roof. It contained a table and chairs, four cots, a stove, and a sliding curtain that divided it into sleeping compartments. Ike wrote, "This contrivance Uncle Abraham christened a 'gospel wagon.'"[35]

Ike added that his uncle had a "streak of carnival barker" in him. During one of his stops, Uncle Abraham encountered a Fourth of July celebration. He decided to divert the public from the bands and speeches at the assembly by forcing his team of horses and his gospel wagon in the parade. Ike wrote that when Uncle Abraham turned down a side street, he yelled at the top of his lungs, "This way to heaven!" The crowd turned away from the rest of the parade and followed Abraham to a back lot, where he "delivered a soul-rousing sermon," that Ike said he could never figure out.[36]

Having quit the store, and thereby losing the income from it, David continued to struggle and ended up moving to Denison, Texas, where he took a job as a "wiper," cleaning engines and machinery and earning about forty dollars a month.[37]

The Eisenhower family's time in Denison was brief, but it was here, on October 14, 1890, that their third son, Dwight David Eisenhower, was born. Ida originally named him David Dwight, but after he was born, she decided to switch the order of his names to avoid the confusion of having two Davids in the family.[38] David and Ida chose the name Dwight for their new boy in honor of the famous Christian evangelist of the era, Dwight L. Moody, who would pass away nine years after Ike's birth after becoming ill while conducting a crusade in Kansas City, approximately 150 miles east of Abilene.[39]

Just two years later, with only $24.15 in his pocket, David and his family made the trek back to Abilene.[40] David took a job as a refrigeration engineer at his father's creamery in Belle Springs.

Through the ups and downs of hopes and disappointments, financial difficulties, and the move to Denison and then back to Abilene, the Eisenhower home still centered around the Bible, with prayers in the morning and evening as well as throughout the day. Once a week, the family held an evening Bible study, reading from three versions of the Bible. David would read aloud from a Greek Bible and then from Jacob's German Bible. Finally, Ida and the children would read from the King James Bible.[41]

Dwight and his brothers also attended Sunday school classes at the Church of the Brethren in Christ in Abilene, and they would see who could read the Bible aloud with the most precision. Ike had read the entire Bible by the time he was twelve, and then read it again.[42]

Late in life, Ike and his brothers would surprise their associates by quoting the Bible verbatim to bolster their arguments.[43]

Ida's background in Bible memorization from her days in Virginia enabled her to use the Scriptures to instruct her sons constantly in the importance of virtues such as frugality, modesty, and fair play.[44] Those values would stick with the Eisenhower boys for the remainder of their lives. Served an enormous steak at a banquet in Chicago after World War II, Ike reportedly cut it in half and sent it back to the kitchen. He said that as long as there were starving people in the world, he could not stand to see food wasted.[45]

The Eisenhower family's love of the Scriptures and many of their River Brethren beliefs remained important to each of the Eisenhower boys for the rest of their lives. However, significant differences in beliefs arose between the Eisenhower parents and their sons. While Ida remained one of Ike's greatest influencers, he abandoned one of her core values: her pacifism and opposition to military service. Also, David's and Ida's faith—particularly Ida's—began to diverge from the River Brethren community. This would eventually force Ike to deviate from many of Ida's deepest convictions.

2

The Watch Tower

For most children, the greatest influence on their spiritual journey is the faith of their parents. That includes times when that faith wanders away from its original moorings, and Ike's journey was no exception. His parents' faith, and struggles with faith, left a strong and clear mark on his entire life.

For years, David and Ida Eisenhower were both committed members of the River Brethren community, including during their time in Denison and in the first years after their return to Abilene. However, at some point in Ike's early childhood, David and Ida Eisenhower began to question some of the church's orthodoxy.

Their gradual withdrawal from the River Brethren community began in 1895. That year, they had their seventh son, Paul. Paul was not as robust as the other Eisenhower boys. Sickly from birth, he would live only ten months before dying of diphtheria in March 1895.

David, Ida, and the other six boys turned to their church for support and solace. The tragedy drove David and Ida to question teachings they had previously accepted without difficulty. The doctrine that caused David and Ida to start reconsidering the River Brethren faith was the explanation from the church that their baby would be awaiting them in heaven. Though it was grounded in Scripture, the Eisenhowers did not find that the teaching eased their heartache, and the grieving couple—especially Ida—began to look elsewhere for seemingly more tangible and immediate comfort.

Ida had begun making friends with her neighbors, a group that included three women named Carla Witt, Mary Holland, and Emma Holland. The Witt and Holland families were not part of the River Brethren community, and Ida grew close to her new companions. These three women saw the grief of their friend as an opportunity to introduce Ida, and then David, to a new religion, one that they all passionately embraced and that seemed able to give the Eisenhowers the comfort they found lacking in the River Brethren faith.

That new religion was a nascent movement inspired by the teachings of Charles Taze Russell, a charismatic and controversial minister who preached restorationism. Russell and his followers believed that stripping Christianity of its modern trappings would lead to the restoration of the simplicity of the early apostolic era. In 1895, when the Eisenhowers experienced their crisis of faith, Russell's followers were referring to themselves as Bible Students, but a faction of the movement later morphed into the more modern-day Jehovah's Witnesses.

Russell and the Bible Students taught that the Eisenhowers would be reunited with their son at the arrival of the resurrection and the end of the world—a teaching that might not have inspired much comfort, except that Russell and his followers determined the end of the world would occur in 1914, if not earlier. As the Eisenhowers' friends explained, the rule of Christ would begin immediately after this. At that point, everyone would reunite with dead loved ones—and David and Ida would see Paul again. To the Eisenhowers, this new "hope" meant they would not have to wait too long to be reunited with their son.

While that "hope" turned out to be false, it was enough to pique the Eisenhowers' interest in this new religion. Ida's friends provided the family with copies of *Millennial Dawn*—a seven-volume set of books written by Russell as a Bible study aid—and issues of *Zion's Watch Tower*, the movement's monthly magazine. These resources, combined with the promise that they would see their baby boy again in the very near future, swayed the Eisenhowers away from the River Brethren.

Russell and his followers' claims about the end of the world were soon proven to be wildly inaccurate (adherents of Russell's religion first predicted the end in 1910, then 1914, then 1918, and continued to make predictions to 2000 and beyond), but Ida never lost interest in the Bible Student movement and the beliefs of the Jehovah's Witnesses.

As of 2015, the worldwide number of Jehovah's Witnesses was around eight million, encompassing nearly 250 nations.[1] These relatively low numbers might explain why their beliefs, or at least their values, remain a mystery to many Americans, who only know them as the people ringing their doorbell to leave copies of the *Watchtower*.

In his scholarly history of the movement, M. James Penton describes the Jehovah's Witnesses as a sect or a religious movement often at odds with the society of which it is part. In Penton's words, they are "alienated from the world."[2] Penton labels the Jehovah's Witnesses as a sect because its adherents dedicate their allegiance to a theocratic kingdom and believe they do not owe deference to the civic institutions and governments in the societies they inhabit.

As a result, Jehovah's Witnesses prohibit military service, the salutation of flags, any political involvement, and even the pursuit of a college education, as all of these things involve associating oneself with an organization that demands some form of loyalty.

The Eisenhowers turned to the Watchtower Society with the same enthusiasm they had applied to the River Brethren community. Though initially only Ida was interested in the Bible Student movement, the whole family soon drifted from the River Brethren community. Just as Jacob Eisenhower's house served as a meeting place for the River Brethren in both Elizabethville and Abilene, David and Ida opened their home to the burgeoning group. Also like Jacob, David quickly became a leader within the group. The family's parlor soon hosted regular Sunday afternoon meetings of the Watchtower Society led by David, a tradition that continued for twenty years, from 1896 to 1915.[3]

The year Russell had prophesied Armageddon came and went with no sign of the promised return of Christ or the Eisenhowers reuniting with their late son, Paul. While Ida, like many others in the movement, clung to Russell's teachings, accepting explanations and alternative years for Armageddon, David's convictions were shaken. The 1914 disappointment was only the first of a string of failed prophesies, and David's disenchantment with Russell and his teachings grew. Before his death in 1942, he had abandoned the movement entirely, though according to Ike's brother Milton, David remained an avid Bible reader until the day he died.[4]

Ida seemingly remained a Jehovah's Witness to the end of her life in 1946, even though there are conflicting reports on whether or not she still adhered to their teachings in her last years. Many state that she never left the sect.[5]

The mysterious and unconventional precepts held by the Jehovah's Witnesses later led to a great deal of discomfort for Ike. His family's involvement with the group continues to confound historians looking for clues about his religious background and to fuel criticisms of claims that he was an orthodox Christian. Needless to say, the Eisenhower family's association with what was understood as an anti-American, antigovernment sect became a dividing line between Ike and Ida as he pursued a military career, and eventually presented a significant challenge to Ike's bid for the presidency decades later.

Ike recalled that, despite her own staunch convictions, Ida "refused to try to push her beliefs on us just as she refused to modify her own."[6] And the Eisenhower boys eventually abandoned many of her beliefs. Milton became a college administrator, despite the religion's condemnation of higher education. Earl served a stint as a state legislator, contrary to the sect's prohibition against working in civil government.

Of all the boys' career choices, Ike's decision to join the military caused Ida the most grief. It symbolized a rejection of the teaching of pacifism that was, and still is, so central to Jehovah's Witnesses' beliefs, as well as her prior River Brethren faith. Ike said that the only person truly disappointed by his career choice was his mother, adding that "she was the most honest and sincere pacifist I ever knew," and it "was difficult for her to consider the decision of one of her boys to embark upon military life."[7]

Ike also shared that his brother Milton told him later that when Ike told Ida he had joined the military, it was the first time in his life Milton heard their mother cry.[8]

Four years later, upon his graduation from West Point, Ida presented Ike with an American Standard Version of the Bible, the translation of choice for Jehovah's Witnesses because it replaced the term "the Lord" with "Jehovah" throughout the Old Testament.[9] Ike kept the Bible and treasured it, but did not return to his mother's faith.

Ida's correspondence reveals that even during World War II, when Ike was serving as Supreme Allied Commander, she held to the tenet of pacifism. In 1944, a soldier and Jehovah's Witness named Richard Boeckel wrote to Ida seeking guidance regarding his struggles to reconcile his military service with his beliefs. She reportedly replied ("reportedly" because allegedly her signature was taped under the letter):

My friend informs me of your desire to have a word from General Eisenhower's mother whom you have been told is one of the witnesses of Jehovah. I am indeed such and what a glorious privilege it has been in association with [other Witnesses]. . . .

It was always my desire and my effort to raise my boys in the knowledge of and reverence to their Creator. My prayer is that they all may anchor their hope in the New World, the central feature of which is the Kingdom for which all good people have been praying for the past two thousand years. I feel that Dwight my third son will always strive to do his duty with integrity as he sees such duty. I mention him in particular because of your expressed interest in him.[10]

If this letter was truly from Ida, then it is one of the few existing glimpses into how she reconciled her son's decision to go into military service with her dedication to pacifism.

————————————

Four decades after heading off to West Point, Ike stood on the East Portico of the US Capitol, ready to receive the oath of office as the thirty-fourth President of the United States. He would use two Bibles. The first was the one George Washington used in 1789. The second was the one given to him by Ida.[11] Ida's Bible was open to Psalm 33:12: "Blessed is the nation whose God is Jehovah." However, when Ike read the verse aloud, he replaced "Jehovah" with "the Lord."[12]

Despite David and Ida's drift away from the River Brethren, Ike would retain an affinity for the church. In 1965, he delivered the commencement address at Messiah College, founded in the early twentieth century by the Brethren in Christ Church in eastern Pennsylvania. The college also presented him with an honorary degree and later named the conference center after his grandfather Jacob.[13]

Although the graduating class numbered only thirty-five, hardly a big enough audience for a former President of the United States to address, more than a thousand people turned out to hear Ike speak about his connection with the River Brethren. The college, in the midst of transforming itself from a small Bible college to a four-year liberal arts school, brought numerous community leaders to hear Ike's talk. In his speech, Ike recalled, "The whole [Eisenhower] family was deeply religious. There was never a day that they did not have to face up to the same human problems that we do today." He then tied his childhood faith to American citizenship, which he viewed as "a political expression of a deeply held religious faith."[14]

It is clear that Ike's childhood—surrounded by worship and featuring daily Bible study and recitation—greatly influenced Ike the man. His replacement at his inauguration of the word "Jehovah" with "the Lord" in Psalm 33:12 demonstrates the troubles that his parents' association with a controversial religion triggered as Ike's prominence rose. While Ida's association with the Bible Student movement and the Jehovah's Witnesses brought her a form of comfort, Ike clearly rejected its tenets. What her association did do, however, was give Ike's critics great fodder with which to attack him as he progressed in his career and spiritual journey.

3

The Road from Abilene

As Ike grew into young adulthood, he embarked on his own spiritual journey to discover and embrace his personal faith rather than simply living out his parents' beliefs.

After Ike left Abilene for West Point, his spiritual journey became harder to trace. There is no evidence of him having gone through a time of rebellion only to return to faith later in life when it became politically expedient, as his critics liked to claim.

In 1911, twenty-one-year-old Ike arrived at the West Point Military Academy. His appointment came as a surprise to many. When he was running for president in 1952, the local newspaper in Abilene pinpointed his time at West Point as a turning point for the "boy from the wrong side of the tracks"—both a career turning point and a spiritual one.[1]

According to the article,

West Point furnished the first of the stepping stones that placed Dwight Eisenhower on a path that may lead to the White House. It was a difficult step too. It took a tough, athletic youngster from the "wrong side of the tracks" in Abilene, Kansas, out of an odd, Mennonite-like religious group, in which his family's lot had been

45

cast for generations. It started him along a military road which that group had always despised.[2]

Ike first became interested in entering the military in about 1909. He and his brother Edgar wanted to escape Abilene and agreed that the only way they could do so was through a college education. The two brothers came up with a plan to help them both achieve this goal: one would go to school for a year while the other worked to pay for his education, and then vice versa for eight years, until they both graduated.[3]

Ike's year of working came first, and he did various odd jobs such as baking and selling tamales, growing and selling sweet corn and cucumbers, harvesting wheat, and hammering out steel bins.[4] He then secured a position at the Belle Springs Creamery, where he initially toiled as a fireman, working six days a week from 6 a.m. to 6 p.m. He eventually advanced to the position of second engineer, where he earned $90 a month—double what his father earned when he returned to Abilene from Denison in 1892.[5] With careful budgeting, Ike was able to send Edgar two hundred dollars for his first year of college.[6]

At this time Ike became a frequent visitor at the office of the *Dickinson County News*, where his friend John F. "Six" McDonnell worked part-time. The paper's editor, Joseph W. Howe, kept a back room at the office for the local boys to meet, read, and, if they wanted to, even box. He covered the walls of the office with newspapers from across the country and allowed the boys access to his personal library. The wide world Ike saw on display in Howe's newspapers and books fascinated him. It was an entire world outside of Abilene that was open for him to explore.[7]

Ike's politeness and genuine interest in learning impressed Howe, who, unlike most people of Ike's acquaintance, was in a position to give the young man a leg up in the world because of his connections as a newspaperman. Howe was a member of the school board, a state senator, and the head of the Dickinson County Democratic Party Committee. Howe encouraged Ike to seek an appointment either to the Naval Academy at Annapolis or to the Military Academy at West Point. Either academy would put him on the path to a free college education.[8]

Ike recounted later that he was at first interested in going to Annapolis, largely because a friend, Everett "Swede" Hazlett Jr., had received an appointment to the Naval Academy through their local congressman, Rep. Roland R. Rees.[9] In his memoir, *At Ease*, Ike wrote that it was not difficult for him to be persuaded that this was a wise decision. Ike had a longstanding interest in military history, and he realized it would take far too much time to finish his college education, as the accumulation of money was going too slowly.

Ike was also aware that his parents, with their limited means, were also helping his older brother Edgar through college, and there was the education of his younger brothers still to come. Ike felt that by entering the Naval Academy, he could lessen the burden on his family's finances.[10]

Ike took a bold step and wrote to Congressman Rees to inquire about an appointment, but Rees wrote back that all the positions were filled. He suggested that Ike contact Senator Joseph Bristow, who still had a vacancy. Here, Ike's famous persistence exhibited itself. He began a serious campaign, asking friends and influential citizens to write letters to support his effort to secure an appointment, contacting not only Howe but also other local political leaders and journalists. Those he sought help from included the local postmaster, a prominent jeweler, and a first cousin of General George S. Custer.[11]

There were two steps to securing an appointment. The first was a physical examination to ensure that the candidate was eligible for appointment, and the second was the entrance exam competition.

Ike's efforts paid off. He received an invitation from Senator Bristow to take part in a competition with seven other candidates. The top two would win an appointment to one of the two military academies, or at least that was what Ike thought.[12] Ike passed the physical and finished second in the competition, securing his appointment.

But soon after taking the entrance examination, Ike learned that due to a misunderstanding, the Naval Academy had already disqualified him, and he would not be able to go to Annapolis with his friend Swede. The entrance regulations for the Naval Academy specified that candidates be between the ages of sixteen and twenty. Ike and his friend Swede read this to mean that they were eligible until they turned twenty-one. They were wrong. Because Ike had already turned twenty and would be nearly twenty-one when the next class enlisted, he was ineligible.

Ike took this blow hard. He had pinned his hopes on attending a military academy alongside his buddy. In addition, after the examinations, he was the number-one candidate for Annapolis before he learned he had been disqualified, but number two for West Point. He could only get into West Point as an alternate.[13]

Ike soon learned that the young man who had finished first for the West Point appointment had failed the physical examination.[14] As a result, since Ike was next in line for the appointment, Senator Bristow appointed him to the Military Academy at West Point instead.[15]

Despite the disappointment of not getting into Annapolis, Ike was thrilled. But Ida was not. Her only consolation was that she had some admiration for West Point because one of her favorite instructors at Lane College had been a cadet there.

Ike told Ida that she did not have to worry, because even though he had received the appointment, he still had to pass the final examination and there was a chance he might fail. That did not satisfy her. She did not want to see her son fail, regardless of how much she disagreed with the path he was taking. But she kept her feelings to herself, because she and David had always insisted that each of their boys should be "the master of his own fate."[16]

In the spring of 1911, Ike traveled to the Jefferson Barracks, just outside of St. Louis, Missouri, to take his final exam. He then returned to Abilene to await the results. Ike recalled that the waiting was almost unbearable. He had passed the physical examination with no problem, but the mental tests were, in his words, "something else again."[17] Nevertheless, Ike passed and was directed to report to the United States Military Academy on June 14, 1911.[18]

Ike would be part of the class of 1915—perhaps the most famous and decorated West Point class in history, dubbed "the class the stars fell on." Fifty-nine members of Ike's class went on to become generals: twenty-four brigadier generals (one star), twenty-four major generals (two stars), seven lieutenant generals (three stars), two generals (four stars), and two generals of the army (five stars).[19]

Amid all these shining stars, many of whom would serve under Ike in the coming decades, Ike did not excel at West Point. He was academically average and, in his words, acquired a "staggering catalog of demerits." He suffered from a lack of motivation but was resolved to get a college education.[20] Ike openly admitted that one of his prime reasons for going to the Academy was to continue participating in athletics, particularly baseball and football.[21] However, to Ike's dismay, competitive athletics ended soon after he entered West Point when he hurt his knee badly in a 1912 game against Tufts College. He later aggravated the injury even more when he twisted that knee while leaping off a horse in the mandatory equestrian classes.[22]

For Ike, the Academy's highly repetitive teaching style was monotonous, and he struggled to focus on the long, tedious lessons. Though he regularly attended the mandatory chapel services, some of Ike's demerits were for tardiness to chapel.[23] However, according to West Point's annual yearbook, the *Howitzer*, Ike was an active member of the Young Men's Christian Association, better known as the YMCA. Ike later told interviewers that he taught at the Academy's Sunday school.[24]

Ike graduated in 1915, placing sixty-first out of his class of 164—barely in the top 50 percent. Yet he still made a positive impression. Writing in *At Ease*, Ike recalled, in his self-deprecating manner, "One report on my early performance even said . . . that I was 'born to command.' The man who wrote that was either a reckless prophet or he had relaxed his standards."[25]

Ike would eventually receive a commission in the Infantry. He also decided to rededicate himself, recalling in an interview late in life with CBS reporter Harry Reasoner, "I made up my mind, [that henceforth] I was going to make myself as good an Army officer as I could. Out of whatever I could do, it wasn't going to be a lack of work that kept me from doing it."[26]

Always hungry for adventure, he applied for an assignment in the Philippines, but the Army denied his request and sent him to guard America's southern border instead. Almost everything was considered better than the border by most officers, so foreign service requests, even to the remote Philippines, outnumbered the requests for domestic assignments.[27] But due to deteriorating relationships with Mexico, the Infantry had to guard the border.[28] And so, after spending the summer in Abilene, Ike went to Galveston, Texas, to join the 19th Infantry, which was patrolling the tense situation there.

Ike recalled that he found this service disagreeable, and the living conditions were rough. Many of the barracks dated back to the Civil War, or even before, and they had not aged well. However, by the time Ike arrived, disastrous flooding had made the Galveston base unlivable. He found himself reassigned to Fort Sam Houston, an army post near San Antonio,[29] where he would soon meet the fetching young lady who would become his wife.

On a breezy Sunday afternoon in October 1915, Ike set out from Fort Sam Houston to nearby San Antonio, where the wife of a fort officer was hosting a small gathering of military men and young women from town. Ike, always reserved, was reluctant at first to attend the gathering, but when he arrived, one of the hostess's friends caught his eye. Ike described the young lady as a "vivacious and attractive girl, smaller than average, saucy in the look about her face and in her whole attitude."[30]

That young woman was Mamie Doud, the daughter of a prosperous Denver meatpacker, whose family was spending the winter at their second home in Texas to get away from the seemingly endless Colorado winters.

Mamie had been born in Boone, Iowa, in 1896, and baptized as an infant in the local Evangelical Free Church. The Douds left Boone, first going to Colorado Springs, Colorado, before deciding to settle farther north in Denver's fashionable Cherry Creek neighborhood. Mamie attended Corona School, and the family joined the nearby Corona Presbyterian Church.

Her family's Presbyterian roots would eventually play a prominent role in Ike's faith journey. Later in life, Ike and Mamie often vacationed in Denver, staying at the Doud family home on Lafayette Street, later called the First Couple's "Summer White House." The couple also maintained a great deal of affection for Corona Presbyterian, regularly attending services there when they were in Denver, even after leaving the White House. In the 1950s, Ike and Mamie helped raise funds for a new church building, which was finished in 1954. The following year, the Eisenhowers gifted the church its pulpit, with the following inscription:

> Dedicated to the preaching of the Gospel of Jesus Christ. "If ye continue in My Word, then ye are My disciples indeed, and ye shall know the truth and the truth shall set you free" John 8:31–32.[31]

Ike and Mamie became engaged in February 1916, and just a few months later, in July, they were married in the Douds' home in Denver. Fifty-six years later, in 1972, Mamie said about her marriage to

Ike: "I'd say to God every day, 'I'm so thankful'. . . . I don't know how to explain it, but everything was a pattern, like it had been planned. But it wasn't planned by us. God planned it."[32]

However, both Ike and Mamie acknowledged that the early days of their marriage were far from easy.

Their lifestyle expectations differed because their backgrounds were so different. Mamie, raised in privilege from one of the most affluent areas of Denver, had never suffered from want. Ike, on the other hand, had lived through relative poverty. The Eisenhowers' ramshackle house on the plains of rural Kansas stood in stark contrast to the Douds' house in Denver's Cherry Creek area. Mamie had been a debutante, described as one of the city's "most captivating belles."[33] She was also used to having servants to manage the housekeeping. Ike had grown up doing chores and also doing his own cooking.[34]

After their marriage, Mamie found herself dealing with not only managing the housekeeping for the first time in her life but doing so in dilapidated and uncomfortable military housing. As one of Ike's biographers, Michael Korda, wrote, "Even these days, base housing is a constant source of complaint; and in the days before World War I life on an army post was not very different from what it had been in the time of US Grant, with the addition of electricity and indoor plumbing."[35]

Despite all this, Mamie and Ike discovered something they did have in common: determination. In the face of these difficulties, Mamie managed to adjust, and soon she was keeping immaculate homes for Ike wherever they went, and often entertained his military friends as befitted a military wife of the era. However, the years ahead would test that determination.

4

Little "Icky"

When America became involved in World War I in 1917, Ike received a promotion to captain. This began a succession of assignments that he hoped would launch his military career. In September 1917, the Army dispatched Ike to Fort Oglethorpe, located on the Georgia-Tennessee border. The fort stood on the site of the Civil War battle of Chickamauga, fought in 1863, and had been built when the federal government turned the battlefield into a national park in 1895. Ike spent three months there training reserve officers on trench warfare tactics, while Mamie remained back at Fort Sam Houston.

The separation was an especially trying one because on September 17, 1917, just a few days after arriving at the fort, Ike received word that Mamie had given birth to their first son, Doud Dwight Eisenhower, whom they affectionately called "Little Ike" or "Icky."[1] Icky's birth and life transformed Ike and Mamie's marriage. Ike wrote to Mamie immediately after receiving word of the birth in a playful and affectionate tone that was not his custom.

> I understand that Mr. Ike Jr. has my feet, hands, and shoulders. That must certainly take up the biggest part of him, for it certainly does for

me. Just wait until I come home, if we don't have more fun with that boy than with a barrel full of monkeys, then I don't know a thing. . . . I'm sending you loads and loads of loves and kisses. Then I'm sending more for "Ikey" [sic] and barrels more for Mother. Tell her I love her so much I'm going to break all her ribs when I come home.[2]

Ike was not at Oglethorpe for long. The fort closed just three months after Icky's birth. His new assignment was Fort Leavenworth, Kansas, for training duty at the Army Service School, but thankfully, on his way to Kansas, the Army gave him three days to see his wife and new baby boy.[3]

Icky brought out a side of Ike that others, including Mamie, had never seen. At just a few months old, the little boy hung on to his father's finger, giving Ike hopes that he would grow up strong and play football, and perhaps enter West Point, just like his dad.[4] The normally stern and silent Army trainer would come home and un-ashamedly clown around and act like a little boy with his son, utter-ing gibberish to Icky while crawling around on his hands and knees.

As he left Mamie and Icky and headed to Fort Leavenworth, Ike was undeniably frustrated to be receiving another training mission instead of a combat mission. He perceived, correctly, that the Army saw more value in him as a trainer of soldiers, but this went against his long-held desire to lead troops into combat.[5] Despite his frustrations, there was one positive aspect of the transfer to Fort Leavenworth: the proximity to San Antonio meant Ike could spend Christmas with Mamie and Icky.

However, after Christmas was over, Ike had to return to Fort Leav-enworth where, much to his disappointment, he learned that his request for another potential combat assignment was denied. Ike recollected that the War Department did not approve of young men applying for overseas duty, seeing such requests as presumptuous. He was furious, and he would later write, "The message was loud and clear. A man at a desk a thousand miles away knew better than I what my military capabilities and talents were."[6] But he continued to serve with dedication, and shortly thereafter found himself transferred to Camp Meade, Maryland.

There he received yet another training assignment. He was to prepare an engineer unit with the mission of organizing eleven thousand troops to serve overseas in the newly formed Tank Corps. But he was excited this time. Though he was still training troops, Ike hoped the assignment might finally lead to an opportunity to serve in overseas combat. And, as a bonus, it brought him through San Antonio to see Mamie and his beloved Icky.[7]

Ike poured himself into the training assignment at Camp Meade, hoping that he would have the chance to lead his trainees, the 301st Tank Battalion, into battle in France. Although he deeply impressed his superiors at Camp Meade with his attention to detail and his leadership skills, Ike did not receive the assignment he hoped for.

Instead of Ike leading his men into combat, his superiors, enamored with his organizational ability, shipped him to another training assignment, this time at Camp Colt in Pennsylvania, near the Gettysburg battlefields and the site of Pickett's famous charge.[8] Ike strove to do the best job he could and exceeded expectations despite the squalid conditions he and his men faced at the dilapidated Camp Colt. Ike rose from the rank of captain to lieutenant colonel in less than seven months.[9]

The best part of the new assignment at Camp Colt for Ike was that Mamie and Icky were able to join him, though the situation was less than ideal for the little family. Mamie and Icky endured a four-day train journey across the country in which Icky fell ill with a fever that eventually became the chicken pox. When they arrived, they moved into a tiny, ramshackle, stench-ridden frame home. Since the house was only equipped with a coal stove to heat it, Ike had to teach Mamie how to operate the stove, as she had not needed to do so before.[10] Despite the squalid housing, Ike's reunion with his wife and his little boy was happy, and Mamie again showed great strength of character as she made the best of an unfortunate situation.

Ike found himself with plenty of time on his hands training soldiers with a shortage of tanks and tank fuel; reinforcements would not arrive until the summer of 1918. Ike and his men would use the recreation room at St. James Lutheran Church as a way to blow off steam.

He also dealt with a Spanish flu epidemic when two sick military inductees arrived and infected the entire camp. In 1918 the Spanish flu would infect more than five hundred million people and kill fifty million people around the world.[11] Dealing with this medical emergency, Ike had to create makeshift bedding and isolate any man who had even the slightest symptom. Ike also used churches as hospitals to deal with the epidemic, but unfortunately, some men were lost.

Ike was terrified that Mamie and Icky might get the disease. He wrote,

> My duties required getting up early in the morning but it was fun to have the chance to see my son growing up and spend the evenings with my wife. Now, of course I was desperately worried.[12]

Lieutenant Colonel Scott, a doctor from Oklahoma, arrived at the camp and used strong and pungent sprays on the throats and nostrils of everyone at the camp, including Ike and Mamie. The treatment was not pleasant, but it seemed to work.[13] However, later on, Ike could not recall if the doctor treated Icky, despite normal medical concerns about the effects of such epidemics on young children.

The Army intended to send Ike and his troops to Germany in November, but then World War I ended. Though he had been promised a promotion to full colonel if he remained in the States to train troops, Ike's desire for an overseas assignment was so strong that he had been willing to take a demotion if necessary.[14] Now, with the retraction of the Army, Ike received a demotion regardless, as did many others, as a matter of routine at the end of a war. He reverted back to the permanent rank of captain, and again found himself being shuttled from one assignment to another.[15]

He went first to Fort Benning, Georgia, and then to Camp Meade, where he marked time waiting for his next assignment.[16] Ike volunteered, as he said, "on a lark and to learn" as a Tank Corps observer to lead a promotional cross-country trek of US army vehicles at the lightning speed of six miles per hour.[17] While Mamie and Icky stayed in Denver, the caravan traveled approximately fifty-eight miles per day, mostly over dirt roads, dealing with constant breakdowns, collapsing motorways, and the need to repair bridges before the heavy vehicles could cross them.[18]

It took three treacherous months to cross the country. The official report of the trek, compiled by Captain William C. Greany, one of the participants, is available in the Eisenhower Library archives. It states that the company consisted of twenty-four expeditionary officers, fifteen War Department staff observation officers, and 258 enlisted men. There were also twenty-one casualties. The report adds, "[There was] much inconvenience and at times, even hardship was experienced due to the almost continuous and excessive amount of strenuous work, insufficient rest and sleep, lack of shelter, ration difficulties, lack of bathing facilities, and at times the scarcity of drinking water."[19]

However, the trip did serve its purpose. The report concluded that nearly one-third of the US population became aware of the trek through local publicity efforts, and in a number of the towns "refreshments were served to the personnel" as the convoy passed through.

As Ike would write in *At Ease* about the trek through rain, mud, and searing heat, "The trip would dramatize the need for better main highways."[20] Later in life, when Ike saw the German autobahn system firsthand, the contrast with his grueling experience on the 1918 tour inspired his advocacy of the Interstate Highway Act of 1956 and resulted in our modern-day interstate highway system.[21]

During the trek Mamie suddenly lost her younger sister Eda Mae, affectionately known as "Buster." According to Ike, the two girls had been close, and he loved Buster as well.[22] Mamie had already lost her older sister Eleanor to heart problems five years before. Mamie and Icky went back to Denver to be with family.

Mamie, Icky, and her parents drove from Denver to North Platte, Nebraska, to meet the convoy.[23] Ike had been separated from his family for nine months, so by the time he met up with Mamie and Icky, he was overjoyed to spend a few days with them.

Once the cross-country trek was over, Ike returned to Camp Meade. Much to Ike's disappointment, Mamie and Icky stayed with her parents, because there were no housing provisions at the camp even for married couples, let alone ones with children.

Ike was determined to make it possible for his family to live at Camp Meade with him in reasonable comfort. He and a friend, an officer named George S. Patton, converted some rundown barracks into rough but livable family housing at significant personal expense. For Patton, who was wealthy, the expense was not a problem, but for Ike and Mamie, who struggled along on meager Army pay, it took great sacrifice. Though the situation remained less than ideal, once the apartments were finished the Eisenhower family was reunited. This renovation project was also the beginning of a longstanding friendship between Ike and Patton, one that became pivotal decades later when the American military entered World War II.

Ike was overjoyed to have his wife and little Icky with him at Camp Meade. Icky was a very happy child, adored by his father and the junior officers at the camp, who outfitted him with a replica of a Tanks Corp uniform and made him the camp mascot. Ike and Mamie, for their part, were grateful for the chance to be an intact family at last. Despite the cost of renovating the barracks, they scraped up enough cash to hire a part-time maid, a local girl who helped Mamie keep up their new living quarters, which relieved a great deal of stress for the young family. For Ike and Mamie, it seemed the years of struggle were coming to an end.

Years later, Ike recalled how much Icky loved being the center of attention at Camp Meade. He loved the noises of the tanks, the football scrimmages, and the martial music. For Mamie, it was an idyllic time.[24] And Ike, now thirty years of age, had finally found contentment and peace.

The Eisenhowers were particularly looking forward to spending Christmas 1920 together, engaging in activities such as getting a Christmas tree and making up for the lost time when Ike had been off on one assignment after another. A few days before Christmas, despite their financial struggles, the young couple purchased a small red tricycle for Icky and put it under the tree they had chosen. Ike and Mamie, like most parents, looked forward to seeing Icky's delight when he unwrapped his present and discovered his gleaming new toy.

As Christmas Day drew nearer, however, little Icky developed a fever, as most children do from time to time. No one thought much about it. The Army doctor dismissed it as nothing more than an upset stomach, and everybody expected Icky to be well enough to ride his tricycle come Christmas morning.

However, Icky's fever continued to rise, and Ike and Mamie grew concerned. As a precaution, they took Icky to the base hospital to confirm that it was nothing more than the upset stomach the doctor had diagnosed. At the time, in the era of post–WWI cutbacks, base hospitals were hardly a model of efficient health care. To compound the situation, no one at the hospital had any experience with pediatric medicine. Even though Icky was the only patient, the staff, who clearly did not have any idea what to do for him, largely ignored him.[25]

Despite the staff's indifference, Icky started to improve. In typical little-boy fashion, at the first sign of feeling better he escaped from his room and started playing in the corridors. Ike and Mamie breathed a sigh of relief. It seemed that their little boy was out of the woods.

Then things turned for the worse. Icky's health spiraled downward at a rapid pace. Alarmed, the hospital staff referred Icky to the Johns Hopkins Medical School in Baltimore, and the doctor who came to examine Icky told the Eisenhowers that their little boy had scarlet fever, a deadly infectious disease that developed from strep throat. Ike and Mamie later found out that little Icky had contracted the disease from the young lady they had hired as their part-time house cleaner.[26]

In the early part of the twentieth century, scarlet fever was rampant in America. It was the leading cause of death in children.[27] The very mention of it must have deeply frightened Ike and Mamie. When Ike was in high school, his brother Milton had nearly died of the disease.[28] Now, one hundred years later, it is no longer a major threat, due in the most part to antibiotics and vaccinations. However, in 1920 there was no cure. The doctor informed the distraught couple that he could do very little to treat scarlet fever patients. "Either they get well or we lose them," he said.[29]

The hospital quickly put little Icky in quarantine, where Ike and Mamie could not even hold his hand. All they could do was help-lessly watch through the glass as their beloved little boy got sicker and sicker by the hour. Ike later wrote about his frustration that the doctor would not allow him into Icky's room and that he could only sit on a porch where he could look into the room and wave to his little boy. Every once in a while, he was allowed to come to the door to speak to Icky. In Ike's words, he "haunted the halls of the hospital," and "hour after hour, Mamie and I could only hope and pray."[30]

Ike may have also thought of his little brother Paul and recalled how his early death affected his parents' life. Now he feared that he was reliving the same trauma.

The Eisenhowers held vigil, hoping and praying that against all odds, Icky would recover. For a while, things started to look up, as the doctor finally allowed Ike to spend a little time with Icky, and Mamie's mother arrived to comfort and support the young couple. However, as the New Year approached, Icky quickly deteriorated, and in the early morning hours of January 2, 1921, the little Camp Meade mascot, the son who had brought Ike and Mamie such joy, breathed his last in his father's arms.

Meanwhile, under the Eisenhower Christmas tree sat the red tricycle, unridden. Ike and Mamie would never experience the look of joy on Icky's face as he saw his new toy for the first time.

Nearly fifty years after Icky's death, Ike would write that Icky's death was the greatest disappointment and disaster in his life, saying it was "one I have never been able to forget completely," which was quite a statement for the man who would later see the horrors of WWII.[31]

The Eisenhowers took Icky's coffin from Baltimore to Denver for a funeral service held in the Douds' home. They buried him near Mamie's two sisters, Buster and Eleanor, in the Doud family plot.[32] In 1966, Ike secretly transported Icky's remains to Abilene,[33] and today he lies in state next to Ike and Mamie, who passed in 1969 and 1979, respectively.

Ike and Mamie never fully recovered from Icky's death. After the first few difficult years of marriage, they had begun to grow closer as a couple during their time at Camp Meade. After Icky's death, they retreated into solitude to grapple with their grief. Ike, like his parents after Paul's death, turned inward. He became a workaholic and rarely spent time at home, the home now haunted by memories of Icky and of the tranquil family life he and Mamie had enjoyed for so brief a time. Years later, Ike admitted that in the months after Icky's death, he nearly had a nervous breakdown.[34]

Compounding Mamie's grief, which was as terrible as Ike's, was her grave concern for her husband. Mamie's biographer, Dorothy Brandon, wrote in 1954, "Ike's grief, as all-consuming as her own, was pitched to a frightening intensity . . . causing her to fear for his health. They have never put aside their sorrow."[35] Mamie attributed two of Ike's numerous heart attacks, one in 1955 and one in 1968, to his ongoing grief over Icky's death.[36] Ike and Mamie's granddaughter-in-law Julie Nixon Eisenhower later recalled that half a century later, Mamie still could not say how much Icky's death impacted her and Ike's relationship. Julie wrote that the pain was too deep, and there was no doubt that Icky's death "closed a chapter" in their marriage. According to her, their "unblemished first love" was lost and never to be regained.[37]

Mamie later said:

> Throughout all the years that followed, the memory of those bleak days was a deep inner pain that never seemed to diminish much. We never talked about it. I did not ask him, because it was something that hurt him so badly.[38]

According to Ike's post–World War II aide and speechwriter, Kevin McCann, Icky's death "changed Ike's character."[39] Ike's biographer, Carlo D'Este, wrote that after Icky's death, Ike's "charming grin" was gone, as well as his outgoing personality, replaced with an emotional wall to "shield himself from further anguish."[40]

If the couple turned to religion or faith in this time of deepest sorrow, they kept it to themselves. Icky's death was a crisis for Ike and Mamie, and Ike's inward turn to deal with the pain stayed with him for the rest of his life.

5

Perseverance

cky's death ushered in a long season of disappointments, both personally and professionally, for Ike and Mamie. These years were not kind to them, though they were critical in preparing Ike for what lay ahead.

Ike was not alone in struggling through the years after World War I. The entire US military was struggling as well. Postwar budget cuts, or "peacetime dividends," as some politicians called them, dropped the US military from being the finest in the world to seventeenth, right behind Romania. Pulitzer Prize–winning author Rick Atkinson wrote, "[American] equipment and weaponry were pathetic. Soldiers trained with drain pipes for anti-tank guns, stovepipes for mortar tubes, and brooms for rifles."[1]

Historian Russell F. Weigley added, "The Army during the 1920s and 1930s may have been less ready to function as a fighting force than at any time in its history. It lacked even the combat capacity that the Indian campaigns had forced on it during the nineteenth century."[2]

Things were hardest for career officers like Ike. During World War I, there had been something to aspire to, a mission to accomplish.

Ike's dream of leading men into combat had buoyed him through the drudgery of his many training assignments. Now even the possibility of combat leadership was gone, and Ike found himself trapped in one tedious assignment after another. Ike was a victim of his own success: his giftedness at training troops had convinced his superiors that he was more valuable in that role than leading troops into battle. Because of this reputation, during the peaceful days following World War I Ike received assignments that had nothing to do with warfare . . . such as coaching football. Instead of devising military strategy, he found himself in sweats, with a whistle around his neck, drawing up football plays rather than battle plans.

Ike received the football assignment at Camp Meade from Brigadier General Samuel D. Rockenbach.[3] Then, unexpectedly, an escape route appeared to open up: Brigadier General Fox Conner, upon the recommendation of George S. Patton, specially requested Ike serve as his executive officer on a mission in Panama, an "overseas" opportunity that interested Ike.[4]

Conner had been impressed with Ike after a dinner he had with the Eisenhowers and the Pattons at Camp Meade, and after the dinner, Patton confided to Ike that he had recommended Ike for the executive officer position, and he encouraged him to accept the job. When the formal offer arrived a few weeks later, Ike took it.[5] It is likely that however interesting the idea of traveling overseas was to Ike, the chance to escape the specter of Icky and of the family's brief, happy days at Camp Meade was the stronger motivation.

But Rockenbach was reluctant to release Ike from his football duties to join Conner in Central America. After a long delay, he reluctantly sent Conner's request to the War Department, who denied it, much to Ike's frustration.[6] Mamie later remarked, "This just irritated him beyond words."[7]

Conner eventually went over Rockenbach's head to the new Army Chief of Staff, John J. "Blackjack" Pershing, and personally requested Ike's services in Panama. This was finally successful. While pre–air conditioned Panama might not have been the most appealing place, Ike and Mamie were enthusiastic about the move, since it would enable the young couple to escape the tragic memories of Camp Meade. This was especially significant to Mamie, as she was now pregnant with their second child.

Unfortunately, Panama turned out to be too much for Mamie, despite the discomforts she had suffered through elsewhere. Things started out badly when she and Ike set out on their journey in a cramped ship cabin after several generals commandeered the comfortable cabin they had originally been assigned. Ike wrote later that the cabin they ended up in was like a "sardine can."[8] Conditions only worsened when they arrived in Panama.[9]

Ike and Mamie found that their derelict quarters came "equipped" with cockroaches, bedbugs, bats, and rats, while lizards, snakes, and other large insects lurked immediately outside.[10]

Mamie described the housing they received as "a double-decked shanty, only twice as disreputable."[11] On their first night at their new "home," Mamie listened to a rat gnaw on the leg of a chair all night.[12] Later Ike described the infestation of bats that inhabited the house and, in his words, "seemed to thrive in the Turkish bath our house became after every storm."[13] The damp, unsanitary camp was also a breeding ground for dysentery and malaria, so meals consisted mainly of canned goods instead of fresh food.

This may well have been the low point in Ike's life and faith. While the horrible living conditions were definitely taking their toll, the heaviest drag on the Eisenhowers, both as a couple and as individuals, was the death of Icky. Ike and Mamie had each internalized it to the point where they were emotionally and spiritually numb. Their mutual isolation grew. Ike coped with his pain by working longer and longer hours and going off to explore Panama with General Conner, which left Mamie to face the decaying house, the bats, the bugs, and her own anguish all on her own.[14] The emotional wall that Ike built after Icky's death was now firmly in place.

In the spring of 1922, just a few months after the couple moved to Panama, Mamie's parents came for a visit. When they saw the appalling living conditions, they demanded that she return to the States with them for the baby's birth. Mamie did not argue. When the Douds returned to Denver, she went with them, escaping the sweltering heat of Panama—along with her increasingly distant husband—for the cool air of Colorado and the comfort of her family home. Ike's notorious temper, inherited from his father, was particularly fiery as he felt Mamie was choosing her parents over him, leaving him isolated and alone to suffer in the Panamanian quagmire.[15]

———

Even in the midst of the darkest times in Ike's life, God was seemingly preparing Ike for the challenges ahead of him. After Mamie left for Colorado, he spent the majority of his time with General Conner, a highly educated, engaging man with an abiding passion for history, especially military history. At West Point, Ike had lost his earlier interest in history due to the dull way it was taught, but here in the jungles of Panama he at last met a teacher who could bring the subject to life for him. The art and science of war became his obsession and provided a distraction from the tragedy of his personal circumstances.

Conner had filled his quarters with books on military history and strategy, and he taught Ike how to read and think about history, then talk about what he had read. He also gave Ike full use of his library.

Conner first had Ike read military fiction, and after Ike finished each book, they would discuss it. He then had Ike move on to more serious topics, especially books on the American Civil War, and in particular Civil War generals and their strengths and weaknesses. He would ask Ike why he thought Robert E. Lee invaded the North for a second time, why General Meade was successful, and what Lee's alternatives were at Gettysburg.[16] Their conversations often went long into the night.[17]

Conner asked probing questions, challenging Ike to consider what he would have done differently in a given historical scenario. Ike also endlessly studied maps of various wars and military campaigns.

General Conner became Ike's most influential teacher. Ike considered his time with Conner as a postgraduate education in military history.[18] The time the two spent together had a profound impact on Ike's thinking about the military and history as a whole. General Conner opened Ike's eyes to, as one account put it, "the real meaning and value of military history."[19] Ike had a new enthusiasm and motivation for his Army career and an important booster in Conner, who described Ike as "one of the most capable, efficient, and loyal officers I have ever met."[20]

This understanding of military history—its successes and failures, and all that was involved in battle—became the foundation for Ike's brilliance as a military strategist and tactician. Perhaps most significantly, Conner explained to Ike his belief that the Treaty of Versailles, which ended World War I, would eventually lead to a second world war because it had left Germany and its allies gutted, demoralized, and in eventual economic chaos. These conditions made these nations ripe for despotic leaders who would play upon the emotions of a downtrodden people to gain power. Conner thought that war would happen in less than a quarter of a century, and the next war would truly be a multifront "world war" rather than a series of single fronts.[21] As Ike listened to his logic, he eventually came to agree with this conclusion, which would, as history would prove, be validated.[22]

———

On August 3, 1922, Mamie gave birth to the Eisenhowers' second son, John Sheldon Doud Eisenhower. The military granted Ike a few days' leave to be present when John was born in Denver, but he then had to return quickly to Panama. John's birth brought some slight solace to the Eisenhowers, but as Ike wrote fifty years later, the pain of Icky's death lingered, even though John's arrival did much to fill the gap that he and Mamie had felt so poignantly and deeply since Icky's death.[23]

John's birth may indeed have taken Ike's mind off the loss of Icky, but soon Ike returned to his assignment in Panama and settled back into his routine. A few months later, Mamie and John joined him in Panama, where she was disappointed to find that, despite John's presence, Ike continued to isolate himself from his family. Living conditions had not improved much, and she soon found herself dealing with insomnia and the intestinal problems that came with life in Panama, in addition to caring for her newborn son. The physical and emotional strain began to take a severe toll. She later recalled of those days in Panama, "I was down to skin and bones and hollow-eyed. . . . My health and vitality seemed to ebb away. I don't know how I existed."[24]

After only a few weeks, Mamie decided she could not take the conditions and Ike's emotional distance any longer. Ike's biographer, Michael Korda, wrote regarding comments Mamie later made to her granddaughter Susan Eisenhower: "[Mamie did] not say outright that she was contemplating divorce, but when one reads between the lines it seems likely that the thought had crossed her mind."[25] While we may never know the specifics, the fact that their granddaughter would say this would indicate that their marriage, in the wake of Icky's death and their way of dealing with the tragedy, was in serious trouble. Within a few months, Mamie and John had returned to Denver.

Since Icky's death, Ike had begun experiencing health difficulties as well. He had lost fifteen pounds and, like Mamie, was dealing with serious gastrointestinal problems. While the squalid living conditions and unclean water in Panama likely contributed to his health issues, Ike was convinced there were other problems as well. In 1923, during another leave in Denver to visit Mamie and John, doctors removed his appendix, but there was no evidence of disease. Ike was so isolated at this point in his life that he did not even tell Mamie about the surgery until it was over.[26]

Whatever physical ailments he endured, Ike was likely affected the most by the emotional scars left by Icky's death. His new son would never know the playful father Icky had experienced. John could not climb over the emotional wall his father had set up. Instead, John grew up knowing Ike as a stern, distant workaholic who suppressed his emotions in fear of a second tragedy. The father John remembered was "a terrifying figure to a small boy."[27] It is possible that Ike's emotional wall also served as a coping mechanism for the difficult decisions he would have to make later, when he issued orders sending America's sons into battle.

Not much has been written or discovered about Ike's faith during these years, as his characteristic reticence to speak about it became even more pronounced in these difficult days. His parents' faith had experienced a dramatic change after the death of Ike's brother Paul, and perhaps Ike's faith was going through a change as well. It seems safe to conclude that in these years, Ike was wrestling silently and fiercely with his beliefs.

In September 1924, Ike's tour of Panama ended, but not as he had hoped. This first non-training assignment whet his appetite for adventure, and he dreamed of leaving the less-than-idyllic camp in Panama for other, more exciting places. Instead, he returned to Camp Meade to resume his football coaching. Ike was less than pleased, later writing, "Why . . . I was moved from Panama to Chesapeake Bay to join three other officers in a football coaching assignment is still a cosmic top-secret wonder to me."[28]

Ike, with Mamie and John, went back to Camp Meade, where the memories of Icky's death were still fresh, to serve as backfield coach. To add to his aggravation, Ike learned that someone at Army head-quarters had written a letter stating that Ike had informally expressed interest in coaching the team, which he had not done.[29] Finally, the success or failure of the team would affect his service record.[30]

Ike could hardly contain his contempt for the assignment, writing that it was probably thought up by an ambitious young junior officer trying to impress his seniors by saying, "Wouldn't it be dandy to get an Army team together that could play an undefeated, untied season and smear the Marines?"[31]

If the idea was to smear the Marines, then the plan was a dismal failure. While the Army had successfully recruited a team of excellent coaches, it had not followed the same standards when it came to recruiting players. The coaches found themselves with a decided lack of selection, as they were told they could only use players stationed at Camp Meade and could not recruit from other assignments to build their team (though apparently the Army could do so for coaches, to Ike's chagrin).

The Army team had a miserable season, which ended with a humiliating shutout by the rival Marine team. Ike concluded, "If, in my semi-professional failure, the War Department never again showed interest in me as a football coach, the season was a huge triumph."[32]

Thankfully, with the end of the football season, Ike's time at Camp Meade also ended. In early 1925, the Eisenhower family planned to move to Fort Benning for another training post—commanding the 15th Battalion—another disappointing move Ike accepted.

He had been hoping for an invitation to attend the prestigious Command and General Staff School at Fort Leavenworth, Kansas. As he prepared himself to go to Fort Benning, he received a telegram from General Fox Conner. It read, "No matter what orders you receive from the War Department, make no protest. Accept them without question."[33] Ike soon found out what Conner meant when he learned that he was now to be sent to Fort Logan, Colorado, to serve as a recruiting officer. He trusted Conner and dutifully took the family to Colorado to carry out the assignment, which came with a great deal of time to spare. The one person who was happy was Mamie.[34]

Conner's telegram would actually turn out to be the opportunity Ike had been seeking. His old mentor from Panama had manipulated Army regulations to arrange for Ike to attend the school at Fort Leavenworth, and Fort Logan was nothing more than a safe and temporary place to bide his time until an appointment for him to attend the school came through, which it did in April 1925.[35] Ike later wrote when he heard the news, "I was ready to fly—and needed no airplane!"[36]

The Eisenhowers arrived at Fort Leavenworth in August 1925, and life finally started to improve for the Eisenhower family. Ike wrote in *At Ease*, "I found the school itself to be exhilarating."[37]

Ike had a taste of career success, finishing first in his class. The living situation was downright luxurious compared to the ramshackle, vermin-infested housing the family had experienced in the past. Unlike his experience at West Point, Ike found the teaching challenging and was buoyed by the camaraderie of other officers at the school. He would later write that his time at Fort Leavenworth was the "watershed" of his career.[38]

At this point, both Ike and Mamie remained reticent about their faith and their marriage, but it is likely that the improved living conditions and Ike's contentment in his situation eased some of the tensions that had developed since Icky's death. Though they continued to grieve for the rest of their lives over the little boy they had lost, this time at Fort Leavenworth provided a much-needed respite for them, both as individuals and as a couple.

After Fort Leavenworth, Ike took another assignment that, at the time, again did not make much sense for an ambitious officer. He accepted a position with the new American Battle Monuments Commission in Washington, DC. General Pershing, the famed World War I military leader, had urged Congress in 1923 to create the commission to build and beautify the cemeteries containing America's war dead abroad. Although it was not an exciting position, the post was in DC, bringing Ike into proximity with military leaders—including the prestigious General Pershing.

But before Ike could begin working with the commission, the War College at Fort McNair in Washington, DC, selected him as a student. This was another prestigious appointment. Ike attended the college, where he wrote a paper on the need to develop an enlisted Army reserve for fast mobilization. This was particularly pertinent given the gutting of regular Army forces after World War I.[39] By the early 1940s, it was clear that this paper was prophetic in its analysis of the major weaknesses of the American Armed Forces, and served as a testament to Ike's prescience on strategic matters.

Upon graduating in June 1928, Ike resumed his duties with the commission. For his first assignment, he agreed to revise a guide-book of World War I battlefields. He chose the assignment because it would give the Eisenhower family a chance to move to France, an opportunity that excited Mamie very much. Even though another assignment with the War Department General Staff would have been more prestigious, Ike wanted to get to know a European country and enjoy the French countryside.[40] For Ike and Mamie, a possible side benefit would be time away in a pleasant destination that could potentially help heal the breach that had come between them.

One month later, the Eisenhower family sailed for France, where Ike and Mamie placed John in a private American school. For the next year, Ike trekked from one battlefield to another along the entire Western front of World War I, extending from Switzerland to the North Sea, and in the spring of 1929 he took Mamie and John along with him.[41] At each battlefield, he catalogued, mapped, and took careful notes of the terrain and the strategies involved.

Ike and Mamie also gained many insights into the life and culture of provincial France. Soon, Ike became more familiar with the French coast, countryside, and rural culture than perhaps any other individual in the US Army. This knowledge of the geography and culture of northern rural France equipped Ike with unique expertise— expertise that would be essential when the Allies began considering how to establish a beachhead in German-occupied France during the later years of World War II.[42]

For Ike and Mamie, this time in France also seemed to be the healing balm that their marriage needed. Ike took leave in the middle of his duty, and as Ike's biographer Carlo D'Este would write, "Eisenhower's year in France, particularly the summer of 1929, was by far the most relaxed, idyllic period of Ike and Mamie's lives."[43] In his memoir, Ike waxed eloquent (for him) about their time there, writing about their trips to Belgium, Switzerland, and the German autobahn, as well as Mamie's enjoyment of Paris shopping.[44]

Though the road ahead would still have twists and turns, they had come through the most challenging years of their marriage intact, and never again would they experience, to such a degree, the particular pain that comes from marital difficulties.

After their idyllic time in France, the Eisenhowers returned to Washington, DC, in November 1929, where Ike received another assignment that relied on his writing skills: revitalizing the very dry memoirs of General Pershing, who had the reputation of being quite difficult to work with.[45] Once again, Ike's assignment did not make much sense in terms of career advancement. But working on the general's memoirs put Ike within Pershing's orbit and on the radar screen of the rapidly rising Lt. Colonel George Catlett Marshall, a name General Conner had told Ike to remember.[46]

George Marshall was perhaps the only officer Pershing really trusted. This trust came about when Marshall, serving as operations officer of the 1st Division in World War I, confronted Pershing after the general had rather bluntly criticized the performance of the unit's commander. Marshall challenged the general's comments and, as a result, grudgingly earned his respect. The two dissimilar men would, in the words of Carlo D'Este, have "a curious but lasting friendship." Pershing could discern Marshall's professionalism and use it effectively. Marshall, for his part, protected Pershing through his actions.[47]

Marshall had a keen eye for talent and a staunch conviction that the American Army was in danger of being left behind as a military force because of its reluctance to embrace modern technology, such as the tank. Unless the American Army modernized, it would rapidly become obsolete, and he was constantly on the lookout for fresh talent to help shape the new US military.

When Pershing asked Ike to present Marshall with his suggestions for how to revise the memoir, Marshall recognized that Ike's ideas of how to restructure the manuscript were good, but he knew what Pershing really wanted.[48] Marshall, as wise aides do, felt he had to protect his leader and keep him happy, even if it meant putting his personal opinions aside. Thus, he rejected Ike's ideas in favor of the dry format desired by Pershing. However, that did not keep him from noticing that Ike had great potential as a leader.[49]

While Ike toiled away at the arid text of General Pershing's book, Marshall had been quietly observing him, and liked what he saw. Ike's biographer, Michael Korda, wrote that Ike's intelligence, patience, hard work, and willingness to be a team player, even with the most difficult of bosses, caught Marshall's eye. Marshall always looked for self-effacing men with good minds who would see a difficult job to completion while putting aside thoughts of personal fame or fortune.[50]

Marshall added Ike's name to his list of "rising stars," a list that included future leaders such as Omar Bradley, George S. Patton, Walter Bedell "Beetle" Smith, and Matthew B. Ridgway, among others.

Ike continued to serve ably, if otherwise indistinguishably, throughout the early part of the 1930s. However, Ike's time with Pershing was not his last experience with a challenging superior; in 1933 he accepted an offer to become the executive aide to the notoriously difficult Army Chief of Staff Douglas MacArthur. MacArthur's oversized ego and unreasonable demands on his subordinates were well known. He expected those who worked under him to be available at all times, with no regard for their personal lives.[51]

Soon after Ike took the position, he and MacArthur found themselves assigned to a posting in the Philippines, ostensibly to help equip the Philippine army to defend their nation against potential attacks from other Asian nations. However, there was more to the story.

President Franklin Roosevelt, who repeatedly clashed with MacArthur, had finally reached the end of his patience with the irascible general and replaced him with a new Army Chief of Staff. MacArthur's role in the infamous "Bonus Army March" of 1932 likely served as an excuse for Roosevelt and his allies to get MacArthur as far away from Washington, DC, as possible.[52] MacArthur had allegedly ordered the Army to burn down the shanties of destitute World War I veterans who had marched on the Capitol to demand early payment of the $1,000 bonuses they were to receive—in 1945. Ike, who witnessed what had happened, called the whole incident "pitiful."[53] He would write, "The veterans, whether or not they were mistaken in marching on Washington, were ragged, ill-fed, and felt themselves badly abused. To suddenly see the whole encampment going up in flames just added to the pity one had to feel for them."[54]

Even as the boat left American shores, it was clear that MacArthur was essentially exiled and taking Ike with him. Thus, the Philippines was not a plum assignment, and in some ways it was a banishment, given Roosevelt's antipathy toward MacArthur. Horrified by the possibility of a repeat of the ghastly conditions in Panama, Mamie chose not to go. In addition, she strongly disliked MacArthur and his overbearing ways. It quickly became clear that the best, though still highly undesirable, situation was for Mamie and John to remain in DC while Ike went abroad.

This separation was heartbreaking for Ike, as he had finally begun to grow closer to John just as the boy was entering his preteen years. Ike's frustration with the situation is clear from a letter he wrote to Mamie's parents.

I hate the whole thought and I know that I'm going to be miserable. On the other hand, Mamie's so badly frightened both for John and herself, at the prospect of going out there that I simply cannot urge her to go . . . I can only hope for the best, as the idea of being separated from my family has nothing for me but grief.[55]

To make matters worse, MacArthur refused to provide Ike with a definite date that the assignment would be over, leaving the Eisenhowers unsure of when they might be reunited. This only deepened Mamie's dislike of MacArthur, and she did not hesitate to voice her strong disapproval of the assignment.

When Ike sailed, Mamie told a friend, "Ike is ruined. He has gone off to the Philippines with that man MacArthur."[56] The DC gossip mill had also made Mamie well aware of how the powerbrokers loathed MacArthur, and she was likely fearful that Ike would now be tarred with the same brush simply because of his association with the general.

Ike remained reticent about his faith. While it is clear that he continued to serve faithfully wherever assigned, and that he stayed true to the moral compass instilled in his youth, there is little information about the state of his faith during this time. He may have spent this period in deep reflection about what he believed, confronted as he was by tragedy and disappointment. If this is the case, and Ike was wrestling with his faith, it would explain his reticence about religion during this period of his life.

It is also possible that Ike chose not to speak openly about religion and faith because he did not sense that it was necessary. The mood of the country at the time was generally favorable to cultural Christianity, and the Cold War—that titanic struggle between religious faith and atheism—was still a few decades away. While the political situation in Europe was deteriorating, its turmoil had yet to affect America. Perhaps Ike simply did not feel a strong pull to be vocal about America's spiritual condition in the 1930s.

6

From MacArthur to Major General

From his vantage point on the muggy island country of the Philippines in 1936, it probably would have shocked Ike to know that just eight years later he would be General Dwight D. Eisenhower, directing one of the largest assaults on an enemy that had risen again from a fortress in central Europe. Despite his years-long silence on the subject of faith, it probably would not have shocked him to learn that in the hours before the D-Day assault, he would be praying.

Ike's correspondence from that era gives few indications of a strong, personal faith. That all changed dramatically with the onset of World War II and the great responsibilities thrust upon Ike. The ease with which Ike began speaking about religion—both frequently and fluently—indicates that he had long been turning over faith-based questions in his mind and heart.

While Ike was in the Philippines serving the autocratic and exiled General Douglas MacArthur, both Europe and Asia were entering a tumultuous time. As General Conner had predicted to Ike in the early

77

1920s during their assignment in Panama, the Treaty of Versailles was rapidly breaking down along the France/Germany border.

In 1933, an economically devastated and demoralized Germany had elected Adolf Hitler and the National Socialist Party—the Nazis—to power, and Hitler quickly consolidated his control over the entire apparatus of the German state. Soon after becoming chancellor, he openly violated the limitations imposed by the Treaty of Versailles after World War I. He authorized a massive increase in German military power, ostensibly in pursuit of "parity" with other European powers. Hitler was not the only totalitarian dictator rising to power in Europe; in Italy, fascist leader Benito Mussolini seized control of the country and, in an attempt to assert Italian significance on the world stage, invaded Ethiopia in October 1935.

Half a world away, the Japanese expanded their plans for conquest. In 1931, the Japanese Army captured Manchuria, and one year later invaded China, sparking a war with the Nationalist Chinese Army and its noteworthy general Chiang Kai-shek. In the aftermath of the war, Japan left the dying League of Nations, former president Woodrow Wilson's utopian vision that he hoped would lead to lasting world peace. Throughout the 1930s, Japan continued to strengthen its army, solidifying a cultural drive for conquest and preparing for its coming onslaught on the South Pacific.

When Ike and MacArthur set sail for the Philippines in late 1935, they were heading into very rough political seas with very little backing. Their mission was allegedly to provide American support and expertise to the Philippine army, but the deployment was a thinly veiled banishment for MacArthur and the ego that had earned him plenty of enemies over the years. In this attempt to get MacArthur as far away from Washington, DC, as possible, several other top-notch officers were isolated as well, including the ever-dutiful Ike and his friend Lt. Colonel Jimmy Ord.

In the years leading up to World War II, the Philippines proved to be a strategic key to the entire Pacific theater—a fact of which the Japanese were well aware. Ike and MacArthur both knew they had an impossible job to do. They recognized the increased aggressiveness of the Japanese, and, despite MacArthur's optimistic public statements to the contrary, neither of them had any illusions that the Philippine army in its present form could defend the island in the face of a coordinated, large-scale attack.[1] MacArthur's group was to provide the training and strategic support necessary to make the Philippines defensible—with few resources to accomplish the task.

Ike and Ord were responsible for drawing up a budget for the assignment, and they devised a plan for a conscripted army that would receive one year of intensive training at a cost of 25 million US dollars, or 50 million pesos in Philippine currency. Though Roosevelt had promised that MacArthur would receive the money and supplies necessary to train and equip the Philippine military forces, those promises turned out to be empty. This was due in part to the Roosevelt administration's desire to rid themselves of MacArthur, the overall lack of funding for the US military, and the ongoing national isolationist movement that opposed any foreign military intervention by the United States.[2] Trying to get Washington to increase the meager Philippine budget became virtually impossible as a result.[3]

In addition, the Philippine government reneged on its initial financial commitment, and by the time they reached Manila, Ike and Ord found their budget slashed to 16 million pesos, forcing them to gut their original plan.[4] Though Ike, MacArthur, and Ord all saw that the tide in the region was turning, without financial backing from the United States they found themselves crippled, unable to do much to prepare for the Japanese assault they knew was coming.

Beside the frustration of seeing an impending disaster and being unable to avert it, Ike's new post put him in nearly constant contact with MacArthur, whose unceremonious relocation to the Philippines had increased his already legendary temper. The years in the Philippines would be difficult for both Ike and Mamie, but like so many

79

of the previous events in Ike's life, they helped build the leadership skills he would need later.

MacArthur's infamous ego led him to treat his subordinates quite poorly, which upset Mamie, and the never-ending task of catering to his commanding officer's slightest whims began to take its toll on Ike. He eventually learned, much to his irritation, that as part of MacArthur's acceptance of the Philippines mission, the general had insisted on a promotion to the rank of field marshal of the virtually nonexistent Philippine army, complete with a ceremony where he received a gold baton.[5]

Besides this, MacArthur received a nearly $4,000 pay raise, making him the highest-paid military officer in the world—money that came out of the minimal Philippine military budget. Ike strenuously objected to all of this, saying that he thought it was "pompous" and "ridiculous."[6] MacArthur also ensured that his living quarters consisted of a lavish, air-conditioned six-room penthouse at the Manila Hotel, while Ike received a small room without air-conditioning—a miserable situation indeed in the hot, humid Philippine climate.[7]

MacArthur's escalating demands, fixations on his own personal aggrandizement, and erratic schedule soon led to a rift between the US base and the Philippine government. The president of the Commonwealth of the Philippines, Manuel Quezon, eventually began bypassing MacArthur altogether and turning to Ike for advice. Quezon gave Ike an office in the Malacañan Palace to have him nearby, as MacArthur was often inaccessible since he would not come to work until 11 a.m., took a late lunch, and then worked late into the night.[8] Ike soon found himself in the unenviable position of regularly having to challenge MacArthur's ego while simultaneously repairing the damage MacArthur had done to other strategic relationships.

The confrontations with the difficult and demanding MacArthur were a dress rehearsal for dealing with the dueling egos of generals who would serve under his command in World War II—particularly his old friend George S. Patton and British General Bernard Montgomery, whose rivalry became the stuff of legend. In the Philippines, Ike was learning skills that would be critical in maintaining the delicate alliance necessary to defeat the Axis powers of Germany, Italy, and Japan.

Ike now began to learn how to stand up for himself as well as how (and when) to confront those he thought were in error. This combination of character traits became a vital tool that served him well in his future roles of both general and president.

Mamie and John finally joined Ike in the Philippines in late 1936. It had been a long and lonely year for Ike. He was not pleased that Mamie had chosen to stay back in the comfort of Washington, DC, while he toiled away under the difficult MacArthur. His letters to her had been less than joyful.[9]

Mamie had hoped that Ike would escape MacArthur and the Philippines and return to Washington. When it became evident that he would not, she decided that she had little choice but to join him there, despite her antipathy toward MacArthur and her dislike of another tropical climate.[10]

While the situation in the Philippines was nowhere near as miserable as what the Eisenhowers had faced in Panama, the cramped room in the Manila Hotel was very different from the comfort of the Doud family home in Denver or the apartment in Washington, DC. Life in the Philippines also meant regular encounters with enormous bats and bugs, as well as torrential rains, earthquakes, and endless mosquitos, accompanied by all sorts of diseases.[11] In perhaps a testimony of how faith was growing in importance to the Eisenhowers, the family chose to enroll John in a private Episcopalian mission school in Baguio, a mountain resort city located in Northern Luzon, Philippines.[12]

The military mission to strengthen the Philippine army had bogged down. The relationship between Quezon and MacArthur grew increasingly frigid, and Ike began spending more and more time with the Filipino president—an unexpected preparation for Ike's future of regular interactions with various world leaders. The two men shared a mutual love of fishing and playing bridge, and Ike sometimes spent weekends on the Filipino president's yacht.[13]

Mamie didn't like Quezon.[14] While she marveled at the social life in Manila, which included seemingly endless poker, mahjong, and bridge parties, she still felt lonely as Ike was frequently away, and was, according to her granddaughter Susan Eisenhower, "desperately homesick."[15] Nevertheless, despite these difficulties, the time in the Philippines was a healing balm to the Eisenhower marriage, and an incident would cause Ike to realize that he could not take Mamie for granted.

Mamie decided to take an automobile trip, without Ike, to visit John at the mission school—a nearly two-hundred-mile journey. Once at the school, she suffered a ruptured blood vessel in her stomach, resulting in her vomiting blood and eventually slipping into a coma. The cause of the hemorrhage was never precisely determined, but a combination of stress, altitude, and the rugged journey might have been the cause.[16] She received immediate medical attention at the Baguio hospital, which saved her life.

Ike rushed to her bedside and kept a somber vigil, much as he had done for Icky, until it was clear that she was going to be all right. This near-death experience brought the couple closer together, and both acknowledged how they had withdrawn from each other in recent years. Ike's emotional wall started to crack once he realized how close he came to losing Mamie, and Mamie, in turn, recognized that she was not guiltless in their marital difficulties, especially when she had initially refused to accompany Ike to Manila.[17]

Mamie would subsequently write a letter to her parents on Easter Sunday, 1938, in which she had admitted she had "made a terrible mistake in not coming out here with Ike."[18]

This new closeness became evident in a letter that Ike would write to Mamie from London in 1943, while he was serving as the leader of the Allied troops in Europe. In that letter, Ike also reiterated his love to her. Mamie had grown concerned about rumors circulating about Ike's relationship with a female staff member, even though no eyewitnesses ever came forward with conclusive evidence proving the allegations true, and later research has done more to dispute rather than affirm them.[19] Ike emphatically wrote at the end of the letter, "Lots of love my sweet . . . I love you—so much—and you only!!"[20] Ike's statement, which was in many ways out of character for him, is a clear demonstration of his love and commitment to his wife.

———————

Soon after Mamie's brush with death, another tragedy struck Ike. For the first several years in the Philippines, Ike worked closely with his friend Jimmy Ord in devising the plans for training and equipping the Philippine army. Ord was Ike's confidante and ally in dealing with the nearly daily confrontations with MacArthur, and he helped Ike get through the lonely and difficult days before Mamie and John arrived. Jimmy Ord was not only a dear friend and an esteemed colleague but was like a brother. Ike remembered Ord as a congenial fellow as well as a top-flight officer who helped to make light work of the heavy chore of building defenses, in Ike's words, out of little or nothing.[21]

Sadly, on January 30, 1938, Jimmy Ord was killed in a freak plane accident. Ike described the fateful day:

[Jimmy] had to make a trip to Baguio one day . . . he mentioned that he was taking one of the Filipino students as pilot. "No, you won't," I said. "Get one of the American flight instructors. They'll be more than glad to do it." He laughed and said "Our Filipino boys are doing really well. I'll use one of them. I won't be gone for more than a few hours. See you late this afternoon."

As they neared the air strip in Baguio, up in the mountains of northern Luzon, Jimmy decided to drop a note near the house of his friends, the Fairchild family. He told the pilot to circle the place. In circling, the pilot lost speed and crashed. The pilot and the plane were not badly damaged. But Jimmy, who was leaning out of the back seat, had his body whipped around so violently that his injuries were grave. He died within a few hours.[22]

Ike later wrote, "From then on, more of the planning work fell on my shoulders, but without my friend, all the zest was gone."[23]

Adding to Ike's ambivalence toward the project after Ord's death was his strained relationship with Ord's successor, Major Richard D. Sutherland. Ike resisted saying anything negative about Sutherland in his memoir, but he could not conjure up anything warmer than this: "As a companion and comrade, no one could fill the void left by Jimmy's death, but Sutherland was capable and I appreciated his help."[24] Ike's curtness told the story of their relationship.

In fact, Sutherland was the antithesis of Ord, and Ike took an immediate dislike to him. The dislike was mutual. In fact, very few people liked Sutherland; many saw him as "ruthlessly ambitious." One of MacArthur's biographers referred to him as "an unpleasant S-O-B."[25] In 1942, MacArthur would cable the War Department to tell them that, in the event of his death, Sutherland would replace him. Ike wrote in his diary, "He picked Sutherland, showing he still likes his bootlickers."[26]

General Marshall also disliked Sutherland, at one point writing a letter (that went unsent) to MacArthur saying that Sutherland was

totally lacking in the facility of dealing with others. . . . He antago-nized almost every official in the War Department with whom he came in contact and made our dealings with the Navy exceptionally difficult. Unfortunately he appears utterly unaware of the effects of his methods, but to put it bluntly, his attitude in almost every case seems to have been that he knew it all and nobody else knew much of anything.[27]

Obviously, many shared Ike's feelings about him.

Sutherland thought that by getting rid of Ike he could advance his own career.[28] At every turn, he sought to undermine Ike while buttering up MacArthur and his ego whenever he could. As a result, the loyal but blunt and honest Ike plummeted in the general's esteem.[29] During the summer of 1938, while Ike was away in Washington, DC, pleading for more war material to bolster the Philippine defenses, MacArthur stripped him of his role as chief advisor and chief of staff and replaced him with Sutherland, who later stated proudly that he had "gotten rid of Eisenhower."[30]

This, along with the deteriorating situation in Europe as Hitler's armies started to march across the continent, convinced Ike (now nearly fifty) to bring his time in the Philippines to a close, though neither he nor Mamie had any idea what their future would look like. At this point, the pieces of Ike's life began to fall into place, and he soon found himself called upon to use the skills and character he had developed through years of disappointment and difficulty.

In September 1938, British Prime Minister Neville Chamberlain signed the tragically misguided Munich Agreement, handing Czechoslovakia to Adolf Hitler on a platter in exchange for what Chamberlain infamously stated as "peace in our time."[31]

Within months, the whole continent, and much of the world, would be alight with war. After the disastrous assignment in the Philippines, Ike reentered the regular Army just in time for the world war that he and Fox Conner had both predicted was coming.

In December 1939, Ike, Mamie, and John set sail from the Philippines to return to America. Ike had received permission to return to the United States from both MacArthur and President Quezon, whom Ike described as "far more emphatic" than MacArthur in trying to convince him to stay. Quezon went as far as offering to allow Ike to determine his pay if he signed a new contract to remain in the Philippines.[32] However, Ike knew his place was elsewhere. He told MacArthur, "General, in my opinion the United States cannot stay out of this war for long. I want to go home as soon as possible.

I want to participate in the preparatory work that I'm sure is going to be intense."[33]

The country Ike returned to was woefully unprepared for war. Two decades of neglect had taken its toll on the US military, both materially and tactically. The military had been so unpopular during the late 1920s and early 1930s that officers serving in Washington, DC, were encouraged not to wear their uniforms.[34]

To start cleaning up the mess, President Roosevelt promoted Ike's old colleague, Brigadier General George C. Marshall, who had been advocating for the modernization of the military, as the new Army Chief of Staff. His first task was to create a fighting force, and it was soon clear that he had to start almost from scratch.[35]

In total disregard for the obvious technological superiority of the German Army, development of the US military had continued to sputter along like a 1917 Model T. Many military leaders persisted in their reluctance to invest in technology. In 1940, there was a contingent of military leaders who were still wedded to the idea of a cavalry, arguing that it was cheaper and more efficient to find grass for horses to eat than to secure fuel for tanks, despite the mounting evidence that Hitler had at his command a war machine unlike anything the world had ever seen.[36]

Roosevelt had conducted his 1940 campaign for reelection under the promise that he would continue to keep America out of the war. Prescient leaders like Marshall knew that American involvement was inevitable. In order to whip the Army into shape, Marshall worked with his handpicked leader, Major General Lesley McNair, to streamline the infantry division, create the armored division, and introduce modern weaponry to replace the Army's World War I–issue equipment.[37]

Marshall also knew that it would be impossible for him to succeed in building a working American military if his commanding officers were still preparing for the wars of yesterday. At heart, Marshall was still the keen-eyed talent scout who had collected a list of promising officers during his time working with Blackjack Pershing—a list that included the name Dwight D. Eisenhower.

Ike was unaware of Marshall's plans when he, Mamie, and John arrived in San Francisco on January 5, 1940. The Eisenhowers disembarked only to find that Ike's scheduled assignment to Fort Lewis (near Tacoma, Washington) had been changed. Instead, Ike was to report to temporary duty with the Fourth Army located at the Presidio of San Francisco, under the command of Lt. General John L. DeWitt. This change in plans once again disrupted the Eisenhowers' lives, as Ike and Mamie had already enrolled John for his senior year of high school. John ended up going to Tacoma to temporarily live with Ike's brother Edgar, for school, while Ike and Mamie stayed in San Francisco.

This disruption was only the first of many for the Eisenhower family during the whirlwind years of 1939–41. Impressed with Ike's attention to detail and careful judgment, DeWitt released him with reluctance to return to the 15th Infantry at Fort Lewis, at least temporarily reuniting Ike and Mamie with John. Less than a week later, which was barely time to get Mamie settled, new orders came sending Ike to Camp Ord in Monterey, California, named after his deceased friend's grandfather. Here Ike would serve as the executive officer in charge of training.

Though he was separated once again from Mamie and John, Ike enjoyed this assignment. He was in his element of training the troops. In July 1940, he wrote his old West Point classmate, Lt. Colonel Omar Bradley of the War Department General Staff, that he was having the "time of his life."[38] After a hiatus of nearly twenty-five years, Ike's dreams of leading a group into combat looked like they might come true. When the 15th Infantry was to deploy to Fort Lewis later in the year, Ike, now a lieutenant colonel, expected that he would receive command of a battalion, which could consist of anywhere from three hundred to eight hundred soldiers.[39]

As America's involvement in the war became inevitable, Ike was completely unaware of how valuable he was becoming. He continued to enjoy his role training troops at Fort Lewis when Patton, who was commanding a brigade of the 2nd Armored Division, offered him his pick of appointment as either chief of staff or regimental commander—a combat command position at last.[40] Patton was well aware of the conflict that was coming, and was training his troops long and hard, in a manner that only Patton could do.[41]

But Ike also received a request to come to Washington, DC, and serve in the War Planning Department. Though this was a prestigious position, Ike did not relish the prospect of working in an office. He felt that taking this position would doom him to be a career bureaucrat and would end his dream of becoming a general. Ike wrote that when he received the telegrammed request, the "roof fell in on me."[42] He contacted Lt. Colonel Mark Clark, who had been part of Ike's West Point class of 1915 and had remained a close friend. Through his connection with Clark, who now served under Major General Walter C. Sweeney, the commander of the 3rd Division, Ike requested that the invitation be withdrawn, which it was.[43]

But in the meantime, the chance to serve with Patton was lost, and Ike remained at Fort Lewis, where he was still enjoying his assignment. Ike had also given up his longtime desire for promotion. He later wrote in *At Ease* that he was happy in his work, and "ready to face, without resentment, the bleak promotional picture." He had resolved to become the person who was known for doing the best he could, and whom people would regret losing after he moved on to a new assignment. It was a statement of personal pride and confidence in his abilities, but also one that showed Ike had resigned himself to his station at this point of his career.[44]

In late November 1940, General Charles Fullington Thompson, the new commander of the 3rd Division, replacing Sweeney, would appoint Ike to be chief of staff. This did not please Ike. While he was glad to have "escaped Washington," he said, "I'm weary of these eternal staff details. I'd like to get a command of my own, even if just a squad."[45] (Perhaps no more than a dozen or so soldiers.)

Marshall continued his efforts to purge the military of the old guard who stood in the way of building a modern fighting force. He forced several retirements and started promoting officers from the list he had compiled over decades. While Ike and George S. Patton were older than others on Marshall's list, they both benefited from his slash-and-burn efforts to rapidly reshape the US military and equip it for the grim new reality it would face on the battlefields of World War II. Without Marshall's aggressive and visionary approach to the role of chief of staff, both Ike and Patton may have found themselves once again passed over.

At this point, Ike could not have known that within four years he would be commanding the Allied military forces. He also probably did not know that during that same time he would confront face-to-face the horrors of modern war and the depth of human evil. In response to these developments, Ike's faith, which had been a very private matter for the previous two decades, was about to become much more outspoken.

As Christmas 1940 arrived, what Ike did know was that another world war was right around the corner. John Eisenhower later recalled singing, "Peace on earth, good will to men," and Ike saying to him, "Be glad for peace while you've still got it."[46]

In the last months of 1940, news had trickled back to Washington, DC, about the effectiveness of Ike's troop training skills at Camp Ord and Fort Lewis. At Fort Lewis, Ike met and began working with Lt. Colonel Lucian K. Truscott Jr., who eventually served as the architect of the Army Ranger force that played a critical role in the D-Day invasion three years later.[47]

In March 1941, Ike received a promotion to full colonel, which at first seemed as if it would spell the end of his training career. However, in July 1941, at the request of Major General Walter Krueger, the new commander of the 3rd Army, Marshall dispatched Ike from Fort

Lewis to one of his former homes, Fort Sam Houston in San Antonio, to serve as Krueger's chief of staff.[48] It was a providential assignment.

Ike's new commanding officer was an excellent match for him, and quickly realized that Ike had more to offer than staff work. Krueger, like Ike, shunned the limelight and cared deeply for his men, while holding a reputation for maintaining high standards and strict discipline. He was also one of the US military's most accomplished tacticians.[49] During World War I, Krueger served in France as the Assistant Chief of Staff for the 26th Infantry Division, the 84th Infantry Division, and finally the Tank Corps, which Ike had served in, training the troops at Camp Colt.[50]

Krueger and Ike started to work together on a massive war game operation—the "Louisiana Maneuvers." General George Marshall described the maneuvers as "a combat college for troop leading,"[51] designed to prepare the troops for the upcoming battles of World War II.

During 1940–41, the US Army more than doubled in size. Most of these recruits were young and green, and it became imperative to test these new troops' combat abilities before America was deeply embroiled in the war. The Louisiana Maneuvers, developed by Krueger and Ike, provided the backdrop to see if the Army could rise to the challenges presented by modern warfare.

The maneuvers were a series of war games staged in the southern part of the United States. They stretched across nearly 3,500 square miles and pitted nearly 400,000 troops against each other in "battles" that lasted months. Through the backwoods and swamps of rural Louisiana, the newly fledged American Army crawled on its bellies, swam through the infested waters, maneuvered tanks, and tested itself against what it knew about the German war machine—and came up woefully short at first.

During the Louisiana Maneuvers, Ike and Marshall saw two things right away. First, the young American troops were strong, dedicated, and intelligent, but they were completely unprepared for combat.

Second, they watched firsthand the profound failures of the old-line Army leadership, who insisted on conducting the maneuvers as if they were still fighting in battles against the 1918 German Army. It was immediately clear that despite the massive growth in the size of the Army, America was utterly unprepared for war. Ike called for a "weeding out" of officers who, in his view, "have not the iron to perform the job."[52]

Marshall and McNair concurred with Ike's judgment and cleaned out the senior leadership, replacing them with the officers whose names Marshall had kept for over a decade in his black book—including Ike, who had outmaneuvered one of the old-line commanders in one of the games.[53] The praise for Ike's leadership was so great that his accolades even overshadowed Krueger, which led to some personal resentment over Ike's "rising star" status—a scenario that would play itself out repeatedly in the years ahead.[54]

In Louisiana, for the first time, Ike had a chance to demonstrate his abilities as a tactician, and he rose to the occasion adeptly. The Louisiana Maneuvers were the testing ground for the tactics Ike would later use in the D-Day invasion. During these months in the sodden backcountry, Ike and his fellow officers experimented with armored divisions, testing their capacity to maneuver quickly across rough ground in unpredictable weather.

They began developing divisions of paratroopers for dropping deep into enemy territory and spending weeks undercover, performing sabotage and intelligence-gathering missions. Years later, this training proved vital when the Allied troops landed at Normandy.

In one of the final maneuvers, Ike found himself pitted against Patton's armored divisions, which rushed in to break Ike's line in another foreshadowing of D-Day and the Panzer divisions bearing down on Normandy in mid-June 1944. Ike's cool-headed leadership, combined with his knowledge of the technology involved and his attention to timeless elements of warfare like terrain, prevailed. His soldiers surrounded and neutralized Patton's tanks.

Patton later executed a stunning surprise maneuver, slipping out of Ike's net and barreled his way up through nearly two hundred miles of rough Louisiana backcountry in just three days.[55]

The leadership of both men deeply impressed military leaders. They noted that Eisenhower had a canny and inventive strategic mind while Patton demonstrated brilliant aggressiveness that stopped just short of audacity. Though the Louisiana Maneuvers exposed the grim state of the American fighting forces, they allowed Ike and Patton, as well as Clark, to rise to the top and display their skills to the entire military.[56]

At the end of the maneuvers, General Mark Clark received the list of officers nominated by President Roosevelt for promotion to Brigadier General. The whole group gathered to hear the selections, Ike waiting nervously to see if his name was to be called.

General Clark read out the names, which did not include Ike's, and then said, "That's it," and dismissed the group. As handshakes and backslaps abounded, Ike could not hide his deflation of being passed over again, and had already started to exit the room. Then, suddenly, Clark banged the gavel again and announced that he had "forgotten" one name—Ike's.[57]

One of Ike's life dreams had at last come true: he was a one-star general in the American Army. The promotion that he had seemingly come to peace with never receiving had come true. The others in the room gathered around Ike and offered heartfelt congratulations. Mamie later said that Ike's promotion was the biggest thrill of their military married life.

However, Ike aspired to more than simply the title of general, and he was concerned that the promotion might keep him stuck behind a desk rather than opening the door for the combat command he had so long desired. That concern would turn out to be unnecessary.

In Europe, the situation had quickly deteriorated from bad to worse. The winter and spring of 1939–40 were some of the darkest days of

World War II, as the Allies continually lost ground across Europe, and the German army seemed invincible. In May 1940, the famed French Maginot Line—designed to protect France and the western coast of Europe from German invasion—collapsed. Hitler's troops marched into Paris, and the whole of France fell to the Nazi occupiers.

Dispatched to France in early 1940 to help hold the line, the British Army, nearly obliterated at Dunkirk, only escaped through the miraculous and heroic evacuation efforts of the entire British people. The British Army and the remnants of the French Resistance, led by Charles de Gaulle, drew back to London only to have the war follow them. From July through the middle of October, 1940, England faced daily aerial bombardments from the Nazis in what Prime Minister Winston Churchill famously called the Battle of Britain.

In the North African theater, Nazi General Erwin Rommel's Afrika Korps were racing across the continent and soundly defeating the British 8th Army. In June 1941, Hitler launched his attack on the Soviet Union, opening an entirely new front of the war. "Peace on earth," as Ike had warned John the previous Christmas, had indeed become a distant dream. On December 7, 1941, that distant dream became a rude awakening with the Japanese surprise attack on Pearl Harbor. A few weeks later, the foment continued to spread across the globe as an increasingly aggressive Japanese Army marched into Hong Kong, and the Japanese Navy began moving toward Burma and the Philippines.[58]

Ike was at Fort Sam Houston in San Antonio when he learned of the attack on Pearl Harbor.[59] As the situation unfolded and the military found itself called upon to spring into action, Ike had to "hold everything together and coordinate the hourly directives from the War Department to shift units, provide security for Gulf Coast ports, and act on a rash of other urgent requirements."[60]

It was time for the American military to call upon the lessons they had learned in the war games just a few months earlier. On the morning of December 12, Ike's phone rang. On the other end was Colonel

Walter Bedell Smith, the secretary of the War Department General Staff. Smith informed Ike that he was to come to Washington, DC, immediately, where he would receive his formal wartime orders.[61] Ike was to replace Colonel Charles Bundy, the senior War Plans division planner for the Pacific operations, who had died in a tragic plane crash in the Colorado Rockies while on an investigative mission to Hawaii on the day of the Pearl Harbor attack.[62]

Ike felt sure that a summons to DC probably meant that he would spend the war working a desk job, which was the initial plan. That was something he dreaded. His outlook did not improve when General Marshall told him,

> The men who are going to get the promotions in this war are the commanders in the field, not the staff officers who clutter up all of the administrative machinery in the War Department and in higher tactical headquarters. The field commanders carry the responsibility and I'm going to see to it that they're properly rewarded so far as promotion can provide a reward.[63]

As Ike wrote, "The frustration I felt in 1918 because of my failure to get overseas now returned briefly. By General Marshall's word, I was completely condemned to a desk job in Washington for the duration."[64]

After Ike angrily expressed his frustration to Marshall for sticking him behind a desk and telling him that no promotions would be forthcoming, he was stunned when Marshall sent a recommendation to President Roosevelt for Ike's promotion. He would now serve as Marshall's subordinate commander—and under Marshall's direction would be responsible for all Army forces on a global scale—including the Army Air Corps (now the Air Force). And with the new assignment came a new rank: major general.[65]

General Marshall asked Ike to draft a directive for a commanding general for the forces in Europe. Marshall then followed that up by requesting Ike's recommendation for who should be that commander, and Ike suggested General Joseph T. McNarney of the Army Air Corps.

But instead of McNarney, Marshall sent Ike to London to command the European Theater of Operations. As Ike would later write, "This brought me much closer to the war—and the desk job in Washington was behind."[66]

The time of preparation, which had begun decades ago in the streets of Abilene, was over. After all those years of faithfulness in difficulty and disappointment, it was time for Ike to step into his destiny as the military leader of the free world—a role that would prompt him to finally begin speaking freely, openly, and boldly about his faith.

7

Nothing We Can Do but Pray

The story of the next few years is well known: the American military soon entered the war in Europe and Africa in addition to the Pacific theater. Ike's responsibilities continued to increase, as he organized and executed massive military operations including Operation Torch (the Allied invasion of North Africa), Operation Avalanche (the Allied effort to seize the Italian peninsula), and eventually Operation Overlord, the Allied invasion of Normandy on D-Day: June 6, 1944. Lesser known is that, during these years, Ike was not only a brilliant military leader but also a man of spiritual strength who, in the midst of the most challenging decisions he had ever made, turned consistently and openly to prayer.

In 1943, Gerald Mygatt, a major in the US Army, wrote to Ike asking for a contribution to *The Soldiers' and Sailors' Prayer Book*, a collection of prayers and hymns selected for American servicemen. Ike eagerly supplied his favorite prayer. He wrote:

> [I] once heard a company commander repeating [this prayer] to his men, on a wet, cold night, just before starting a march to the front line. It struck me more forcibly than almost any other I have heard. Possibly the drama of the occasion had something to do with my

reactions, but in any event, it was a better prayer than I could compose. While I cannot repeat it verbatim, I am sending you the words that approximate the original.

"Almighty God, we are about to be committed to a task from which some of us will not return. We go willingly to this hazardous adventure because we believe that those concepts of human dignity, rights, and justice that Your Son expounded to the world, and which are respected in the government of our beloved country, are in peril of extinction from the earth. We are ready to sacrifice ourselves for our country and for our God. We do not ask, individually, for our safe return. But we earnestly pray that You will help each of us to his full duty. Permit none of us to fail a comrade in the fight. Above all, sustain us in our conviction in the justice and righteousness of our cause so that we may rise above all terror of the enemy and come to You, if called, in the humble pride of the good soldier and in the certainty of Your infinite mercy. Amen."[1]

One commentator said of Ike's contribution to the book, "[The prayer] is remarkable for two reasons. First, it ties the work of war to the teachings of Jesus. Second, it shows an American officer of the highest rank identifying his service with the principles of the Son of God."[2]

This prayer demonstrates that, for Ike, religious faith went far deeper than a merely civic or deistic appreciation of the divine. It contains profound and explicitly Christian doctrine: theology of Christ, the Incarnation, and the necessity of the Christian life being lived in accordance with Christ's teachings. This prayer puts Ike squarely within Christian orthodoxy.[3]

During his time as a leader in World War II, Ike spoke elsewhere about the importance of prayer. In 1943, during the preparation stages of Operation Avalanche, the emotional strain on Ike was enormous. He described his stomach as being a constant knot, like a "clenched fist." When he finally gave permission for the invasion to proceed, Ike said there was nothing he could do but to turn to heaven and say a "silent prayer for the safety and success of all the troops under his command."[4] Ike later wrote to Mamie, "There was nothing we could do but pray, desperately."[5] Ike clearly lived within the Christian paradox that people must constantly strive to live with virtue while acknowledging in faith that all of our efforts are useless without God's grace.

Shortly after Operation Avalanche, Marshall promoted Ike to Supreme Commander of European Operations.[6] This placed him in charge of Operation Overlord, the Allied assault on Nazi-occupied France. On June 6, 1944, as over 150,000 Allied troops prepared to move on the Normandy countryside, both by air and by sea, Ike commissioned his troops with the following words:

Soldiers, Sailors, and Airmen of the Allied Expeditionary Forces: You are about to embark upon the Great Crusade, toward which we have striven these many months. The eyes of the world are upon you. The hope and prayers of liberty-loving people everywhere march with you. In company with our brave Allies and brothers-in-arms on other fronts you will bring about the destruction of the Nazi war machine, the elimination of Nazi tyranny over oppressed peoples of Europe, and security for ourselves in a free world.

Your task will not be an easy one. Your enemy is well-trained, well-equipped, and battle-hardened. He will fight savagely.

But this is the year 1944. Much has happened since the Nazi triumphs of 1940–41 [including conquests of Norway, Denmark, Belgium, Holland, France, Luxembourg, Yugoslavia, Greece and North Africa, plus the invasion of Russia, nearly bringing Great Britain to its knees at Dunkirk, and previous victories in Poland, Czechoslovakia, and Austria[7]]. The United Nations has inflicted upon the Germans great defeats, in open battle, man-to-man. Our air offensive has seriously reduced their strength in the air and their capacity to wage war on the ground. Our home fronts have given us an overwhelming superiority in weapons and munitions of war, and placed at our disposal great reserves of trained fighting men. The tide has turned. The free men of the world are marching together in victory.

I have full confidence in your courage, devotion to duty, and skill in battle. We will accept nothing less than full victory.

Good luck! And let us all beseech the blessing of Almighty God upon this great and noble undertaking.[8]

Filled with Christian imagery, from his portrayal of good versus evil to his calling upon the blessing of God, Ike's charge shows that he knew what was at stake on that fateful day. The consequences of failure went far beyond the lives needlessly sacrificed. If Operation Overlord failed, it would take at least another year to plan and execute a second attempt at an invasion.

In 1944, Nazi Germany was on the ropes, with whole armies trapped in the Soviet Union and crumbling defenses in Western Europe. A D-Day failure would buoy the Nazi system, and the war would drag out indefinitely as the Nazis advanced with the extermination of the remaining Jews in their concentration camps, as well as possibly develop nuclear weapons. The whole world knew that this was a turning point in the war; back in America, millions listened to President Roosevelt's D-Day prayer and flocked to their places of worship to beseech the Lord's blessing on the young men storming the beaches of Normandy.

Roosevelt's prayer, broadcast live, was not bashful. His words, in many ways, echoed Ike's on the gravity of the mission upon which the Allied forces had embarked.

Almighty God: Our sons, pride of our Nation, this day have set upon a mighty endeavor, a struggle to preserve our Republic, our religion, and our civilization, and to set free a suffering humanity.

Lead them straight and true; give strength to their arms, stoutness to their hearts, steadfastness in their faith.

They will need Thy blessings. Their road will be long and hard. For the enemy is strong. He may hurl back our forces. Success may not come with rushing speed, but we shall return again and again; and we know that by Thy grace, and by the righteousness of our cases, our sons will triumph.

100

They will be sore tried, by night and by day, without rest—until the victory is won. The darkness will be rent by noise and flame. Men's souls will be shaken with the violences of war. . . .

Some will never return. Embrace these, Father, and receive them, Thy heroic servants, into Thy kingdom.

Roosevelt continued, calling for the American people to do their part:

And for us at home—fathers, mothers, children, wives, sisters, and brothers of brave men overseas—whose thoughts and prayers are ever with them—help us, Almighty God, to rededicate ourselves in renewed faith in Thee in this hour of great sacrifice.

Many people have urged that I call the Nation into a single day of prayer. But because the road is long and the desire is great, I ask that our people devote themselves in a continuance of prayer. As we rise to each new day, and again when each day is spent, let words of prayer be on our lips, invoking Thy help to our efforts. . . .

With Thy blessing, we shall prevail over the unholy forces of our enemy. Help us to conquer the apostles of greed and racial arrogancies. Lead us to the saving of our country, and with our sister nations in a world unity that will spell a sure peace, a peace invulnerable to the schemings of unworthy men. And a peace that will let all of men live in freedom, reaping the just rewards of their honest toil.

Thy will be done, Almighty God.

Amen.[9]

While Roosevelt was calling the nation to prayer, Ike shouldered the burden of the invasion entirely on his own. On the night of June 5, he even drafted a message taking full responsibility if the mission failed and, perhaps nervously, misdated it July 5. Thankfully, he never had to send it. God would answer Ike's prayer and the prayers of the free world. The invasion succeeded, though the human toll was horrific: from D-Day, June 6, through August 21, the Allied troops suffered approximately 209,000 casualties.[10] While the war in Europe dragged on for months, even with the very costly Battle of the Bulge, the Nazi war machine's back was broken, and Hitler's troops never regained the confidence that had helped make them seem invincible for five years. Less than a year after the D-Day invasion, Germany surrendered.

On April 12, 1945, with the Allied forces on the march to Berlin, Ike went with fellow generals Omar Bradley and George S. Patton to visit the Ohrdruf camp, an annex of the infamous concentration camp at Buchenwald. Another man was also there: Army Chaplain Edward L. R. Elson. There, camp survivors showed the men the more than three thousand naked, emaciated, and rotting corpses scattered across the ground. General Patton, who had fought in some of the bloodiest battles of both World War I and World War II, vomited as he looked out over the horror. Observers wrote that Ike's face was white and frozen.[11] Years later, General Bradley recalled the scene in haunting detail, writing, "The smell of death overwhelmed us even before we passed through the stockade."[12]

The experience at Ohrdruf shook Ike to the core. After his visit, seeing the depths of human evil firsthand, he ordered that every nearby unit not on the front lines visit the death camp. Ike said, "We are told the American soldier does not know what he is fighting for. Now, at least, he will know what he is fighting against."[13] Later, Ike wrote to Mamie, "I never dreamed that such cruelty, bestiality, and savagery could really exist in this world!" He went on to call it an "indescribable horror."[14]

In his book *Crusade in Europe*, Ike would write,

> I visited every nook and cranny of the camp because I felt it my duty to be in a position from then on to testify at first hand about these things in case there ever grew up at home the belief or assumption that "the stories of Nazi brutality were just propaganda."[15]

There can be little doubt that what Ike saw—and photographers fully documented at Ohrdruf—bolstered his conviction that a world without faith would lead to horrific consequences for humankind.

On May 8, 1945, Ike accepted Germany's surrender. Roosevelt had died a month earlier from a cerebral hemorrhage, not living long enough to witness the surrender himself, and Vice President Harry S. Truman assumed the presidency.

In the summer of 1945, the new president had to make a difficult decision. He ultimately chose to have American planes drop atomic bombs on Hiroshima and Nagasaki. This unequivocal threat of total destruction helped end World War II but ushered in a new age with new terrors: the Atomic Age, fraught with the fear of imminent extermination. In November of that year, Ike, now serving as Army Chief of Staff, addressed the American Legion in Chicago about this new worldwide atmosphere of dread and uncertainty. Talking to the veterans in attendance, Ike spoke of the destruction he had seen unleashed on the world during World War II, while also offering hope for humanity, saying that the world had entered into a scientific age that contained "unimaginable threats for civilization." He included a spiritual component, saying that if such a day came when science had made humans capable of mass destruction, "the only hope for the world as we know it will be complete spiritual regeneration" and "a strengthening of moral fiber that will place upon all men self-imposed determination to respect the rights of others."[16]

In the following months and years, Ike continued to develop and articulate a philosophy that positioned faith and religion as a central part of American democracy and a counterweight to the terrors of the twentieth century, particularly the coming Cold War with the Soviet Union.

In October 1946, as Army Chief of Staff, a year after his address to the American Legion, Ike was even more vocal about the importance of faith and religion in a message to the sixteenth annual convention of the Chaplains Association in Washington, DC. He told the chaplains that they had a great responsibility and that "religion has always been the most effective process of developing human character strong enough to forget the motivation of selfishness and act on the larger concept of duty to God, humanity, and to country." He concluded that religion nurtured "men of faith, men of hope, men of love," and such men would be needed to build a "new world reflecting the glory of God."[17]

A month later, in a speech to the Congress of Industrial Organizations in Atlantic City, Ike talked about his "rooted belief in our democratic way of life." He spoke of how Americans enjoyed that way of life because of the suffering, privation, and courage of those who went before and who established it as the basis of American government. He concluded,

> It insures our right to meet here together; to express our individual views; to work in a calling of our own choosing; to worship our God according to our consciences. The basic justification of the United States Army is your determination and mine that we shall live undisturbed in that democracy.[18]

In this speech, Ike clearly stated that the right of conscience was the foundation for all our other freedoms, such as freedom of speech, freedom to work, and, in particular, freedom of religion. In addition, Ike deemed that this right was so essential to America's founders that they suffered and in some cases put their very lives on the line to ensure that the new republic could survive.

At a meeting of the Jewish Theological Seminary of America on September 27, 1948, Ike (by this time serving as president of Columbia University) reasserted the importance of the "freedom for each of us to worship God in his own way." In these fascinating remarks, he also traced democracy back to the Old Testament and linked freedom to the existence of the soul, saying, "We believe because men have been born with a soul they have inalienable rights and none can take them away. These rights can never be destroyed." He concluded, "Free government cannot be explained in any other terms but religious. Our founding fathers had to refer to the Creator in order to make their revolutionary experiment make sense."[19]

Finally, in 1950, a year before he would assume the position of Supreme Commander of the North American Treaty Organization (NATO) in Europe, Ike gave a speech directed straight at Eastern Europe, where the Iron Curtain, as Churchill called it, had descended and state-forced atheism was spreading. In his remarks, Ike made the bold claim that "no human, whatever his position . . . merits more respect than any other animal of the woods or fields unless we accept without reservation the brotherhood under the Fatherhood of God."[20]

So, after years of silence on the subject, Ike became increasingly vocal about religion and matters of faith through the 1940s and 1950s. The question that arises is this: Was Ike commenting on faith from his own personal convictions, or was he simply expressing a civic sentiment that faith played a key role in stabilizing and strengthening society?

The second explanation—that Ike's rhetoric on religion during these years was a result of his increased political and civil standing rather than his own personal faith—has long been popular. Biographers and writers such as Kevin Kruse and Jean Edward Smith have championed this view.[21] One piece of evidence that advocates of this theory often cite is the fact that, though Ike acknowledged prayer as a central part of his life and never lost the Bible knowledge developed in his youth, he did not formally join a church or get baptized until after his presidential inauguration in 1953.

But these speeches and rhetoric reveal more than a general cultural sense that religion is a good thing. They are the carefully considered thoughts of a man who believed firmly that religion was at the center of the American experiment—that the whole system hinged on the belief that humans are not mere animals but creatures of dignity created by the Almighty. This belief and the respect for life that accompanied it gave the United States the moral strength to stand up to the atheistic Soviet Union during a time of terror, when the potential of another, even more brutal war loomed constantly.

In 1951, Ike contributed again to a prayer book, this time for servicemen stationed in Korea. He originally planned to select Psalm 23, but another contributor had already made that choice. He then submitted the words to his favorite hymn, "Lead, Kindly Light," a choice that speaks beautifully to a soldier's experience in any war but was particularly fitting to the early days of the Cold War.

> Lead, kindly Light, amid th' encircling gloom;
> Lead thou me on!
> The night is dark, and I am far from home;
> Lead thou me on!
> Keep thou my feet; I do not ask to see
> The distant scene—one step enough for me.
> I was not ever thus, nor pray'd that thou
> Shouldst lead me on.
> I love to choose and see my path; but now,
> Lead thou me on!
> I loved the garish day, and, spite of fears,
> Pride ruled my will. Remember not past years.
> So long thy pow'r hath blest me, sure it still
> Will lead me on.
> O'er moor and fen, o'er crag and torrent, till
> The night is gone.
> And with the morn those angel faces smile,
> While I have loved long since, and lost awhile![22]

Speeches and favorite hymns notwithstanding, Ike's religious beliefs remained unclear to many for some reason. This lack of clarity became more pronounced as Ike's public profile rose and his responsibilities increased. By the early 1950s Ike, now serving as Supreme Allied Commander of NATO while on leave from Columbia University, found himself increasingly mentioned as a potential president. With this speculation came heightened scrutiny, and reporters, citizens, and political foes and allies began to wonder what, if anything, Ike believed in.

8

The Approach to the Presidency

After World War II, America was unequivocally the most powerful nation on earth. The war effort had reinvigorated the US economy and its manufacturing sector after the Great Depression of the 1930s. American infrastructure remained unscathed while six years of devastating war had left Europe in shambles.

Even though the Allies emerged victorious, both England and France had a massive rebuilding job on their hands. Simultaneously, a new threat was rearing its head in the east as America's ally of necessity, the Soviet Union, quickly made its expansionist plans known. Just a few months after the end of World War II, the USSR swallowed up the Eastern European countries the Allies had liberated from the tyranny of the Nazis and locked them away behind the Iron Curtain.

This was the situation when the leaders of the Allied Powers met in 1945 in Potsdam, the capital of the German state of Brandenburg, to plot the future of postwar Germany. One of those leaders was Ike.

It was in the back of a car at Potsdam, riding to and from the meetings with General Omar Bradley and President Truman, that Ike received an astonishing offer. Truman, the sitting president whom everyone assumed would eagerly run for reelection, told Ike directly that if he decided to throw his hat into the ring in 1948, he would step aside and the presidency would be Ike's to have.[1]

Truman's proposition was a testament to Ike's stateside status as one of the great heroes of World War II, if not the greatest. The Washington, DC, rumor mill, which ran nonstop even in those days before the internet and 24/7 news networks, was full of chatter about Ike's political future. Ike did nothing to dispel the chatter because, for the most part, it was true: he was becoming interested in a political career. Nevertheless, Ike replied to Truman's tempting offer by saying, "Mr. President, I don't know who will be your opponent for the presidency, but it will not be [me]."[2]

Later, on July 25, 1947, Truman would write in his diary about another conversation he had with Ike:

> Ike and I think MacArthur expects to make a Roman triumphal return to the US a short time before the Republican Convention meets in Philadelphia. I told Ike that if he did that he (Ike) should announce for the nomination for President on the Democratic ticket and that I'd be glad to be in second place, or Vice-President. I like the Senate anyway. Ike and I would be elected and my family and myself would be happy outside this great white jail, known as the White House. Ike won't quot [sic] me and I won't quote him.[3]

Nevertheless, Ike ultimately chose not to run, and in one of the great political upsets in American history, Truman was reelected in 1948, narrowly defeating front-runner Thomas Dewey, the Republican governor of New York. Truman had to deal with numerous defections from Southern Democrats, led by Strom Thurmond, over the inclusion of civil rights in the Democratic platform, and progressives, led by Roosevelt's former vice president Henry A. Wallace, who felt Truman was too "hawkish" in his conduct of the new Cold War. This made Truman's victory even more stunning and demoralizing for the Republicans.

As 1952 approached, Ike's name was once again on the lips of political operatives around the country, especially after the bitter taste of Dewey's defeat, just when the GOP thought they could finally end the Democrats' sixteen-year stranglehold on the White House. The Republicans wanted—and needed—an American hero such as Ike.

Ike's supporters had also been quietly stoking the fire of a "Draft Ike" movement, and Ike, while not actively seeking the presidency, did nothing to deter their efforts.

It is likely that one of the reasons Ike considered a run in 1952 was his opposition to the staunch isolationism of the presumed GOP front-runner, Senator Robert Taft of Ohio.

Taft, the son of former President and Supreme Court Chief Justice William Howard Taft, had first tried for the GOP nomination in 1940, losing to Wendell Willkie. He tried again in 1948 but came up short against Dewey. Despite these losses, he was widely viewed as the strongest GOP candidate for 1952, largely because in those days candidates secured nominations through backdoor deals between party brokers—the so-called "smoke-filled room"—rather than by earning votes in the primaries. As a result, a few losses in a candidate's record did not then spell certain defeat as they do today.

Taft and other Midwest Republicans were fearful that the stationing of American troops in Europe would quickly lead America into another European conflict.[4] Ike, on the other hand, felt very strongly that America needed to maintain the World War II alliance, which had evolved into the North Atlantic Treaty Organization (NATO), and embrace its new international role as leader of the free world.[5]

Taft's isolationist views troubled Ike, especially Taft's refusal to endorse and advocate for American postwar international engagement in Europe and the rest of the world. Ike, as Supreme Allied Commander of NATO in Europe, was well aware of the seething atmosphere of the continent and of the imminent threat posed by the Soviet Union. Contrary to Taft's isolationism, Ike believed that American involvement in Europe was essential to ensure that another world war did not break out. For him, the liberation of Europe for which he fought in World War II was at stake.

111

In 1951, shortly after becoming the Supreme Allied Commander of NATO in Europe, Ike met with Taft. At first, Ike was encouraged. He hoped that because of the meeting, the United States would be solidly supporting NATO by the time he got to Europe. He said plainly that if he received forthright assurance that this would happen, he was ready to "kill off any speculation about me as a candidate for the Presidency."[6]

Ike recalled that he asked two staff officers to draft a statement, which he would issue that evening, "on the assumption that Senator Taft would agree that collective security should be adopted as a definite feature of our foreign policy."[7] He continued, "My statement was so strong that, if made public, any political future for me thereafter would be impossible."[8]

He told Taft that he would gladly continue in his new role without seeking office if the Senator would answer yes to Ike's question, "Would you, and your associates in the Congress, agree that collective security is necessary for us in Western Europe—and will you support this idea as a bi-partisan policy?"[9]

But the meeting became increasingly tense as it quickly became evident that Taft was not going to give Ike the assurances he wanted. Ike wrote that he used "all the persuasion I could," but Taft would not commit to supporting NATO, and his lack of assurance "aroused [Ike's] fears that isolationism was stronger in Congress than [he] had previously suspected."

Once the meeting ended, Ike called in his assistants, took out the drafted statement that he would not run for president, and tore it up in front of them. Ike realized that he might have no other choice but to throw his hat into the ring for the 1952 GOP nomination.[10]

———————

The battle for the 1952 GOP nomination was a struggle between sharp contrasts: the internationally minded, pragmatic Ike and the idealistic, isolationist Taft. Taft had long been an opponent of American involvement in foreign affairs, only supporting World

War II after the attack on Pearl Harbor. In addition, Taft's "chilly" demeanor was well-known, making the normally reticent Ike seem warm and fatherly in comparison.[11]

Like many other national elections, the battle quickly became ugly. When Ike stepped onto the public stage as a potential presidential candidate, the press and his political opponents turned their attention to digging up all the details they could about his past. Much of his family history and his personal life, which he had kept out of the public eye for decades, began to be analyzed, scrutinized, and soon criticized, as the details of Ike's past provided fuel for his political opponents. Supporters of Taft and other isolationist candidates launched an attack alleging that Ike was a communist sympathizer, among other things.[12]

Ike's record as a devoted American and a defender of democracy made it impossible for the allegations of communism to stick, so Taft's supporters turned to another line of attack: Ike's faith. Thanks to his mother's adoption of the controversial Jehovah's Witnesses movement, they found plenty of material ripe for picking.

Though Ida had passed away in 1946, Ike's own reticence had left the door open for wild speculation, the spread of misinformation, and potential embarrassment, especially since, as the primaries approached, he had yet to join a church or identify with a particular denomination. Some have speculated that the transitory nature of Army life had made it impossible for him and Mamie to make a long-term commitment to any church body. Others said that Ike disliked what he viewed as the propensity of mainline Protestant churches to talk more about politics than faith.[13]

This speculation about Ike's faith was not new. As far back as the early 1940s, Ida's devotion to the Jehovah's Witnesses movement had gained the attention of the press. In the spring of 1942, the *Wichita Beacon* reported that Ida, along with six hundred others, had traveled to that city to attend a Jehovah's Witness assembly.[14] This small-town newspaper story spread far enough to come to Ike's attention, even as he was in the midst of fighting World War II.[15]

113

Even though he was far from Kansas, Ike was well aware that Ida's beliefs included doctrines that would strike Americans as not only unusual but even dangerous, and her adherence to them could cause problems for Ike's public image as the leader of the Allied forces in Europe.

During the height of the war, the Jehovah's Witnesses, backed by the American Civil Liberties Union, went before the US Supreme Court to opt out of performing the Pledge of Allegiance to the flag in public schools. On June 14, 1943, the Court upheld their right under the First Amendment to do so.[16]

Nearly a decade later, in the midst of the Cold War as the national atmosphere was thick with fear verging on paranoia, the Jehovah's Witnesses' prohibitions on saluting the flag and serving in the military were dramatically outside of the American mainstream. Thus, any proof that Ike possessed such beliefs could potentially disqualify him as a presidential candidate.

Ike was not the only Eisenhower male who was aware of the risk posed by Ida's faith and beliefs. Shortly after Ida's death in 1946, Milton discreetly removed five decades' worth of *The Watch Tower* issues from the Eisenhower home in Abilene and left them in the care of one of the women who had originally introduced Ida to the Jehovah's Witnesses.[17] However, not all Ida's ties to the Jehovah's Witnesses could be concealed as easily, and in 1952, Ike's critics unleashed all kinds of allegations based on her religious convictions in an effort to discredit him.

In February, even before Ike officially declared his candidacy and a month before the critical New Hampshire primary, the rumors began to swirl. An Army-intelligence-officer-turned-journalist named Robert Williams dug up and reprinted the 1942 *Wichita Beacon* article in his political newsletter, *The Williams Intelligence Summary*. In his commentary on the article, Williams openly questioned Ike's suitability for the presidency, and for evidence pointed to Ida, whom he described as a "crusading Jehovah's Witness" who had worked with "other members of that strange sect, handing out their literature on street corners."[18]

He continued:

The fact that [Ike's] mother was one of that particular sect who refuse to fight for their country, refuse to recognize national sovereignty, and thus would negotiate the very existence of our very country, cannot fail to be of extreme interest to every American. This is indeed a strange background for a man who aspires to become President of the United States.[19]

Williams's own beliefs were quite far out of the mainstream; he was a Holocaust denier who later suggested that Ike was head of a Zionist cabal. Nevertheless, he was not alone in circulating unsubstantiated rumors about Ike's religious beliefs. His opponents also circulated a photo of Ike from the 1915 edition of the West Point yearbook, the *Howitzer*, along with the yearbook's caption describing Ike as a "terrible Swedish Jew." At the time, the caption was considered a class joke, but in the heated atmosphere of the primary election, Ike's opponents reported it as fact, using it as ammunition for their attacks on his religious views, especially since anti-Semitism was still an issue in many areas of the country.

Gerald L. K. Smith, known for anti-Semitic views, also spread the "Swedish Jew" falsehood and therefore declared Ike was unfit for office.[20] Gerald Burton Winrod, a pro-Nazi writer out of Wichita, went as far as to proclaim that Ike was the "choice" of the International Jewish Banking Fraternity in the 1952 presidential election.[21]

While many of these individuals, just like the conspiracy theorists of today, operated on the fringes of society, their rumors continue even to this day, as a quick internet search will pull up a number of references to Ike's alleged Jewish ties. In addition, their constant drumbeat of these charges was loud enough to cause many Americans to speculate about what Ike's beliefs really were.

Other equally improbable rumors began to circulate that Ike was Catholic. This rumor would have severely damaged his candidacy, especially after the disastrous presidential runs of Al Smith in the 1920s, in which his Roman Catholic faith had become an issue, especially in rural areas of the United States. It would not be until the election of John F. Kennedy in November 1960 that Roman Catholicism would no longer be a disqualifying factor for a potential presidential candidate.

The source of these rumors was the 1946 book *San Antonio: City in the Sun*, written by a reporter named Green Peyton, which chronicled San Antonio's history, including Ike's time at Camp Sam Houston back in 1916.[22] Peyton inaccurately, and without malice, wrote that Ike was Catholic because he had coached the St. Louis College (now St. Mary's University) football team after he graduated from West Point. To his credit, Peyton acknowledged the error and set the record straight in 1952, saying,

> Like many Army officers, General Eisenhower has taken pains in the past not to mention either his political preference or his religious affiliations in biographical reference books. Until circumstances brought him into public life, he considered that they were his own business. But army men with whom I've talked tell me that it's well known in the service that Eisenhower always worshipped in a Protestant church.[23]

As those early rumors began to swirl in the first months of 1952, Ike had not yet decided if he was even going to run for the Republican nomination for president. While the meeting with Taft resulted in his serious consideration of the idea, ultimately it was through the encouragement of a small, informal group of advisors, referred to affectionately as the "gang," that Ike finally decided to run.

The "gang" included notables such as Clifford Roberts, a banker and avid golfer like Ike who also happened to be the chairman of the Augusta National Golf Club (home of the Masters and cofounded by famous golfer Bobby Jones), and William E. Robinson, an executive with the *New York Herald-Tribune*, who later became president of the Coca-Cola Company.

Roberts recalled Ike was the most patriotic American he had ever known, and he had never forgotten that he had been educated at public expense. In Roberts's words, despite his continued indecision about running for president, Ike's duty to country came ahead of all other considerations in his life. Roberts wrote, "That is why he could not take the easy way out by issuing one of those 'If elected, I will not serve' statements."[24]

Roberts also remembered that Ike had been shocked by Dewey's defeat and believed that the socialistic trend, in Ike's view, of the Roosevelt administration needed to be curtailed.[25]

The gang also included Henry R. Luce, the founder of *Time* magazine, and his wife, Clare Booth Luce, the formidable former Congresswoman from the state of Connecticut, both deeply enamored with the idea of Ike as president. It was Clare Booth Luce who took note of Ike's silence on his religious beliefs and wondered if it would become an electoral liability.

According to her recollections, Mrs. Luce met with Ike in the spring of 1952 to discuss his potential candidacy. She brought up the issue of Ike's faith and how his silence, regardless of his speeches, about more specific matters was a potential obstacle to his prospects. It was widely known that this topic touched a nerve with Ike. One of Ike's aides warned Clare,

> He goes through the roof when people ask him what his denomination is, what church he belongs to. We've tried to discuss it with him, and he bawls us out and says it's not any of our damn business, [because] religion is an absolutely private matter.[26]

Despite this warning, Mrs. Luce raised the issue with Ike during their conversation. When she broached the topic, he exploded in anger, just as his aides predicted. She recalled, "[Ike] jumped to his feet, and got red to the roots of his hair."[27] Ike then openly talked about his faith, saying,

> Clare, do you think I could have fought my way through this war, ordered thousands of fellows to their deaths, if I couldn't have gone

down on my knees and talked with God and begged him to support me and make me feel what I was doing was right for myself and the world? Why, I couldn't live a day of my life without God.[28]

Mrs. Luce learned that Ike was not hostile to being part of a church. Rather, he was deeply opposed to the possibility that if he began to speak more openly about religion and associated himself with a particular church, people would perceive it as a political move. In his mind, by maintaining his lifelong habit of reticence about faith, he was remaining consistent to his beliefs. He did not want anyone—even himself—to suspect that he was using religion to promote himself. He told her, "I would have nothing but contempt for myself if I were to join a church in order to be nominated president of the United States. I think it would be an unbearable piece of hypocrisy."[29]

Mrs. Luce would not back down. She pressed him, asking, "What would happen on Sunday mornings when the young were told that they have to go to church and they responded with, 'Why do I have to go to church? The President of the United States . . . refuses to go to church'?"[30]

That question struck a chord with Ike. He mulled over it, and eventually agreed that joining and more regularly attending a church was a "constructive and necessary thing you have to do for the morals of and religion of the rising generation, not to mention your own contemporaries."[31] Mrs. Luce, according to her recollection, suggested that Ike attend services at a Presbyterian church in which Mamie, raised in that denomination, would find herself naturally comfortable. Ike was open to the idea and, as circumstances would play out, he would eventually take her up on her recommendation.

This is not the only account of how the presidential campaign prompted Ike to consider becoming more expressive about his personal faith and not just a collective American faith. Before Ike's conversations with Robert Taft and Clare Booth Luce, another key figure in Ike's faith journey entered his life: Rev. Billy Graham.

— 9 —

Spiritual Renewal

n 1951, Ike began corresponding with a youthful evangelist from North Carolina named Billy Graham. They met through a mutual friend, the reclusive Texas oil baron Sid Richardson.

Richardson, who had first met Graham during Graham's 1951 Fort Worth crusade, shared a letter from him with Ike outlining why Graham believed Ike should run for president.[1] Graham, who might have been familiar with Ike's speeches after the war, wrote, "The American people have come to a point where they want a man with honesty, integrity, and spiritual power. I believe the General has it. I hope you can persuade him to put his hat in the ring."[2]

Ike's interest was piqued, and he wrote back to Graham, marking the letter "personal and confidential" because he did not want it quoted in the press. Ike congratulated Graham on his successful efforts to "fight for the old-fashioned virtues of integrity, decency, and straightforwardness in public life." He added, "I thank the Almighty that such inspired persons as yourself are ready and willing to give full time and energy to this purpose."[3]

These initial conversations with Graham came at a time when Ike remained reluctant to run. He told Graham that his role as Supreme

Commander of NATO was too important. Graham persisted. Nancy Gibbs and Michael Duffy, in *The Preacher and the Presidents*, write that Graham responded to this letter and continued to press his case. Graham conveyed to Ike that a district judge had "confided in me that if Washington is not cleaned out in the next two to three years, we are going to enter a period of chaos that could bring about our downfall." Graham then added that the judge went on to say, "Sometimes I wonder who is going to win the battle first: the barbarians beating at our gates from without, or the termites of immorality from within."[4]

Graham told Ike that he would be praying for him, specifically that God would guide him in the "greatest decision" of his life, a decision on which, in Graham's words, "could well rest the destiny of the Western world."[5]

Ike was uncertain about what to do with Graham's letter. He wrote to Richardson, "That was the damnedest letter I ever got."[6] Richardson sent Graham to meet Ike, and an alliance quickly formed between the fiery Southern Baptist evangelist and the taciturn Ike.

As Supreme Commander of NATO and the leader of the Allied forces in Europe in World War II, Ike, perhaps more than anyone else, was keenly aware of the geopolitical climate of the Cold War. That awareness brought him to the conclusion that if America was to win the Cold War, it would have to be on spiritual terms. The religious faith that shaped America—in contrast with the atheistic Soviet Union—would be the key to victory. The difference was that faith not only brings hope but also provides a source for people to turn to in difficult times, while nothing in the Soviet system could provide anything similar. He also understood that it is faith that brings out people's nobler instincts. Ike verbalized these thoughts to Graham, saying,

> In spite of the difficulties of the problems we have, I ask you this one question. If each of us in his own mind would dwell more upon those simple virtues—integrity, courage, self-confidence, and unshakeable

belief in his Bible—would not some of these problems tend to simplify themselves? Would not we, after having done our very best with them, be content to leave the rest with the Almighty?[7]

Graham and Ike met in person for the first time in early spring 1952, while Ike was in Paris, still in his role as the Supreme Commander of NATO. Graham recalled that what he remembered most was Ike's smile, his handshake, and the "curious" way Ike looked at him, as though Ike really did not know what to do with the handsome North Carolinian evangelist.[8]

The meeting came about through the efforts of Richardson, who was still trying to convince Ike to run for president. In his comments at the Eisenhower Centennial Celebration in October 1990, Graham recalled, "I did not know whether he was a Republican or a Democrat, but I told him that I thought that any man who was loved and respected by so many Americans should at least offer himself."[9]

The two men talked candidly about the spiritual health of the United States. Ike was perhaps more open with Graham about his faith than he had ever been with anyone else, even touching on the nature of his spiritual life during those long and difficult early years in the military. Graham recalled, "I talked to him about religious faith. I'll never forget that he looked down and seemed embarrassed to say that while he had been in the military he had rarely attended chapel or had much spiritual life."[10]

Despite the closeness of their friendship, Ike still found it unnatural to speak freely about his beliefs, and much remained private. Gibbs and Duffy wrote that while Ike had a more strict religious upbringing than other modern presidents, his story was difficult to tell because of his mother's embrace of the Jehovah's Witnesses. It would take careful explanation, and Ike never wanted to come across as disrespectful toward his mother, especially since her beliefs rejected much of what Ike stood for. As a result, he never did tell the entire story to Graham.[11]

Though Ike had kept some things close to the chest, Graham greatly impressed him, and he took their conversation very seriously. Two days after the meeting with Graham, Ike wrote a long, confidential letter to the famous newspaper columnist Drew Pearson. In the letter, Ike wrote, "The more intimately I become familiar with the desperate difficulties that abound in the world today, the more convinced I am that solutions must be firmly based in spiritual and moral values."[12]

Graham and Ike did not meet again face-to-face until August 1952, after Ike had secured the GOP nomination. This next meeting took place at Denver's famous nineteenth-century landmark, the Brown Palace Hotel, which Ike had made his team's headquarters. Ike requested that Graham come see him to assist with his speeches, to which Ike wanted to add "a religious note."[13] Even now, nearly seventy years later, the Brown Palace Hotel looks much as it did in the 1950s. When one walks through the front door of the beautiful old hotel and sees the expansive and classic Victorian-era interior, it is easy to visualize Ike and Graham sitting at one of the tables or on a couch discussing matters of faith.

During this time, Graham tried to encourage Ike to share more about his faith in preparation for the rigorous questioning on the subject that he was sure to receive during the campaign for the general election. He asked Ike directly, "Do you still respect the religious teaching of your father and mother?" Ike admitted, "Yes, but I've gotten a long way from it."[14] Graham later wrote, "He told me that he had become disillusioned with the church early on when some preachers seemed to detour from spiritual essentials to merely social or secular matters."[15]

It was during a conversation with Graham that Ike finally consented to joining a church. At the same time, Ike reiterated that he did not want his decision to join a church perceived as a political move. He was quite sure that such a move would be the height of hypocrisy. Graham recalled that Ike told him, "If I join a church now, people will think I'm doing it to get votes, but I promise I will join a church whether I win or lose."[16]

Echoing Ike's feelings on the matter was his speechwriter, William Ewald, who recalled,

> He was not a hypocrite. He was not trying to display something that wasn't there, for the sake of votes or appealing to a constituency. He said he didn't see how in the world he could bear the burdens of the presidency without a belief in divine providence and leadership. It couldn't be done. That was a very genuine feeling of his.[17]

Once Ike had decided that he would join a church after the election, it did not take him long to choose a denomination. During that same meeting in Denver, Graham recalled that Ike asked him about churches in Washington in particular. Graham, who had recently held a crusade in Washington, DC, was familiar with the churches in the area and asked Ike what denomination would interest him. Ike replied, "Well, I don't have any particular denomination, but my wife is a Presbyterian, so I suppose we would feel at home with the Presbyterians."

With that information, Graham recommended two Presbyterian churches where he felt Ike could worship freely, and in Graham's words "be nourished with solid preaching from the Bible." Graham would later recall, "After his inauguration, he joined the National Presbyterian Church pastored by one of his former chaplains in Europe, Dr. Ed Elson."

Then Graham shared how that decision would lead to the most important personal decision Ike would ever make:

> Dr. Elson met with him on several occasions to talk with him about what it meant to be a member of a church and what it meant to be a Christian and to follow Christ. And I believe it was during these

sessions that Eisenhower made a personal commitment to Jesus Christ.[18]

As he left the Brown Palace Hotel that day, Graham presented Ike with an inscribed red Moroccan leather Bible, in which he carefully marked the margins and left notes about specific Scriptures for Ike to study. Ike kept that Bible by his bedside throughout his entire presidency.[19]

Graham would also recollect another encounter with Ike, about three years later, while Graham was visiting the Eisenhowers in Gettysburg. Mamie had not been feeling well, and Graham prayed for her. Afterward, they went to the den, and Ike asked Graham, "Billy, could you explain to me how a person can be sure when he dies he's going to heaven?"

According to Graham, he pulled out his New Testament and walked Ike through the passages that explained how salvation came through grace and "not by anything we can do for ourselves." Graham said later, "It was an interesting visit. And a very humbling one for me. I didn't feel that I could answer his question as well as others could have."[20]

Fourteen years later, when Ike was lying on his deathbed, Graham had another opportunity to answer his question.

———

In the days leading up to the election, Ike seemed to have at last reconciled himself to speaking more openly about his faith, and he began to flavor more of his speeches with a religious tone. He insisted that the essential difference between the United States and the Soviet Union was not economic or political but spiritual. This was a sentiment that Ike's Democratic opponent, Adlai Stevenson, did not convey, and Ike's rhetoric struck a chord with the electorate.

On November 4, 1952, Ike, in a landslide victory, became the thirty-fourth President of the United States, defeating Stevenson by an Electoral College margin of 442–89. The next several weeks included appointing his cabinet and preparing for the inauguration. Things were tumultuous. And as he had promised Graham, he would join a church just after the inauguration, National Presbyterian, scheduling his baptism for February 1, 1953.

The pastor of National Presbyterian, Edward L. R. Elson, was born on December 23, 1906, just outside of Pittsburgh in Monongahela, Pennsylvania. His father, LeRoy, was an engineer for the Pennsylvania Railroad. Edward described his father as an amateur philosopher and theologian, musically inclined, a regular Bible reader, and a churchgoer.

Edward studied music at Asbury College, a small Christian college in central Kentucky, where his sophomore class's motto was "100 percent for Christ." After graduation, he continued his studies at the University of Southern California, where he pursued a master's degree in theological studies.

In 1930, Dr. Elson was ordained and began a pastorate in Santa Monica. Eventually he served at La Jolla Presbyterian Church and was also a reserve chaplain in the Army. In 1941, he entered active duty. According to his wife, Helen, the day after the capture of infamous Dachau concentration camp, Dr. Elson entered it and saw firsthand the incredible brutality of the Nazis. The shattering experience haunted him for the rest of his life.[21] His daughter, Eleanor Elson Heginbotham, also recalled how the gruesome events of World War II affected Elson.

> He was also at the Battle of the Bulge, [and] in the Colmar Pocket. . . . All of that, particularly the death camps at which there were Christians as well as Jews, gave him nightmares all his life. He never forgot. The war was a terrible thing for a sensitive person like him. He had a physical ailment (a stomach problem) the rest of his life. . . . He had a drawer in which he had the pictures from Dachau. Although he had hidden the sad and terrible pictures from us, we knew where they were. They were just horrifying, as were the stories about

watching someone run toward him and fall down dead at his feet from the excitement of the release.[22]

Perhaps the most crucial of Elson's wartime duties was representing Ike at a meeting of the old German churches after the war. Helen Elson remembered,

> Edward had been [Ike's] senior chaplain in Germany at the end of World War II. He had represented General Eisenhower as his emissary at the convocation of the old German churches that were in existence during Hitler's time. The church leaders wanted the permission of General Eisenhower to hold their church meetings once again. General Eisenhower talked it over with Edward who knew the whole story of the German churches and knew who sacrificed their freedom in resistance to Hitler and who supported Hitler. . . . He wrote a notable article about the clergy at Dachau that was widely circulated. He [Elson] was in no mood to tell the German church leaders they could hold their services at that time.[23]

Dr. Elson described the aftermath of World War II as "a world in convulsion" which could only be healed by a "reawakening of the true human spirit"—a spiritual regeneration or renewal.[24] Once he returned stateside in 1946, Elson became the pastor of the Church of the Covenant (also known as Covenant Presbyterian) in Washington, DC, which a year later became, through a merger, National Presbyterian Church.

When it was time for Ike to choose a church, Dr. Elson's presence as the pastor of National Presbyterian likely had some influence on his decision. Billy Graham had also come to know Elson in the days leading up to his January 1952 Washington, DC, crusade.[25]

Beside Elson, many of Ike's professional colleagues and friends also attended the church. These individuals included FBI Director J. Edgar

Hoover; General Harold Bull, Assistant Chief of Staff under Ike; John Foster Dulles, Ike's Secretary of State (who served as an elder at the church); and Lt. General Willard Steward Paul, who served under Ike during the war and later served as a director of personnel and administration for the Army.[26]

Dr. Elson openly encouraged Ike to join National Presbyterian. On November 23, 1952, Dr. Elson wrote to Ike, who was staying at the Hotel Commodore in New York City, and personally invited him and Mamie to become members. He outlined the church's historical significance, tracing its origins to a congregation begun on the White House grounds in 1795, and expounded on the significant role the church had played in serving key federal leaders over the years. Elson also made a personal pitch, reminding Ike of his military service and of their shared experiences overseas during the war. He wrote candidly, "I am the only Presbyterian pastor in Washington having personally served you in the past."[27]

Ike soon received letters from other National Presbyterian congregants such as Paul Wooten, an elder at the church and the president of National Conference of Business Papers and Editors. Wooten also happened to be a friend of Ike's brother Milton. Senator Edward Martin of Pennsylvania, also a congregant of National Presbyterian, wrote to Ike as well and encouraged him to consider joining the church.[28]

Only days after his initial letter, Elson wrote to Ike again. In this letter, Elson restated his invitation for Ike and Mamie to attend National Presbyterian. He even offered to bring Hoover, Bull, and Wooten to New York to meet with Ike and talk to him about the church.[29]

Elson followed up with a number of calls and inquiries about Ike's church preference in DC and plans for preinaugural prayer activities. On December 2, 1952, Senator Arthur Vandenberg of Michigan, an Ike supporter and confidante, wrote to Elson at Ike's request, thanking the reverend for his interest but stating that a decision regarding a church was still under consideration.[30]

Also on December 2, Mamie's assistant Anne Wheaton wrote her the following memo:

> There have been several letters from Washington clergymen in reference to a Pre-Inaugural service and continued attendance at a chosen church. It is assumed that your choice would be a Presbyterian church.
>
> Dr. Edward R. Elson, Pastor of the National Presbyterian church has telephoned and written to the General (and he tells us he has written to you) urging the selection of his church.
>
> It would seem to be a logical choice. It is the recognized National Presbyterian Church, chosen by the General Assembly. It is located at 18th Street and N Street N.W. on a corner and has a side entrance, which is very helpful in establishing security. This church also has a brief 9 o'clock Sunday morning service which would allow time for other Sunday activities.
>
> Dr. Elson, the Pastor, was a military chaplain during the war and served at the post church which the General attended while in Europe. He has one of the most outstanding churches in Washington, is personally popular, and conducts an excellent church program.[31]

Ike apparently made his decision shortly thereafter, and word got to Elson that the Eisenhowers would join National Presbyterian. On December 9, Vandenberg received a letter from Elson, in response to one he had sent seven days earlier, in which the reverend expressed his joy that Ike and Mamie had chosen National Presbyterian as their church home.[32]

Shortly after the Elson letter to Vandenberg, Ike wrote to Elson to confirm his choice. In his letter, Ike mentioned, "preliminary details have been agreed upon" and promised an in-person conversation in the near future. A number of considerations apparently went into Ike's decision, made in concert with his advisors though likely also influenced by peers who were part of National Presbyterian. On December 21, Elson reassured Ike that, "it will be my purpose to serve your spiritual needs in every way possible; and . . . this relationship will never be allowed to be exploited for any other purpose."[33]

After Ike and Mamie made this decision, inauguration plans moved forward, including a service at National Presbyterian. The outline for this service foreshadowed the emphasis Ike's administration would put on nondenominational civil religion, as Ike made sure it included representatives from the Protestant, Catholic, and Jewish traditions.[34]

One thing Ike insisted happen *after* the election was a baptismal ceremony. Ike, being Ike, had requested a memo from Dr. Elson outlining the baptismal procedure.[35] Ike made it abundantly clear that he "would be joining the church in precisely the same way as any other unbaptized person."[36]

In a 2006 interview, Dr. Elson's daughter, Eleanor, remembered the events leading up to Ike's baptism and entry into membership at National Presbyterian.

In 1952, Eisenhower was elected and almost the first thing he did was to join our church. Why he was baptized there [National Presbyterian Church]—the only president in history to be baptized in office—is an interesting story. . . . Eisenhower's youth was spent with a deeply religious Mother. There is a debate about whether his family was River Brethren or Jehovah's Witnesses, which . . . embarrassed at least one of her sons. In any event, both of the religions believe in adult baptism, so Dwight Eisenhower was never baptized as a baby.

She continued about the reasons why Dr. Elson and National Presbyterian were a good fit for Ike:

[Ike] was invited by people in the church, mainly the military people, to join this church where this fine energetic preacher "preached a kind of muscular Christianity." That's what they said about Daddy. In other words, his was not a mamby-pamby, feminized, sentimentalized, rosy, huggy Christianity, but a real, practically militaristic Christianity. . . . And of course, Eisenhower already knew Daddy. So he decided to join the church.[37]

Three weeks before his baptism and entry into National Presbyterian, on January 12, Ike met with his cabinet-elect for a planning session at the Commodore Hotel in New York City. During the meeting, the group reviewed a draft of his inaugural speech, which contained a strong faith component. In a back-and-forth exchange with Harold Stassen, the director of the Foreign Operations Administration, Ike conveyed his intentions:

> I don't want to deliver a sermon. . . . But I firmly believe that our government, and the first thing we must remember about it, is that it is deeply embedded in a religious faith. Our forefathers said we hold that men are endowed by their Creator and unless you accept that sentence our form of government makes no sense.[38]

In New York, Billy Graham also met with Ike, who asked him for advice on the address. Ike told Graham, "You know, I think one of the reasons I was elected was to help this country spiritually. We need a spiritual revival."[39] Graham recommended Ike place his hand on 2 Chronicles 7:14 while taking the oath of office:

> If my people, which are called by my name, shall humble themselves and pray, and seek my face, and turn from their wicked ways; then I will hear from heaven, and will forgive their sin, and will heal their land.

Ike accepted Graham's recommendation but also decided to do something that would surprise even Graham.[40] As he had discussed with Dr. Elson, Ike arranged for a special church service for his incoming administration, held at National Presbyterian. The service opened with the hymn, "Oh God, Our Help in Ages Past." Dr. Elson prayed for Ike, "Grant unto Thy servant Dwight David Eisenhower, now and henceforth, health of body, serenity of soul, clarity of insight, soundness of judgment, a lofty moral courage, a sanctified stewardship of office, and a constant and confident faith in Thee."[41]

130

Dr. Elson wrote that then:

> From [the service] he went to his quarters and wrote a prayer of his own with which he began his address. It electrified the world and revealed a dimension in the new President previously less exposed.[42]

On an uncharacteristically balmy Washington morning, Dwight D. Eisenhower, the boy from the dusty streets of Abilene, stood with his hand on 2 Chronicles 7:14 and took the oath of office from Chief Justice Fred M. Vinson. Then he did what no other president had done before. He asked the crowd to pray with him, saying,

> My friends, before I begin the expression of those thoughts I deem appropriate to this moment, would you permit me the privilege of uttering a private little prayer of my own. And I ask that you bow your heads.

Ike then proceeded to pray:

> Almighty God, as we stand here at this moment my future associates in the executive branch join me in beseeching that Thou will make full and complete our dedication to the service of the people in this throng, and their fellow citizens everywhere.
>
> Give us, we pray, the power to discern clearly right from wrong, and allow our words and actions to be governed thereby, and by the laws of this land. Especially we pray that our concern shall be for all the people, regardless of station, race, or calling.
>
> May cooperation be permitted and be the mutual aim of those who, under the concepts of our Constitution, hold to differing political faiths; so that all may work for the good of our beloved country and Thy glory. Amen.[43]

Billy Graham recalled, "In spite of what a few commentators said, I had no part in his prayer. He wrote that prayer himself, and the whole country was encouraged and blessed by that prayer. He was not afraid to acknowledge God privately or publicly from that moment on."[44]

Ike's carefully composed prayer was only the beginning of the most emphatically religious American presidential inauguration of all time. As Ike delivered his first inaugural address, his entire speech revolved around religious faith and natural law. Some of the most notable references were:

> We are summoned by this honored and historic ceremony to witness more than the act of one citizen swearing his oath of service, in the presence of God. We are called as a people to give testimony in the sight of the world that the future shall belong to the free.

> In the swift rush of great events, we find ourselves groping to know the full sense and meaning of these times in which we live. In our quest of understanding, we beseech God's guidance.

> At such a time in history, we who are free must proclaim anew our faith. This faith is the abiding creed of our fathers. It is our faith in the deathless dignity of man, governed by eternal moral and natural laws. This faith defines our full view of life. It establishes, beyond debate, those gifts of the Creator that are man's inalienable rights, and that make all men equal in His sight.

> The enemies of this faith know no god but force, no devotion but its use. They tutor men in treason. They feed upon the hunger of others. Whatever defies them, they torture, especially the truth.

> No principle or treasure that we hold, from the spiritual knowledge of our free schools and churches to the creative magic of free labor and capital, nothing lies safely beyond this struggle. Freedom is pitted against slavery; lightness against the dark.

> A people that values its privileges above its principles soon loses both.

> The faith we hold belongs not to us alone, but to the free of all the world.[45]

While Ike had grown increasingly comfortable with talking about the role of religion in American society in the years directly after World War II, the 1952 election was a turning point in his faith. As Gibbs and Duffy wrote, "No future president, even the born-again evangelicals, would present themselves as the country's spiritual commander-in-chief in quite the way Eisenhower did."[46] They added, "To Eisenhower, there was a direct spiritual line between 'In God We Trust' and 'E Pluribus Unum.'"[47]

Ike's outspokenness on religious truths that emerged in his inaugural address persisted for the rest of his career as a public servant. It was not merely that Ike had found a winning rhetorical strategy; he had made a carefully considered choice that had its roots in his religious upbringing and his personal relationship with God. Ike would later remark to his friend and World War II correspondent/reporter Virgil Pinkley about his inaugural address:

> God has always been with me, but He had been even more strongly in my thoughts since the election. That is why I emphasized spiritual aspects of living in writing my inauguration address. Yet I didn't want to be preachy.
>
> From the time I was a boy, there was embedded in me a deep and abiding faith in God and His beneficence. . . . I read the Bible from cover to cover before I was nine—my mother gave me a gold watch for this—and have read it often since. Throughout my military life— especially before major battles—I prayed long and hard.
>
> My lifelong faith had to be part of my inauguration address. I felt strongly that the nation was becoming far too secular, that God was no longer a part of our daily life.[48]

On Sunday, February 1, 1953, before the formal church service, Dwight David Eisenhower, now the most powerful man in the world, humbled himself, confessed his faith in Jesus Christ, and was baptized in a private meeting. Only Ike, Mamie, Dr. Elson, and the session of National Presbyterian were present.

Dr. Elson's daughter, Eleanor, remembered the day:

> So they came for membership. But lo and behold, they couldn't join because Eisenhower hadn't been baptized. . . .
>
> The baptism was private, attended only by the Session and Mrs. Eisenhower. . . .The baptism was so private that it was almost secret, but his joining the church was very public. He did so with all the other people on the Sunday when new members were received, standing up saying, "I do, I do, I do, and I will" when asked the key questions about belief, then sitting back down. There was no special note of a president among the new communicants, but, of course, everyone knew he was part of that crowd.[49]

Dr. Elson asked Ike,

> Do you, Dwight David Eisenhower, confess your need of the forgiveness of sins, and do you confess your faith in Jesus Christ as Lord and Savior of your life? In this faith do you desire to be baptized, and in dependence upon His grace, do you promise to live the Christian life?

Ike responded "I do" as he knelt. Elson dipped his hand into the water, touched Ike's forehead, and declared, "Dwight David, I baptize thee in the name of the Father and the Son and of the Holy Spirit, and may the Lord defend you with His grace."

The session notes from February 1, 1953, noted,

> There appeared before the Session as candidate for membership in the Church Dwight David Eisenhower, who having confessed his Christian Faith and received the Sacrament of Christian Baptism, was upon motion duly made and seconded, admitted into the membership of the Church.[50]

After Ike's baptism, the 9:00 a.m. worship service started. Dr. Elson quickly noted during the service that he had other new members

134

beside the newly elected president and the first lady, so as not to draw special attention to Ike's decision.

A week later, Elson also told *Time* magazine that Ike was "a man of simple faith, who is sincere in his religious doctrine," and that Ike had "staked down his faith—this is his home church now."[51] Dr. Elson later commented on Ike's consistency in attending National Presbyterian, telling a nationwide television audience, "He just doesn't miss church."[52] His daughter recalled, "He came every Sunday he was here in Washington unless there was some major reason not to. He was very, very faithful. Mostly he came with Mamie, although she had some health problems, and sometimes he came without her."[53]

Ike's membership at National Presbyterian and baptism nearly did not happen. The week before, when he had attended church alone because Mamie had a cold, reporters from the Associated Press, *New York Times*, *Washington Post*, and several other news outlets had gathered along the back of the church to chronicle the president's attendance at his new church.

As a result, the *Washington Post* declared on the front page the next day, "Eisenhower Goes Alone to Church."[54] The attention, predictably, infuriated Ike. He had trusted Elson to not exploit his attendance and felt betrayed. He wrote in his diary that his presence at National Presbyterian "was being publicized by the pastor, to the hilt."[55] He reportedly told his press secretary, Jim Hagerty, to "go and tell that . . . minister that if he gives out one more story about my religious faith I won't join his church."[56]

Dr. Elson later denied feeding stories about Ike joining the church or his baptism to the media. He said that the media interest came from the fact that "nothing like this had happened before in American history."[57] Dr. Elson was correct that the spectacle of the baptism of a sitting head of state would rivet the nation. Even in days before social media and 24/7 cable news, such an event was big news and led to wall-to-wall coverage. After all, the last time in known history the leader of a country had been baptized while in office was in AD 496, when the Frankish king Clovis I converted to Catholicism.[58]

In defense of Dr. Elson, there was probably no way to keep Ike's baptism and church membership at National Presbyterian out of the public eye. The public and the press tend to be cynical, and often rightfully so, about candidates who approach their posts with formal, carefully articulated, and sometimes politically expedient confessions of faith. The fact that a head of state, after his election, would formalize his religion was difficult for the press to comprehend and fit into a narrative.

The press and others would never truly understand that Ike did not want people to perceive that his faith was for political gain. This lack of understanding is evident in the conflicting opinions about the genuineness of Ike's faith in the numerous biographies of his life.

It was also difficult to reconcile the Ike of the inauguration and his subsequent baptism with the man who had bitterly turned inward after the death of Icky, had remained silent about his faith for three decades, and had never made a commitment to an organized church.

But in the months and years ahead, it would become increasingly clear that Ike was a man of deep and sincere faith.

10

The President and the Pastor

I n January 1953, Dr. Elson wrote to Ike and reminded him that since the earliest days of the Republic, Congress had opened its daily sessions with prayer. Since Ike, in Elson's words, "symbolized today a moral resurgence and spiritual counter-offensive in our world," it would be appropriate to start cabinet meetings with an "invocation of God's presence and wisdom."[1] Dr. Elson offered to be the person leading the prayer.

Ike's Secretary of Agriculture, Ezra Taft Benson, also raised the idea of beginning the cabinet meetings with prayer. Ike agreed with Benson's suggestion, and from that time forward, all cabinet meetings started with prayer. Benson led the prayer at the first cabinet meeting at the Hotel Commodore on January 12, 1953, eight days before the inauguration.[2] Benson was the namesake of Ezra T. Benson, who was an original member of the Quorum of the Twelve Apostles of the Church of Jesus Christ of Latter-day Saints, also known as the Mormon Church.

Benson did not support Ike's candidacy, but regardless, Ike selected him to serve in his cabinet, the first time in a century that a person in such a high-ranking leadership position with a major religious group served in a presidential cabinet.[3]

While there were very significant theological differences between the Mormon Church and the Presbyterian beliefs of Ike and the majority of his cabinet, Benson often led the morning prayers. Later on in the presidency, Ike chose to start the cabinet meetings with a silent prayer.[4]

Benson's appointment was an excellent example of how Ike sought to be inclusive of all faith traditions in his call to revive religious faith in America. Ike's cabinet also included two active Methodists (Arthur Fleming, Secretary of Health, Education, and Welfare, and Robert B. Anderson, Secretary of the Treasury) and two Presbyterians (Douglas McKay, the Secretary of the Interior, and John Foster Dulles, the Secretary of State, whose son, Avery Dulles, joined the Jesuit order and became a prominent Catholic priest, eventually becoming a cardinal). While John Foster Dulles was not initially enthusiastic about his son's conversion to Roman Catholicism and joining the priesthood, he later found his son's priesthood "very helpful" in dealing with Catholic foreign ministers, chancellors, and premiers around the world.[5] John Foster Dulles's brother, Allan, also served as the director of the CIA.

The opening prayer became central to Ike's leadership and to the life of his cabinet. At one point, Ike accidentally opened a meeting with a discussion instead of the prayer, and White House Counsel Maxwell Rabb slipped him a note reminding him. Ike immediately cut the conversation short and exclaimed, "We forgot the silent prayer!"[6] Or according to another source, Ike actually said, "We forgot the G—d d—d prayer!"[7] Even after his sincere expression of faith and baptism, in moments of great excitement and stress, Ike still struggled with the salty language ingrained in him during his Army days.

Ike's emphasis on prayer went beyond just his cabinet meetings. On February 5, 1953, just two weeks after taking office, Ike helped start a tradition observed by every president since: the National Prayer Breakfast.

It was the founder of Goodwill Industries, Abraham Vereide, along with Billy Graham, who approached Ike with the idea of such an event. Vereide, a Seattle-based minister, had organized prayer breakfasts for political leaders and business leaders to discuss matters of faith since the 1930s. Working with Senator Frank Carlson, who conducted similar prayer breakfasts for members of Congress, he, along with Billy Graham, convinced Ike to speak at one of these occasions.[8]

Diane Winston, an Associate Professor at the University of Southern California Annenberg School for Communication and Journalism, wrote about the importance of Ike's attendance, "[His] legitimating the National Prayer Breakfast was a signature achievement."[9]

On that February morning, Ike addressed a crowd of five hundred attendees at the Mayflower Hotel, owned by the sponsor of the event, Conrad Hilton. In his remarks, Ike looked back to America's founding:

> The very basis of our government is: "We hold that all men are endowed by their Creator" with certain rights.
>
> When we came to that turning point in history, when we intended to establish a government for free men and a Declaration and Constitution to make it last, in order to explain such a system we had to say: "We hold that all men are endowed by their Creator."
>
> In one sentence, we established that every free government is imbedded soundly in a deeply felt religious faith or it makes no sense. Today if we recall those things and if, in that sense, we can back off from our problems and depend upon a power greater than ourselves, I believe that we begin to draw these problems into focus. . . .
>
> Today I think that prayer is just simply a necessity, because by prayer I believe we mean an effort to get in touch with the Infinite. We know that even our prayers are imperfect. Even our supplications are imperfect. Of course they are. We are imperfect human beings. But if we can back off from those problems and make the effort, then there is something that ties us all together. We have begun in our grasp of that basis of understanding, which is that all free government is firmly founded in a deeply felt religious faith.[10]

Another example of Ike's emerging acknowledgment of his faith occurred five days earlier, when the American Legion "Back to God Hour" played recorded comments by Ike in which he expressed thankfulness for prayers on his behalf. He also touched on his desire to see Americans take their eyes off material things and focus instead on spiritual matters. He told the radio audience that their prayers were the "greatest gift" they could give him. He went on:

> As your prayers come from your hearts, so there comes from mine an earnest one—that all of us by our combined dedication and devotion may merit the great blessings that the Almighty has brought to this land of ours.

Then Ike turned from the issue of prayer to that of America's spiritual condition, stating:

> We think often of these blessings in terms of material values—of broad acres, our great factories—all of those things which make a life a more convenient and fine thing in the material sense. But when we think about the matter very deeply, we know that the blessings that we are really thankful for are a different type. They are what our forefathers called our rights—our human rights—the right to worship as we please, to speak and to think, and to earn, and to save. Those are the rights that we must strive so mightily to merit.
>
> One reason that we cherish these rights so sincerely is because they are God-given. They belong to the people who have been created in His image.[11]

Given the incredible economic prosperity the country was experiencing, as servicemen returning from World War II threw their energy into working in factories already running at full capacity, Ike's decision to urge Americans to focus on spiritual things was boldly countercultural. Most political leaders, and especially presidents, tend to celebrate material prosperity, but Ike recognized that this new material prosperity was in fact a mixed blessing, as it could do great damage to America's spiritual condition.

———————

If Ike set himself up as an instrument for spiritual renewal, he was the right man at the right time. Dr. Elson wrote,

> Everywhere new churches were appearing, religious books and magazine articles had wide acceptance and large sales, church membership expanded. There was new evangelistic zeal and missionary outreach—the greatest religious activity in American history. Soon the president by his spiritual sensitiveness, his manly life of prayer, his uninhibited Christian testimony, became a symbol of America's spiritual awakening following the great war.[12]

In June 1953, Billy Graham wrote Ike about the tremendous crowds he was drawing in Dallas. Graham told Ike:

> I am only informing you of these things to indicate the great spiritual hunger there is in America. Your interest in spiritual matters has helped tremendously, and I believe there is a great groundswell of religious revival that must take place if our country is to be spared.[13]

By 1953, religion was booming in America. The American economy was thriving, young families worked hard and began to experience success, and America's cities sprawled with the creation of new suburbs. The Korean War, with its sad legacy of more than forty thousand American deaths and over one hundred thousand wounded,[14] ended in July, six months into Ike's presidency. Americans settled into a new era of prosperity and relative peace. The newfound sense of stability led to the baby boom, which resulted in massive population growth as the population surged from 150 million in 1950 to 180 million by the end of the decade.

This growth and the increasing stability of life in post-Korea peacetime led to the creation of new churches, synagogues, and religious schools and institutions. By the end of the decade, nearly half of all Americans were attending church on a regular basis, a high-water mark that still stands.[15] This growth in religious practice was not just limited to Christianity. In the middle of the 1940s, only 9 percent of Jewish Americans were attending weekly religious services; by the middle of the 1950s, that number had increased to 18 percent.[16]

The religion boom of the 1950s also gave cynics plenty of excuses to brush off Ike's increasingly public faith as mere opportunism, even though Ike went to great lengths to clarify that his faith was not politically motivated.

That did not stop others from accusing Ike of using his faith as a political prop. One of his most vociferous critics was the octogenarian senator Matthew Neely of West Virginia. Neely, described by *Time* magazine as "rabble-rousing" and "Bible-spouting,"[17] made a regular habit of attacking Ike on all fronts, including his faith life. Calling Ike a "publican," Neely complained that Ike's actions in joining a church and including religious language in his public discourse were an attempt to "parade his religious associations or connections for political purposes."[18]

After Neely received harsh criticism for his comments from many corners—private citizens as well as his fellow congressmen—he backed down a bit. His frustration came not from Ike's church attendance, he said, but because "every time he went to church we had a half-page picture in the Monday papers."[19] Ironically, Ike had the same frustration, judging by his anger at the presence of reporters at National Presbyterian worship services, such as when he went to church without Mamie the week before his baptism.

At National Presbyterian, Ike entered his new church with the same wholeheartedness he brought to every other part of his life. Recalling Ike's presence at a particular Sunday morning service, Dr.

Elson wrote, "I looked down from the pulpit during the hymn before the sermon, and there was the president lustily and confidently singing, 'What a Friend We Have in Jesus.'"[20]

After the initial kerfuffle over the *Washington Post* putting Ike's first church service on the front page, Ike found comfort and insight through his friendship with Dr. Elson. Elson remembered Ike lingering by the church door after services, which probably caused heartburn for Ike's Secret Service agents, waiting and eager to discuss a matter the pastor had brought up or to ask for clarification.

Ike and Dr. Elson would develop a strong bond over the years, with the reverend serving as something of a spiritual advisor to Ike. Helen Elson recalled,

> The Pastor and the President were very much alike. I always thought during the war when I saw photos of Eisenhower, "There is Edward." They were both Pennsylvanians. They were both men with military bearing. They came out of the same culture, simple people where patriotism was very important, and the church equally so. . . . Eisenhower knew his Bible very well.[21]

At one point, after a sermon on temperament, Ike, aware of the bad temper he had inherited from his father and his struggles with salty language, waited at the door to request that Elson print fifty copies of the sermon so he could distribute it to his friends and colleagues.[22] The sermon, entitled "Mastery of Moods," offered advice on controlling one's emotions and impulses, with the main point being, "Self-mastery is not enough; only Christ's mastery is sufficient."[23] Ike requested fifty copies of another sermon, "Working under Pressure," as well.[24]

The interactions between Dr. Elson and Ike did not just stop at the church door every Sunday. Dr. Elson met with Ike and his staff on a regular basis, and the two men corresponded frequently. Besides their discussions about theology and Scripture, the two also had to maintain close contact because of the security arrangements that came with having the President of the United States sitting in the congregation of National Presbyterian. Ike's team developed a routine for communicating with Elson on security procedures.

Every Saturday night, the Secret Service would inform Dr. Elson about Ike's Sunday plans. After arriving in a black limousine, Ike would walk to his pew while Secret Service agents would spread themselves out among the congregation. Dr. Elson's family, including his daughter Eleanor, sat near the president.

Eleanor later recalled,

> I was very often the one closest. I could (though I should not have) watch him sideways. . . . I will tell you this about the President. His knuckles were white during prayers. I guess the reason I knew this was because I wasn't praying. I was sneaking a peek. Anyway, he prayed with intensity. He participated in the oral prayers. You could hear him in the singing. . . . He was a churchgoer. . . . Eisenhower's parents were extremely devout. They had daily family devotions and Bible readings. The President said late in life, that he too read the Bible every day. Even during the war, during the worst years. It was very interesting to me.[25]

Eleanor also said that the Eisenhowers' dedication to the community of National Presbyterian Church was clear. This was not a shallow, pie-in-the-sky faith that Ike had developed; he and Mamie recognized the need to be present in church on a regular basis and to be active members of their faith community, participating in fundraising efforts, tithing, and donating items, such as the pulpit at Corona Presbyterian in Denver. Eleanor remembered realizing that Ike needed National Presbyterian more than National Presbyterian needed Ike, and said that she doubted Ike's regular attendance was "for appearances." She added, "I think the Eisenhowers . . . thought that all times in their life they needed a church."[26]

There were numerous other indications that Ike greatly valued his relationship with Dr. Elson. The reverend attended state dinners and addresses to Congress. He also kept Ike apprised of events at National Presbyterian and sent notes of encouragement. Ike and Mamie would send gifts to their pastor, ranging from the secular, such as boxes of dates from California's Coachella Valley,[27] to the sacred, such as a complete recording of the New Testament and book of Psalms.[28]

Ike and Dr. Elson also exchanged letters each Good Friday. Ike's letter from March 23, 1956, had an especially explicit Christian message. He wrote,

> To the individual Christian, Good Friday is an occasion for intensifying his faith and renewing his recognition of the worth of humanity and sacrifice. But because it is a day which commemorates an event central to Christianity, it is of significance to all throughout the free world who strive to uphold the values of a civilization in which the Christian heritage is of immeasurable importance.
>
> As in years past, therefore, this year's observance of Good Friday in the churches of Washington and of communities throughout the land will surely strengthen Americans in their endeavors to live as Christian citizens in their relationships with their fellow men. And in many nations, here and abroad, the observance will fortify the hearts of men and women of good will by deepening their understanding of those spiritual values which guide them in their quest for a just peace and for a better life for human beings everywhere on earth.[29]

Ike even wrote Dr. Elson on November 25, 1956, to let him know that his pledge card for 1957 was enclosed. Ike wrote, "I have chosen to put the pledge on a yearly basis, as you will note,"[30] demonstrating his commitment to the church.

These private and deeply personal letters between the president and his pastor, which played no role in politics and did not appear in the public square until after Ike had passed away, are another clear sign that Ike's faith and his concern for America's spiritual condition were genuine. They also show that cynics' concerns that he was exploiting religion for the sake of politics were baseless.

———

The recollections of Dr. Elson, Billy Graham, and various members of Ike's staff—people who were very close to him—all indicate that Ike's religious awakening upon assuming the presidency was genuine. Ann C. Whitman, Ike's personal assistant for his entire presidency, wrote to her husband in the summer of 1953 that "the president preached religion to me all day long." She said Ike had declared to her, "An atheist is a stupid person. He is the one who won't think."[31]

These recollections also give credence to Graham's belief that Ike made a personal and sincere commitment to Jesus Christ in the days leading up to his election. While Ike had always respected his family's faith heritage, there clearly came a moment rather late in his life, around the time that he became president, when he began to actively and consistently speak and live out his faith, and his convictions undeniably permeated all aspects of his life and leadership.

What is clearly evident, through his correspondence and interactions with Dr. Elson, Billy Graham, and eventually other pastors at Gettysburg Presbyterian Church and other places he worshiped, is that Ike was seeking personal spiritual growth and also sought to ensure that his faith was never seen as self-aggrandizing. As Ike was to tell Billy Graham in 1959, "I have had to lean over backward, in the last six years, to draw a distinction between my official position and myself as a private individual."[32]

And it was becoming increasingly clear, except to his most vigorous detractors, that Ike was a man of genuine faith whose personal and public conduct in office were guided by faith in God, and he was interested not just in his own personal spiritual renewal and growth but in America's as well.

---- **11** ----

Spiritual Weapons for the Cold War

In 1954, FBI Director J. Edgar Hoover wrote an introduction to a short book, *America's Spiritual Recovery*, about the religious renaissance of the 1950s. In that introduction he said, "We are living in one of history's most difficult periods, and in an hour of widespread disruption, confusion, diversion, and aggression."[1]

The author of that book was Dr. Edward L. R. Elson, who dedicated it to the most famous member of his congregation: Dwight Eisenhower. He wrote that Ike, "by personal example and public utterance is giving testimony to the reality of America's spiritual foundations."[2]

In this little-known book, Dr. Elson captured the role that Ike's faith played throughout his presidency, both for Ike personally and for the nation as a whole. By the mid-1950s, it had become evident that Ike's faith was not just a source of personal comfort and strength, nor was it merely a means to reinforce founding principles among the American people. The president's faith—and by extension, the faith he inspired in others—was an important element in the United States' arsenal against enemies abroad, in particular the Soviet Union and the communism creeping through Southeast Asia and Latin America. During his first campaign for president, Ike spoke out clearly

147

about the role that religious faith would have to play in defeating the Soviet Union. Ike's faith was also a key element in dealing with domestic challenges, particularly the struggle for civil rights, which came to a head during his presidency.

When Ike settled into the Oval Office, the Cold War was burning hot and the Korean War, with the mounting American casualties, was dragging into its third year. While World War II with its common enemy had temporarily smoothed over the ideological differences between the Soviet Union and the United States, just days after the end of the war hostilities between the two nations were already beginning to escalate.

Soviet leader Joseph Stalin made no effort to hide his expansionist plans, and in mid-1945 began seizing control over the Eastern European countries just liberated from the Nazis. In response, President Harry S. Truman committed the United States and its allies in the Western bloc to the containment of Soviet expansion. This sparked an arms race, and by the time Ike assumed the presidency in 1953, both nations were in the midst of a massive military buildup, including developing and producing nuclear weapons.

The Soviets detonated their first nuclear weapon during a test in August 1949, escalating the atmosphere of worldwide dread of an impending nuclear holocaust.[3] With the onset of the 1950s, the Federal Civil Defense Association began coordinating air raid and duck-and-cover drills, and by the late 1950s Americans were building concrete bounded bunkers, known as fallout shelters, to survive a nuclear holocaust if one were to occur.

In the early 1950s, the United Nations, with the United States in the lead, began engaging in so-called "peacekeeping" in Asia to block Soviet and Chinese aggression. Those two nations had backed North Korea's "People's Army" invasion of South Korea in 1950, launching the Korean War.

Then, in the late summer of 1953, the Soviet Union had detonated its first hydrogen bomb in Kazakhstan. The explosive power was thirty times that of the US atomic bomb dropped on Hiroshima, and the mushroom cloud it produced stretched five miles into the sky.[4] That detonation set off shock waves around the world.

However, on September 14, 1954, the world changed even more dramatically. The Soviet Union successfully test-fired a 40-kilaton hydrogen bomb, dropping it from a plane near the Russian village of Totskoye.[5] The Soviet Union could now wipe out large American cities with a single bomb. This test further increased worldwide dread.

Though the world was weary of war, there was never a question in Ike's mind as to whether America would resist the Soviet Union's expansionism. Having seen the tragic human toll of a totalitarian regime playing out in Nazi Germany, Ike was a staunch cold warrior, but more than that, a determined peacemaker.

"Look, I am tired—and I think everyone is tired—of just plain indictments of the Soviet Union," Ike told speechwriter and former *Life* editor Emmet Hughes during an Oval Office meeting in 1954. He went on to say that America needed to address the question, "What have we got to offer the world?"[6]

Ike believed that America could offer faith. Contrary to the Soviet Union, America was established on the belief that humans were created in a divine image and endowed by their Creator with rights. This was the very premise that the Soviet Union denied. Simply increasing America's military arsenal, in Ike's view, would not win the Cold War. It had to be won by presenting the American way of life—based in faith and the conviction that humanity's value came from God—as the best way of life.

Ike recognized that there was a stark philosophical contrast between the United States and the Soviet Union. America and the West were locked in not only a military struggle with the Soviet Union and the

East but a moral struggle as well. That moral struggle was between two philosophies: the Soviet Union, through communism, opposed God, and America rested upon the belief in a higher power as the source of human dignity and freedom. Ike believed that America's true advantage was not its material and technological advancements but its faith, or as he put it, America's "spiritual weapons."[7]

In 1953, Ike extolled the virtues of America's churches.

The churches of America are citadels of our faith in individual freedom and human dignity. . . . And this strength is our matchless armor in the worldwide struggle against the forces of godless tyranny and oppression.[8]

This vision of the role of religion in society stood in direct contrast to that of the Soviet Union. In 1917, during the Russian Revolution, the Bolsheviks (the intellectual and political fathers of the Soviets) sought to replace, with brutal violence if needed, the nation's churches—the Russian Orthodox Church in particular—with atheistic nationalism. As early as January 1918, church and state became "separated." In the language of Bolshevism, this meant the church had lost all rights to exist under the state and could be destroyed.[9] Once in power, they quickly set out to eradicate any vestige of religion across the country, persecuting Christians, Jews, Muslims, and other religious minorities.

The leader of this assault on religious faith was Joseph Stalin, who became General Secretary of the Communist Party in 1922.[10] Though he was born and raised in the Georgian Orthodox Church and spent some of his childhood in an Orthodox monastery, Stalin carried out a program of forced atheism, often under the auspices of the League of Militant Atheists, which had millions of members and offices throughout the country. Only during World War II, in an effort to "boost morale," did Stalin allow any degree of religious tolerance. As soon as the war ended, the persecution resumed.[11]

Ike, sensing this deep philosophical conflict both between the Soviet Union and America and within the Soviet Union itself, continued to rhetorically hammer away at the differences between the two nations and assert the superiority of the religious foundation upon which America was built.

Just a month before his election, Ike said of the Soviet Union, "They have no use for religion. They silence the church bells. . . . Here in America, our society, our traditions, the very foundation of our government rest upon the motto 'In God We Trust.'"[12]

Stalin, under whose murderous regime up to twenty million people "disappeared," died on March 5, 1953, less than two months into Ike's presidency.[13] Stalin's death was not a surprise; the fact that he was gravely ill was well known. The day before Stalin's death, Ike released a statement with a pointed religious and conciliatory tone:

> At this moment in history, when multitudes of Russians are anxiously concerned because of the illness of the Soviet ruler, the thoughts of America go out to all the peoples of the USSR—the men and women, the boys and girls—in the villages, cities, farms, and factories of their homeland.
>
> They are children of the same God who is the Father of all peoples everywhere. And like all peoples, Russia's millions share our longing for a friendly and peaceful world.
>
> Regardless of the identity of government personalities, the prayer of us Americans continues to be that the Almighty will watch over the people of that vast country and bring them, in His wisdom, opportunity to live their lives in a world where all men and women and children dwell in peace and comradeship.[14]

Ike's message was sincere but also cleverly juxtaposed the difference between the two rival nations, one where prayer and church

151

attendance were on the rise, and the other where faith had been driven underground and prayer and worship were done in secret.

The juxtaposition set the strategic tone for Ike's use of faith as both an overt and covert means of combating communism. Stalin's antireligion campaign, continued by his successor Nikita Khrushchev, destroyed any objects of religious reverence at a furious clip. The churches were stripped of precious ornaments and statues of historical figures, their gold and silver torn off. The nation's great and historical churches, which had been sources of hope, inspiration, and community to the lower classes, were confiscated and used for storage or outright destroyed. This brutality included architecturally and historically significant places of worship such as Moscow's Saint Paraskevi and Christ the Savior, both destroyed on Stalin's orders.

In the places where churches once stood, the Soviet government often built museums of atheism, making it clear that religion no longer had any part in Russian life. The persecution of religion was so complete that even church bells had their clappers removed, with many of the bells melted down and the metal used for industrial purposes.[15]

Upon taking office in 1953, Ike oversaw the creation of the United States Information Agency (USIA), which enabled the government to coordinate the various efforts of its foreign and national security agencies to promote pro-faith and pro-democracy messages around the world—even to allies in various resistance groups behind the Iron Curtain.[16] Ike also approved of the creation of the Operations Coordinating Board (OCB), part of the National Security Council, which was responsible for implementing national security policies across several agencies.

These and other government initiatives helped block the Soviet Union's attempt to stamp out religion among its subjects by coordinating the State Department, Pentagon, and Central Intelligence Agency (CIA) efforts to support orthodox churches and anticommunist religious leaders in the Middle East and the Mediterranean.[17] Ike recognized, as would future leaders such as President Ronald Reagan, Prime Minister Margaret Thatcher, and Pope St. John Paul II, that providing covert financial and other support to these churches and groups would ultimately undermine the communist foundations of the Soviet system and lead to its eventual collapse.

Ike's faith crept into his administration in other ways besides the practice of regular prayer in the cabinet. In 1953, during the opening of a cabinet meeting, he suggested that those in attendance should watch the recently released biographical film *Martin Luther*, which he had just viewed and found thought-provoking. One of his aides recalled that in conversations about domestic policy, Ike's deeply held religious beliefs had a strong influence on discussions. The aide said, "In Ike's lexicon, the 'spiritual needs' of the US rank ahead of the political or economic ones."[18]

While Ike would not allow his faith to be exploited for political expediency, he understood that public proclamations of faith were essential to address his concerns about what he perceived as the deteriorating spiritual condition of America. He bluntly told Secretary of Agriculture Benson, "We've got to deal with spiritual matters."[19] Ike clearly saw value in using his presidency to promote society-wide, nondenominational religion as a civic virtue.

For example, in his remarks to the First National Conference on the Spiritual Foundations of American Democracy on November 9, 1954, Ike emphasized that rights come from the Creator, not from humankind.

The sponsor of the conference was the Foundation for Religious Action in the Social and Civil Order (FRASCO). FRASCO, formed as a spiritual response to the Cold War, received Ike's full endorsement.[20] It was the brainchild of Dr. Elson and Charles Wesley Lowry. Lowry was an Oklahoma-born and Oxford University–educated Episcopalian minister and served as the organization's chair. FRASCO's mission, as proposed by Elson, was to further the "moral and spiritual revolution" underway in America. Its advisory committee included a cross-section of prominent Americans, including former President Herbert Hoover, Billy Graham, Dr. Norman Vincent Peale, Henry Luce, Charles Wilson of General Electric, and Henry Ford Jr.[21] The objective of the group was to promote religious faith in America while undermining communism.[22]

In his speech, Ike emphasized the need to consider America's spiritual, rather than material, condition, stating,

> [John] Milton asserted that all men are born equal, because each is born in the image of his God. Our whole theory of government finally expressed in our Declaration, you will recall . . . and remember the first part of the Preamble of the Declaration was to give the reasons to mankind why we had established such a government: "Man is endowed by his Creator." It did not assert that Americans had certain rights. "Man" is endowed by his Creator—or "All Men" I believe was the expression used.
>
> So this connection is very, very clear. And no matter what Democracy tries to do in the terms of maximum individual liberty for an individual . . . and identifying the people as the source of political power in that government, when you come back to it, there is just one thing: it is a concept, it is a subjective sort of thing, that a man is worthwhile because he was born in the image of his God.[23]

For months, Ike had anticipated the delivery of these remarks. On April 17, 1954, Ike wrote to Dr. Elson regarding the formation of FRASCO, the sponsor of this conference. The letter read,

> *Dear Dr. Elson:*
>
> *I was pleased to learn that you and Dr. [Charles Wesley] Lowry have been instrumental in forming a Foundation for Religious Action whose purpose is to emphasize the place of religion and moral values in our national life.*

Certainly, there is a need for us constantly to remind ourselves that the American heritage is strongly spiritual. Our government has logically been described as a translation into the political field of a deeply held religious faith. This faith holds that man is created in the image of God, and from this fundamental concept springs our dedication to the principle of and our belief in equality under the law, justice, mercy, and brotherhood of man.

I am informed that the Foundation has already enlisted much support among American leaders and that plans are under way for a National Conference on Moral and Spiritual Recovery. I look upon this purpose as completely laudatory and worthwhile, and hope that its work will benefit from the cooperation and support of all those who will be called upon to help achieve successful results.[24]

The words of Ike's letter, and his subsequent remarks, closely mirrored those from his 1953 inaugural address and illustrate Ike's continued concern with America's spiritual condition and his belief that America was built on the base of deeply held religious faith.

This recurring conviction of Ike's, that American democracy was based on a deep and abiding faith in God, led to two of his best-known and longest lasting contributions to the religious renaissance of the 1950s.

The first of those contributions was Ike's strong support of the inclusion of the phrase "under God" in the United States Pledge of Allegiance. The Pledge of Allegiance, written by Colonel George Bach in 1887 and revised by Christian minister Francis Bellamy, for decades remained an unofficial expression of patriotism. During the early days of World War II, in 1942, the federal government recognized it as the official national pledge. The original pledge made no mention of God, but in 1951, the board and directors of the Roman Catholic organization the Knights of Columbus resolved to have Congress add "under God" to the pledge.[25]

State councils of the Knights of Columbus quickly created their own resolutions, and in August 1953 shared them with Ike, Vice President Nixon, and members of Congress. Michigan Congressman Louis C. Rabaut introduced a resolution at their behest (Public Law 83–396) to insert "under God" into the pledge. It passed both houses.[26]

Ike had fully supported the addition of the words, and he signed the resolution into law on June 14, 1954, which was also Flag Day. At the signing, he proclaimed,

> From this day forward, the millions of our school children will daily proclaim in every city and town, every village and rural school house, the dedication of our nation and our people to the Almighty. To anyone who truly loves America, nothing could be more inspiring than to contemplate this rededication of our youth, on each school morning, to our country's true meaning. . . . We are reaffirming the transcendence of religious faith in America's heritage and future; in this way we shall constantly strengthen these spiritual weapons which forever will be our country's most powerful resource, in peace or in war.[27]

After the ceremony, Ike went to the steps of the US Capitol, where the American Legion had raised a new flag, and, with his hand over his heart, recited the pledge with its new line.[28] He later wrote to the head of the Knights of Columbus, Supreme Knight Luke E. Hart, to thank the organization for their role in having the words "under God" included in the pledge. Ike wrote:

> We are particularly thankful to you for your part in the movement to have the words "under God" added to our Pledge of Allegiance. These words remind Americans that despite our great physical strength we must remain humble. They will help us to keep constantly in our minds and hearts the spiritual and moral principles which alone give dignity to man, and upon which our way of life is founded.[29]

Ike's second nationwide contribution to including religious language in the American public square involved America's currency.

Since 1837, America's coins and currency had borne mottos, but at first there were no religious references on the country's currency. That changed with the American Civil War. The onset of the war prompted a number of Americans to ask the federal government to add a reference to God on the nation's currency. Congress agreed, and in 1864 "In God We Trust" began appearing on all newly minted gold and silver coins. According to then-Speaker of the House Schuyler Colfax, in his eulogy for Abraham Lincoln, signing the legislation into law was one of the last acts performed by Lincoln before his assassination.[30]

In 1953, Matthew R. Rothert, the president of the American Numismatic Society and a member of the American Numismatic Association, delivered a speech to the society's Arkansas chapter in which he proposed that "In God We Trust" be added also to the nation's paper currency. Ike, along with Secretary of the Treasury George M. Humphrey, was receptive to the idea.[31]

On July 30, 1956, Ike signed Public Law 84–14 into law, declaring "In God We Trust" as the national motto. According to the law, this motto would appear on the nation's paper currency starting in 1957.[32] Despite legal challenges from atheist groups, the words "under God" remain in the pledge, and the words "In God We Trust" remain on the nation's coins and paper currency to this day.[33]

Despite the mounting conflict with Russia and the detonation of the hydrogen bomb earlier in the month, the last days of September 1954 were seemingly an idyllic time in America. After a recession, the economy was beginning to turn around.[34] For baseball fans, the hated (outside of New York, at least) Yankees were set to miss their first World Series in six years as the upstart Cleveland Indians swept through the American League, setting a then-record of 111 wins against only 53 losses. Meanwhile in the National League, the New York Giants, led by their exciting new star, Willie Mays, were set to capture the National League pennant. Mays electrified America with an amazing catch in the first game of the World Series, leading the underdog Giants to a four-game sweep of the record-setting Indians.

Innovations in entertainment technology, most notably the home television set, increasingly captivated Americans. By 1950, nearly six million American homes had televisions. Televised for the first time in mid-September 1954, the Miss America Pageant would become an American institution.[35] Each night, families crowded around their televisions to watch top-rated shows such as *I Love Lucy*, *The Jack Benny Show*, *The Texaco Star Theatre with Milton Berle*, *Your Show of Shows*, *You Bet Your Life*, and *Dragnet*.[36]

Despite America's economic prosperity and seemingly idyllic state, a cloud hung over America. Ike was deeply concerned about the Soviet nuclear threat and its ramifications for humankind. He requested that his speechwriters draft a speech about the growing threat of Russian air-atomic power.[37] Beyond this, he launched a formal campaign to educate American citizens about the dangers facing the nation in the Atomic Age, or as Ike described it, "an age of peril," words taken from a White House security information memo dated July 22, 1953.[38]

This campaign, known as Operation Candor, had as its informal mission statement, "Age of Peril demands patience, determination, fortitude. Emphasis on moral and spiritual values in American life worth fighting for and making material sacrifices for," and the strategy called for Ike to deliver, among other speeches and addresses to the nation, a speech specifically emphasizing these values to the American people.[39]

The best remembered aspect of Operation Candor was a speech now known as "Atoms for Peace," which Ike delivered to the General Assembly of the United Nations in New York on December 8, 1953. In this speech, Ike explained how the fearsome technology unleashed by nuclear war had potential beyond killing millions of people. Nuclear technology, he said, could benefit humanity rather than destroy it. In the speech, he admitted that America no longer had a monopoly on atomic power and spoke bluntly about the dangers of the modern world, saying that all technological advances had to consider the "awful arithmetic of today's atomic realities."[40]

This speech remains a well-known piece of Ike's legacy. Another element of the speech, receiving less attention than his insights into the varying roles of technology, was the spiritual component of Ike's reflections on the nuclear age. Ike said,

> Should such an atomic attack be launched against the United States, our reactions would be swift and resolute. But for me to say that the defense capabilities of the United States are such that they could inflict terrible losses upon an aggressor—for me to say that the retaliation capabilities of the United States are so great that such an aggressor's land would be laid waste—all this, while fact, is not the true expression of the purpose and hope of the United States.
>
> To pause there would be to confirm the hopeless finality of a belief that two atomic colossi are doomed malevolently to eye each other indefinitely across a trembling world. To stop there would be to accept helplessly the probability of civilization destroyed—the annihilation of the irreplaceable heritage of mankind handed down to us generation from generation—and the condemnation of mankind to begin all over again the age-old struggle upward from savagery toward decency, and right, and justice.
>
> Surely no sane member of the human race could discover victory in such desolation. Could anyone wish his name to be coupled by history with such human degradation and destruction?
>
> Occasional pages of history do record the faces of the "Great Destroyers" but the whole book of history reveals mankind's never-ending quest for peace, and mankind's God-given capacity to build. . . .
>
> The United States pledges before you—and therefore before the whole world—its determination to help solve this entire heart and mind to find the way by which the miraculous inventiveness of man shall not be dedicated to his death, but consecrated to his life.[41]

In the margins of the original draft of the speech, written by Ike's special assistant Charles Douglas Jackson, Ike's handwriting shows where he penned a different ending, which went unused. One can only speculate why it was not. This alternative ending carried with it a much stronger spiritual statement:

> And if each of us is truly worthy of freedom, our nation will possess such spiritual and material strength that we shall lead the way to an ultimate and glorious solution to the challenge posed at least in part by man's conquest of yet another bit of God's handiwork.[42]

Though Ike's ending was not included, the speech underscored his belief that a spiritual element must be part of any solution to the dangers of the Cold War and the Atomic Age. The intent of the "Atoms for Peace" program was to promote the use of nuclear technology as a means for improving humanity's station on earth rather than a means of its demise. To do this, the United States proposed using nuclear technology to provide energy to parts of the world in poverty. This vision would eventually lead to the creation of the International Atomic Energy Commission in 1957.[43]

The Soviet detonation of the hydrogen bomb in 1954 had been so alarming because it showed the USSR could simply drop a bomb and kill untold millions from an airplane, without warning. It also further escalated the arms race. On September 30, 1954, the US Navy commissioned the world's first nuclear powered submarine, the USS *Nautilus* (SSN-571).[44]

Eight days earlier, Ike had declared September 22, 1954, as a day of national prayer, encouraging Americans to pray for peace. This day of prayer was both spiritually and militarily tactical, as it bolstered the spirits of Americans and helped them pour their fears out to God while simultaneously allowing the USIA to share his declaration via its broadcasts to nations under Soviet control, providing them with the hope the Soviet system could not provide.

Ike asked "the peoples of the Iron Curtain to join Americans in prayer for peace on September 22, 1954. . . . May the world be ringed with an act of faith so strong as to annihilate the cruel, artificial barriers erected by little men between the peoples who seek peace on earth through Almighty God."[45]

Ike based his call for prayer on his belief that faith still had a pulse even in nations where communism had tried to crush it, and that appealing to religious dissidents could undermine the stability of the Soviet regime. Ike's call for prayer was another brick in the foundation of peace future leaders built upon, military strength and the affirmation of faith, that would lead to the eventual dissolution of the atheistic Soviet Union four decades later.

"I hate war as only a soldier who has lived it can, only as one who has seen its brutality, its futility, its stupidity," Ike declared in 1946.[46] Ike had seen the horrors of war in the Nazi concentration camps, the Normandy landing and assault, and the bloody battles in North Africa. He had written orders and devised battle plans that sent young men to their deaths. Too many times, Ike had doffed his helmet and solemnly bowed his head to honor those who had made the ultimate sacrifice for their country. He was well aware of the evil that came from totalitarian regimes that treated human beings as commodities instead of dignified beings made in the image of God.

These personal experiences, and perhaps even some remnant of the pacifistic influence of his mother, pushed Ike to fight for peace even as he prepared for war with the communist bloc. He strove with every means at his disposal to avoid a nuclear holocaust without compromising his convictions about the evil nature of totalitarianism.

The success of the USIA led Ike to use faith to challenge the Soviet regime through the creation of the Office of Religious Information within the USIA, appointing David Elton Trueblood as its chief of religious policy. As a presidential advisor, Trueblood's task was to synchronize government efforts to unite Americans and their allies abroad in the moral struggle between the "free world and atheistic communism." The objective was to remind people all over the world of the connection between "religious truth" and "properly functioning democracy."[47] In layman's terms, this meant that democracy could only function when it recognized the inherent dignity of all people, all of whom were created in the image of God—*Imago Dei.*

Trueblood was an Ivy League–educated member of the Religious Society of Friends as well as a professor of philosophy at Earlham College, a small Quaker-founded liberal arts school in Richmond, Indiana.[48] He was also a prolific author, friends with former President Herbert Hoover, and a protégé of Abraham Vereide, who in 1953 encouraged Ike to launch the National Prayer Breakfast. Trueblood was also a friend of Dr. Elson, who invited him to deliver a sermon at National Presbyterian with Ike in attendance.[49] According to True-blood, his sermon resulted in "friendship [with] President Eisenhower, who, after I had preached the sermon at the National Presbyterian Church with the Eisenhowers present, invited me to the White House and later, after his retirement, to Gettysburg."[50]

In 1954, Trueblood preached a sermon on "Basic Christianity." While this may not have been the sermon Ike heard at National Presbyterian, in it Trueblood preached about how "much of our contemporary Christianity fails because all concerned seem vague in their beliefs." He then went on to answer, in an evangelical fashion, the questions "Who is God?" "Who is Jesus Christ?" and "What is life everlasting?" In the sermon, he made a powerful case for the resurrection of Christ, and that Christ was not just a teacher and revealer but a redeemer.[51]

There was nothing vague about Trueblood's Christian doctrine.

The creation of this office and Trueblood's appointment generated the usual pushback from groups concerned about the so-called "separation of church and state." Ike and his chief of staff, Sherman Adams, quickly dismissed those attacks, with Adams stating, "Our democratic freedoms have a solid religious foundation which must be adequately explained if the true story of America is to be told."[52]

To those concerned about the government engaging in proselytization, Ike was merely making the point that faith in God served as the base upon which America was founded. The predominant faiths in America in 1952 all shared Judeo-Christian roots, and by no means, given the cultural understanding of the time, was Ike being dismissive of other faith traditions.

In fact, Ike's administration recognized that though not all countries shared those Judeo-Christian principles, *any* display of faith, no matter in what religion, could deal a serious blow to the Soviet Union by validating and strengthening the part of life that communism denied existed: faith in a higher power. That is why the State Department worked to cultivate anticommunist feelings among Muslims in the Middle East, using radio broadcasts transmitted to various nations in the region while also strengthening diplomatic ties between Western and Middle Eastern nations. The federal government also assisted Buddhist leaders in Southeast Asia in combating communism by producing and distributing anticommunist literature and films in Burma and Thailand.[53]

In an interview for the *Portland Press Herald* (Maine), columnist May Craig asked Ike, "Are you thinking of mobilizing the religious countries of the world against communism?" Ike responded that the United States was engaged "in a battle between those people who believe that man is something more than just an educated animal, and those who believe he is nothing else. It is atheism against some kind of religion." He explained that it was important to mobilize people of faith because, in his words, the "underlying basic fact is this: that religion ordinarily tries to find a peaceful solution to problems."[54]

Another example of Ike's thoughts on the subject was included in a lengthy and rather extraordinary letter he sent to Dr. Elson on

July 31, 1958, about the peace process in the Middle East and how America and its faith were perceived in the Arab world. Dr. Elson, given his experiences in the Middle East after World War II, was an expert in this area. Ike wrote in part,

> I assure you that I never fail in any communication with Arab leaders, oral or written, to stress the importance of the spiritual factor in our relationships. I have argued that belief in God should create between them and us the common purpose of opposing atheistic communism. . . .
>
> The real strength of America must be described in values that are intangible. . . . By and large you are well aware of the basic purposes, hopes, and efforts of the American government in the foreign field. Those efforts in the Mid East are based upon convictions that largely parallel your own. Yet I feel that all of us must do more, here at home, if we are to be successful abroad. I have made speeches on this subject, three or four of them on nation-wide television. But I believe teachers, business leaders, labor leaders, and, indeed, including and especially the clergy, ought to be active in this work. . . .
>
> We must get down to the fundamentals of human behavior, values, and aspirations. We must be true to our religious heritage in recognizing clearly the basic principles by which we must attempt to guide our nation's destiny.[55]

Until the end of his second term, Ike relied on the power of faith, both personally and strategically, to deal with the realities of the Cold War. As columnist May Craig had anticipated with her questions, Ike contemplated, but never called, a meeting of the world's religious leaders to underscore the "supremacy of spiritual values" and to "alert us to the threat posed by communist imperialism, and to unite us better in the search for peace."[56]

In 1954, Ike wrote to California Senator William Knowland, "The Soviet Union has not succeeded in extinguishing the religious faith and aspirations of the people behind the Iron Curtain."[57] This observation proved prescient, and was in large part the source of Ike's hope that the Cold War would end peacefully. As stated earlier, in many ways Ike was ahead of his time in seeing that the Soviet Union's atheism would ultimately be a major part of its undoing. He was certain that religion lingered behind the Iron Curtain—even if it was hidden.

His belief was proven to be true in the 1980s, when the anti-Soviet movements spreading across Eastern Europe were often led by individuals with strong religious sentiments, such as Lech Walesa and the Solidarity movement in Poland, and Vaclav Havel and the Velvet Revolution in Czechoslovakia. With the encouragement and support of leaders such as John Paul II, Margaret Thatcher, and Ronald Reagan, these leaders helped restore religious faith throughout Eastern Europe, which played a major role in the fall of the atheistic Soviet Union.

12

Spiritual Weapons for Civil Rights

N
ot all was quiet on the domestic front in the mid-1950s either. During Ike's terms as president, the emerging Civil Rights movement rocked America—forcing the nation to confront the sin of racism that continued to plague American society.

In the years after their first meetings in 1952, Ike had developed a deep and lasting bond with Billy Graham. John Steele, a correspondent with *Time Life*, noticed that although the two men seemed very different on the surface, "the common denominator seemed to be, if not a love, an understanding of the heartstrings of the 20th century man. The pastor and the president seemed, indeed, to have much in common."[1] This alliance with Graham the preacher pushed Ike the president to seek to peacefully, but decisively as necessary, reverse the evil of racism in America.

While not remembered as a civil rights crusader, no president between Abraham Lincoln and Lyndon B. Johnson did more to advance the human dignity and civil rights of African Americans than Ike. He signed the first piece of civil rights legislation since the early antebellum period and was the first president to appoint a black special assistant to his presidential staff.[2] Even though President Truman signed Executive Order 9981 in 1948, desegregating the American military, it fell to Ike to implement that order, which he, having seen white and black troops fight together on the battlefield during World War II, did commandingly.[3] In Ike's first State of the Union address, he proposed "to use whatever authority exists in the office of the President to end segregation in the District of Columbia, including the federal government, and any segregation in the Armed Forces."[4]

Paul Hutchinson, in an article published in *The Christian Century* in the early days of Ike's term, wrote:

> One of the prime indications that Washington's morality is improving is its progress towards the elimination of racial segregation. On that, Washingtonians who are fighting for equal rights for all citizens declare they owe much to the forthright support they have received from the White House.[5]

In 1953, Ike established the President's Committee on Government Contracts to ensure antidiscrimination compliance with any organizations affiliated with government contracts.[6] The same year, the Supreme Court upheld the desegregation of the nation's capital in *District of Columbia v. John R. Thompson Co., Inc.*, followed by its 1954 *Brown v. Board of Education* decision regarding desegregation of public schools.[7]

Ike's approach to segregation was informed by his faith and his collaboration with religious leaders such as Graham. Graham had already been active in confronting racism in the South, personally taking down the ropes at his Chattanooga crusade that had separated white and black audiences and calling on Baptist colleges to accept qualified black students. But Graham also understood the mindset of many in the South who upheld segregation. In their numerous interactions on the issue, Graham and Ike concurred that changing hearts and minds would be a long process, and laws alone could not force that change. Graham told Ike, "I believe the Lord is helping us, and if the Supreme Court will go slowly and the extremists on both sides will quiet down, we can have a peaceful social readjustment over the next ten-year period."[8]

Graham's desire to see the issue to a peaceful end did not allay his strong moral opinions on the subject. He added, "There are a lot of segregationists who are going to be sadly disillusioned when they get to heaven—if they get there."[9]

Graham's statement about the Supreme Court going slowly was in line with Ike's beliefs. In fact, it explains Ike's initial concerns about the *Brown* decision. Ike did not oppose the decision because he was a racist, as some of his harshest critics would claim. Ike had lived in the South during his wartime service, and like Graham, who grew up there, he knew how inflamed passions were on the issue.[10] As he did in so many ways, Ike was seeking to find a peaceful solution.

In fact, Ike respected the *Brown* decision morally and indicated that he would implement it to the full extent of his executive power, but he did express concerns that the Court was moving too fast. In his book, *Going Home to Glory*, Ike's grandson David Eisenhower stated that General Lucius Clay, a confidante of Ike, thought that Ike regarded the *Brown* decision not as a blunder but as a burden. It had taken Ike by surprise, as he felt a pattern of legal precedents should have been set first, such as disposing of the governing precedent, *Plessy v. Ferguson*. By not establishing such a pattern, Ike felt, the Court had made it more difficult to defend and implement the decision.[11]

Ike believed that if change was to be peaceful, it had to come gradually, and that desegregation would come both more peacefully and more thoroughly through gradually desegregating colleges and secondary schools rather than through action on the federal level.[12] To those seeking faster change, Ike's desire for orderly and peaceful change came across as indifference or foot-dragging. Explaining his call for a more measured and peaceful method of ridding the nation of racism, he said, "Not enough people know how deep this emotion is in the south. Unless you've lived there, you can't know . . . we could have another civil war on our hands."[13] Given the turbulence to come, Ike's words proved to be prophetic.

———————

By 1956, much of the South had become a powder keg. *Brown v. Board of Education* triggered riots and protests throughout the region. Four state legislatures refused to enforce the Court's decision. More than a hundred senators and congressmen vowed to seek its reversal.[14] Meanwhile, a young African American woman named Rosa Parks refused to move to the back of a Birmingham bus. Her act of peaceful protest led to a high-profile arrest and sparked the Birmingham bus boycott. Leading the boycott was the Rev. Dr. Martin Luther King Jr.

In the midst of the escalating racial conflict, Ike had a meeting with Graham to discuss how best to preserve peace while moving toward justice. After the meeting, he wrote a long letter to Graham, asking him and other religious leaders to assist in diffusing the situation. Part of the letter read,

> Dear Billy . . . I have been urgently thinking about the matters we discussed in our conversation the day before yesterday. . . . Ministers know that peacemakers are blessed; they should also know that the most effective peacemaker is one who prevents a quarrel from developing, rather than one who has to pick up the pieces after an unfortunate fight.[15]

In their book *The Preacher and the Presidents*, Nancy Gibbs and Michael Duffy write that Ike asked Graham to keep abreast of any progress toward improving civil rights and to urge ministers to express approval of "whatever advances were being made on any front."[16] Ike asked Graham to use his influence in the South to advance desegregation in such quiet and effective ways as finding and supporting qualified African American candidates for public office, making entrance to graduate schools merit-based, and keeping applicants' racial backgrounds unknown to admission boards.

For Ike, this issue transcended partisan politics. He wrote to Graham, "I think it is a great pity that this crucial matter will, almost inescapably it seems, be dragged into the arena of partisan politics." Ike added that his moderate approach, based on personal conviction, would lead to real rather than spurious change.[17]

On March 22, 1956, Ike wrote to Graham, "It would appear to me that these things like this could be properly mentioned in a pulpit." He added that Graham should support the efforts of Joseph Francis Rummell, a Catholic archbishop in Louisiana, who had desegregated parochial schools in his archdiocese. Ike stressed to Graham that Rummell's example could show that "one man had the courage to give this kind of integration a good trial to determine the results."[18]

Graham wrote back to Ike a few days later. He concurred that "the church must take a place of spiritual leadership in this crucial matter that confronts not only the South but the entire nation."[19] However, as the unrest in the South intensified and the politics surrounding the situation grew more bitter, a frustrated Ike wrote back four days later, expressing his anger with "foolish extremists on both sides of the question," and again emphasized desire to find a moderate path to justice.[20]

Graham took Ike's words to heart and began working with religious leaders of both races across the South in "calling for desegregation and yet demonstrating charity, and above all else, patience." He spent the next several months following his meetings and correspondence with Ike by meeting with Protestant leaders and speaking at African American universities, promoting Ike's "sensible program for bettering race relations."[21] Graham also encouraged religious leaders across the South to put forth their ideas for implementing desegregation. He remained confident that Ike's gradual, cautious approach would ultimately lead to a peaceful reconciliation of the races.

This approach had its first serious test in 1957. On September 4, the National Association for the Advancement of Colored People (NAACP) enrolled nine African American students, based on their academic achievement, into the previously all-white Central High School in Little Rock, Arkansas. When those nine students tried to enter the school that sunny fall morning, the state's governor, Orval Faubus, ordered the National Guard to block their entry.

This was Ike's "nightmare scenario."[22] To stand by and do nothing was not an option. Ike feared that if he called in federal troops and sparked a clash with the National Guard, the ramifications could be grave. Beyond the immediate danger to the nine students (now known as the Little Rock Nine), Ike worried that some communities in the South would choose to close their public schools rather than integrate, which would deny education to poor children of all races.

Over the next several weeks, Ike tried to resolve the issue peacefully. When Faubus asked to meet with him in an attempt to avoid a prolonged national conflict and stall the use of federal troops to enforce the law, Ike readily agreed.[23] However Faubus, despite intimations to Ike at the meeting, did not remove the National Guardsmen from the school. He only dismissed them under a federal court order stemming from a lawsuit filed by the NAACP.[24]

The departure of the National Guard on September 23 left a mob of angry citizens surrounding the school's entrance, with very little in the way of police to keep the situation from spinning out of control. Woodrow Wilson Mann, the mayor of Little Rock, begged Ike to dispatch federal troops.[25] Ike once again consulted with Billy Graham, who told him bluntly that he had no alternative. Graham's words were, "The discrimination must be stopped."[26] Ike concurred. The next day, September 24, Ike sent one thousand members of the 101st Airborne Division of the US Army—the same division that had been under his command during D-Day's Operation Overlord—to escort the nine students through the school's doors.[27] That same day, he went on television and gave a national address explaining his actions. He concluded his speech with another statement affirming human dignity and concern for America's spiritual authority in the world:

> At a time when we face grave situations abroad because of the hatred Communism bears toward a system of government based on human

rights, it would be difficult to exaggerate the harm that is being done to the prestige and influence, and indeed to the safety, of our nation and the world.

Our enemies are gloating over this incident and using it everywhere to misrepresent our whole nation. We are portrayed as a violator of those standards of conduct which the peoples of the world united to proclaim in the Charter of the United Nations. They affirmed "faith in fundamental human rights" and "in the dignity and worth of the human person," and did so "without distinction as to race, sex, language, or religion."

And so, with deep confidence, I call upon the citizens of the State of Arkansas to assist in bringing to an immediate end all interference with the law and its processes. If resistance to the Federal Court order ceases at once, the further presence of Federal troops will be unnecessary and the City of Little Rock will return to its normal habits of peace and order and a blot upon the fair name and high honor of our nation in the world will be removed. Thus will be restored the image of America and of all of its parts as one nation, indivisible, with liberty and justice for all.[28]

Graham also faced backlash for taking a strong stand against racism and encouraging Ike to send in the federal troops. The governor of South Carolina refused to allow Graham to hold a rally at the State House. Ike rose to his defense and gave his blessing for Graham to hold a crusade at the Ft. Jackson Army Base instead. [29]

On September 25, the day after Ike's speech, he received the following note from Rev. Martin Luther King Jr.:

I wish to express my sincere support for the stand you have taken to restore law and order in Little Rock, Arkansas. In the long run, justice finally must spring from a new moral climate. Yet spiritual forces cannot emerge in a situation of mob violence.

You should know that the overwhelming majority of Southerners, Negro and White, stand firmly behind your resolute action. The pen of history will record that even the small and confused minority that oppose integration with violence will live to see that your action has been of great benefit to our nation and to the Christian traditions of fair play and brotherhood.[30]

Ike replied on October 7:

Thank you for sending me your comments regarding the necessity of the decision I had to make in the difficult Arkansas situation. I appreciated your thoughtful expression of the basic and compelling factors involved.

I share your confidence that Americans everywhere remain devoted to our tradition of adherence to orderly processes of law.[31]

It was a measured response, which was consistent with the restraint Ike had exhibited in his mission to bring about a peaceful end to segregation and racism. A month later, the Southern Christian Leadership Conference, headed by Rev. King, sent the following letter:

> *Dear Mr. President:*
> *The Southern Christian Leadership Conference . . . extends its warmest commendation for the positive and forthright stand you have taken in the Little Rock school situation. You have shown to the nation and the world that the United States is a nation dedicated to law and order rather than mob rule. In an hour so charged with the tragic possibility of world conflict, America can ill afford to be guilty of sins against her own way of life.[32]*

While King and other civil rights leaders wanted Ike to be more vocal and take further federal action to speed up the civil rights process, Ike continued to seek out religious leaders willing to work with him to implement integration with as little unrest and conflict as possible. Ike had "little faith in legislation as a vehicle for promoting better race relations."[33]

Besides Graham and King, Ike frequently met and corresponded with Reverend John P. Markoe, a Jesuit priest whose work to end racism predated the Civil Rights movement by several decades. Markoe, coincidentally, had known Ike at West Point. As early as the 1930s,

Markoe had declared, "Racism is a God-d—d thing. And that's two words: God-d—d."[34] Markoe also encouraged and commended Ike's approach on civil rights, complimenting him on the "tremendous good you have accomplished in this particular area of American life; more good in a few years than the combined efforts of many over the years."[35]

Ike neatly summed up his approach to the Civil Rights movement and the resulting racial tensions in a letter to his childhood friend Swede Hazlett after the *Brown v. Board of Education* decision. He wrote, "When emotions are deeply stirred, logic and reason must operate gradually and with consideration for human feelings or we have a resultant disaster rather than human advancement."[36]

Despite the staunch Southern opposition to *Brown v. Board of Education* that Ike saw, his hesitation to use the federal government to solve America's racial divisions eased enough for him to sign into law the Civil Rights Act of 1957. The act, designed to protect the voting rights of African Americans, was the first piece of civil rights legislation enacted since Reconstruction. Congress passed it at Ike's strong urging. The act empowered federal prosecutors to obtain court injunctions against interference with the right to vote and established a federal civil rights commission to investigate discriminatory conditions and recommend measures to correct them.[37]

Although Ike's actions during these early days of the modern Civil Rights movement lacked some of the urgency or sense of righteousness later associated with the movement, he was undoubtedly committed to the cause of racial equality. Ike deeply believed that legal justice must be accompanied by social and culture justice at the deepest level, and he feared that strong action by the federal government would only lead to further divides. His faith motivated his commitment to racial equality and affirmed the dignity of all people regardless of the color of their skin.

This commitment continued after Ike left the Oval Office. He lent his support to his successor, John F. Kennedy, to advance civil rights for all Americans. In a letter written on June 14, 1963, he told Kennedy that the matter of civil rights encompassed "the conscience of the individual and the nation, and indeed our moral standards."[38] This statement suggests that no matter how reluctant he was to have the federal government intervene in the civil rights struggles of the 1950s and '60s, Ike viewed the cause of racial equality as a moral one. To him, it was vitally important that both the pulpit and the president's desk address this issue.

Throughout the 1950s, Ike continued to attend church regularly. As Dr. Elson had noted, he just "didn't miss church."[39] On one Sunday in 1957, Ike took some special guests with him: Queen Elizabeth II, the head of the Church of England, and her husband, Prince Philip.[40] He even invited Soviet leader Nikita Khrushchev to attend Gettysburg Presbyterian in 1959, but Khrushchev declined.[41]

During his years in the White House and afterward, it is easy to demonstrate Ike's faithfulness in attending church. When he was in DC, he was at National Presbyterian every week. If he and Mamie were at the family farm, they attended Gettysburg Presbyterian Church. After his years in the White House, Ike attended Mamie's home church, Corona Presbyterian, located in the Cherry Creek district of Denver, where Mamie grew up, and also Palm Desert Community Presbyterian Church in Southern California.

Clifford Roberts, chairman of the Augusta National Golf Club, also recalled Ike's devotion to attending church while visiting there. Ike made forty-five visits to Augusta—five before his election as president, twenty-nine while he was in the White House, and eleven afterward.[42] According to Roberts, golf represented complete relaxation for Ike as he dealt with the constant pressures of the presidency, which precluded his ability to shut everything out and take brief naps. Along with painting, golf played an important role in giving Ike the rest and relaxation he needed.[43]

He wrote that after Ike became president, in order to protect Ike's privacy and that of the club members, he had to promise Roberts that he would never leave the grounds—except to go to church.[44] A 2012 article in *The Augusta Chronicle* about Ike's time at the golf course starts with the sentence, "He stayed. He prayed. He played."[45]

Jim Davis, a local television anchorman in Augusta, remembered Ike's visits to Reid Memorial Church, recalling how the church would commemorate those visits. According to Davis, Ike and Mamie sat in the third pew on the left, which now has a historical marker commemorating their place. Across the aisle from the pew, a standing glass window now features a likeness of Ike looking down at the three wise men bringing gifts to baby Jesus.[46] Finally, on the rear wall of the church is the full text of his 1953 Inaugural Prayer.

Davis recalled that Ike attended Easter services at the church on April 18, 1954, and took part in the cornerstone-laying ceremony for the new sanctuary, something he later also did for National Presbyterian. After Ike's death, the church dedicated its Redemption Window, located in the balcony, to his memory, and his widow, Mamie, continued to attend whenever she was in Augusta.[47]

Davis also recalled that Ike "was never one for making way-forward plans. He would decide Saturday afternoon or Saturday evening that he was going to church the next day. That drove the Secret Service crazy."[48]

Though it may have made the Secret Service's job more difficult, Ike's faithfulness in attending church no matter where he was attests to the fact that his faith was far more than just public proclamations to defeat the Soviets or to advance the Civil Rights movement. Even when traveling to India in late 1959 as part of an eleven-nation tour, Ike arose early and departed by car to attend services at the Protestant Church of the India Cathedral.[49] That type of effort was not indicative of someone who held merely a casual faith but of a man who was truly concerned not only about America's spiritual condition but his own as well.

On the same tour in 1959, the people of the world recognized Ike's spiritual leadership. In Italy, one journalist said of Ike, "He represents a moral conscience, a spiritual force."[50]

While in Rome, on December 6, 1959, Ike met with Pope John XXIII, another significant historical figure, in a meeting hailed as "coming together of two scions of peace."[51] Ike was only the second president to visit the Pope at the Vatican (the first being Woodrow Wilson forty years earlier), and he set a precedent that all other presidents have followed.[52] Pope John XXIII, whose grasp of the English language was tenuous at best, stumbled with the language during his opening address to Ike, and in his native Italian proclaimed about his botch up, "Era di Belli!" which translated into English as "That was a beaut!" Both Ike and the Pope roared with laughter, setting the tone for the warmth of their encounter.[53]

The Catholic magazine *America* wrote at the time, "President Eisenhower's call at the Vatican on December 6 set an example of courtesy and mutual esteem for which the entire American nation and not Catholics alone should congratulate themselves."[54] Five decades later, Joseph McAuley, writing for the same magazine, commented,

> In this particular encounter between a general-turned-president and a one-time-army-chaplain-turned-pontiff, the mutual goodwill that was plainly evident gave a glimpse into a humanity that registered in genuine laughter and showed that it was possible to transcend any barrier, even that of language.[55]

That goodwill was also evident when two hundred young Catholic student priests shouted, "We like Ike!" as his motorcade passed.[56]

In India, the people cheered Ike as a "prince of peace."[57] As Clint Hill, one of the Secret Service agents accompanying Ike, would later write,

> Because of all the great things Dwight D. Eisenhower had accomplished, both before and during his term of office, he had earned the respect of people all over the world. He was an ambassador of the highest order, instilling hope and inspiration, a true leader who reflected positively on the American people.[58]

13

A Continued Commitment

On January 20, 1961, seventy-year-old Dwight Eisenhower, at that time the oldest man to have served as President of the United States, turned over the reins of power to forty-three-year-old John F. Kennedy, the second youngest man ever to serve as President.

Over the past decade, Ike had stood toe-to-toe against the expansionist plans of the Soviet Union. He had sought to bring about the peaceful implementation of equal rights for all Americans, regardless of race. During his eight years in office, he had faced significant health challenges, including a heart attack in 1955, abdominal surgery in 1956, and a stroke in 1957.[1] Through all this, Ike had remained both resolute and outspoken in his faith, carrying on the tradition of boldly faithful language that he started during his presidential campaign in 1952. In the last decade of his life, despite his failing health, his commitment to his faith continued to deepen, even though (or perhaps because) he no longer had access to the bully pulpit of the presidency.

In many ways, Ike's final years exemplified the famous statement attributed to many individuals: the true test of a man's character is what he does when no one is watching.

As many people do as they come to the end of life's journey, Ike returned to his roots, moving to Pennsylvania, the land of his ancestors.

In 1950, Ike and Mamie had bought a farm and a dilapidated house in Gettysburg, just miles from where the Battle of Gettysburg took place; they thought it would be for their sunset years. Just down the road from the Eisenhower farm, Robert E. Lee's Army of Northern Virginia had collided with General Meade's Army of the Potomac. The farm also happened to be just seventy miles from Ike's ancestral home of Elizabethville, Pennsylvania, and it was near Camp Colt, where Ike had trained Tank Corps soldiers decades before.

The location's historic and military significance appealed to Ike, but the property's buildings, in Ike's words, "had seen better days." He added, "So had the soil."[2] The stone house on the property, built by a farmer named Robert McCurdle, was dilapidated and desperately in need of repair. But before Ike and Mamie could get started on the renovation project, the White House beckoned. It would be another eight years before Ike and Mamie could finally move permanently to Gettysburg.

The Gettysburg farm also allowed Ike and Mamie to settle in one place after decades of moving from one military post to another and then into the White House. After the presidency, they finally had this place to call their own. The farm was a place they had discussed and dreamed of for years. As Ike put it, he longed to "escape from concrete into the countryside," while Mamie had grown weary of a "lifetime of adjusting herself to other people's housing designs, or lack of them," and "wanted a place that conformed to her notions of what a home should be."[3]

In 1955, five years after purchasing the farm and making renovations based on Mamie's specifications, Ike and Mamie wanted to conduct a house blessing ceremony with Dr. Elson of National Presbyterian Church and Rev. Clyde Raynor Brown, the young pastor of Gettysburg Presbyterian Church.

Before the house blessing could happen, Ike suffered his first heart attack on September 24, 1955, while visiting Mamie's family in Denver.[4] For several weeks, Ike directed Vice President Richard Nixon, suddenly thrust into running the White House, from afar. On November 14, after returning to DC, Ike wrote Dr. Elson the following letter, which with his usual reticence avoids mentioning his recent health challenge.

> Many thanks for your welcome to Washington. The homecoming we received touched Mrs. Eisenhower and me most deeply.
>
> Mrs. Eisenhower may have mentioned something to you yesterday concerning her hope that you and Mrs. Elson might come up to Gettysburg for luncheon on the day after Thanksgiving, and at that time have the little "house blessing" ceremony of which we have sometimes spoken. [5]

Ike added a personal PS that read, "Of course, I would be delighted to see the text of your sermon, 'The Tools of Peace.'"[6]

A follow-up letter to Dr. Elson, dated November 19, 1955, again illustrates how Ike sought to avoid the kind of publicity that could construe his religious life as manipulative. He wrote,

> I suggest that I have a White House car call for you and Mrs. Elson at something like 9:45 a.m. Friday, the twenty-fifth. Such a schedule should bring you to our house about 11:45.
>
> We could have a 12:30 luncheon—probably just the family present—and then shortly thereafter have the little "house blessing" ceremony. The period you would be here before the luncheon should allow you and Mrs. Eisenhower to determine on exactly the kind you would consider most appropriate. I think this would be better than to attempt to plan the ceremony in advance because I am sure that she wants to conduct it in the simplest way possible and with no publicity whatsoever.[7]

Rev. Brown, still alive at the time of this writing and still sharp as a tack, shared some memories of that event in a personal interview.

> We just got a telephone call [about the house blessing ceremony]. [My wife] called me at the church and I said well, of course, we'd

be happy to do that. So plans were made, they gave us instructions, what time, and that we should be at the gates, tell the person at the gates who we were and why we were coming, and they would know to escort us to the house, which is what happened. . . . I was asked to give a blessing.[8]

The house blessing was yet another example of Ike's simple, sincere, and unpretentious faith, as well as a tribute to the relationships he developed with numerous members of the Presbyterian clergy over the last twenty years of his life. Today, when one visits the Eisenhower home, they will see two brass prayer plaques at the front door, another testament to Ike and Mamie's faith, quoting the lyrics of the still-popular hymn "Bless This House."

Gettysburg Presbyterian Church claimed a congregation dating back to 1740. Abraham Lincoln had visited the church the day he delivered his fabled Gettysburg Address in November 1863, and the pew where he sat became known as the Lincoln pew.

The Eisenhowers' first visit to the church was on May 15, 1955. A picture of a smiling Ike and Mamie with the Rev. Brown appeared in the Harrisburg newspaper with the headline, "Ike and Mamie Worship Where Lincoln Did." The article goes on to say,

> The Eisenhowers sat just three pews behind the one Lincoln occupied November 19, 1863. A small American flag and a bronze tablet mark the Lincoln pew. . . . On arrival at the church, the President and his wife . . . were met out front by two old friends, retired Brig. Gen. and Mrs. Arthur S. Nevins. The Nevins, who live near Gettysburg, sat in the same pew with the Eisenhowers. . . . The party was escorted to the Lincoln pew by 81-year-old S. Gray Bigham, senior elder. Bigham had invited the President to attend the service and he proudly displayed a thank you note from the chief executive. Nevins said the original plan was for the President to occupy the Lincoln pew, but it was decided

that would be "too uncomfortable." It is the only pew in the church which has not been replaced with modern ones.[9]

Ike and Mamie, accompanied by their son John and grandson David, first took Communion at the church during their third visit on July 10, 1955. Rev. Brown prayed for "divine wisdom" for Ike. "To our own President," Brown said, "ever give the knowledge that our hope and our prayers go with him." After the service, a crowd gathered in the sweltering summer heat outside the church, and when Ike and Mamie stepped through the front doors, everybody burst into applause.[10]

Rev. Brown was not the Eisenhowers' pastor at Gettysburg Presbyterian for long. In 1957, he took a new pastorate elsewhere, and his replacement was a young minister named Robert MacAskill. The new pastor's first meeting with Ike was on Mother's Day 1957, when Ike and Mamie visited Gettysburg Presbyterian accompanied by famed British Field Marshal Bernard Montgomery. For Rev. MacAskill, who was only in his second Sunday at the church, the thought of three such honored guests must have been a bit intimidating.[11] Nevertheless, MacAskill and Ike would soon develop a strong bond.

In later interviews, Rev. MacAskill looked back warmly at the relationship he had with Ike. His comments show how deeply involved Ike was with the church, even while he was still serving as president. The reverend said,

> Knowing that I was to come to Gettysburg as the pastor, I did have some correspondence with President Eisenhower. . . . The correspondence was of a pretty general nature. He was aware of the committee on ministry being active in pursuit of a new pastor and [the committee] would, through our newsletter and other correspondence and church publications, give reports as to how that committee was proceeding. So he was kept aware of that and when it was known that I had received a call he was notified about that. He sent a letter welcoming me to Gettysburg as pastor of the church.[12]

The letter also expressed interest in striking up a friendship.[13] Ike and Mamie, in their first in-person meeting with the new pastor, were, according to Rev. MacAskill, "very cordial, complimentary, and encouraging, hoping that it will be a long and productive pastorate."[14] Their wish came true, as Rev. MacAskill would serve Gettysburg Presbyterian from 1957 to 1986.

Rev. MacAskill also remembered how Ike did not want to receive any special recognition. Ike greatly disliked being at the center of the necessary security and other logistical issues that he, as a president and later a former president, presented while sitting in the congregation.

Rev. MacAskill recalled that Ike and Mamie had a designated pew. The Secret Service would bring them to the front entrance, where ushers would then escort them to their pew. They would remain in their seats until the end of the service. At that point, Rev. MacAskill would leave the pulpit area, walk down the aisle, and pause to meet the Eisenhowers, who would follow behind him as he left. He then described what would happen:

> The Secret Service would pick them up and take them to their limousine. . . . I was careful not to say, "Well, we're happy to have President and Mrs. Eisenhower with us today." . . . They wanted to be just a part of the congregation and so we tried to deal with them in that manner.[15]

Ike's grandson David Eisenhower spent many of his formative years at his grandparents' home in Gettysburg. David worked at the farm from age ten. On his tenth birthday, Ike presented his grandson with a large, wine-colored family Bible with ten parchment pages to enter the births, deaths, and marriages of David's future sons, daughters, grandchildren, and great-grandchildren.[16]

In his book *Going Home to Glory*, David recalled sitting with his grandfather and listening to Rev. MacAskill's sermons. The pastor was diminutive but spoke with great poise and authority. David wrote that Ike was especially fond of MacAskill and admired his sermons and his command of the language, as well as his sincerity and low-key manner.[17]

According to David, when a larger congregation tried to lure Rev. MacAskill away with a bigger salary and the chance for his children to receive a better education, Ike worked with Dr. Elson at National Presbyterian to arrange for a raise for Rev. MacAskill, enabling him to stay with the Gettysburg congregation.

David described the interests Ike shared with MacAskill, saying that MacAskill found Ike to be "'dynamically' interested in discussing ways of involving the church in improving national and global problems."[18] David added that his grandfather was also interested in liturgy and was not shy about sharing his opinions and preferences for sermon topics and hymns.[19]

The correspondence between the two men shows a warm relationship, even before Ike left the White House. On June 27, 1958, Ike wrote to Rev. MacAskill to thank him for sending him two sermons he had requested, adding, "I appreciate your thoughtfulness in remembering my request."[20] A year later, he thanked Rev. MacAskill for his note of sympathy on the passing of John Foster Dulles, Ike's Secretary of State.[21]

In another letter written on September 2, 1960, Ike sent a rather contrite note about missing the services at Gettysburg Presbyterian based on a time confusion. Rev. MacAskill had apologized for the confusion, but Ike replied, "I assure you there was no necessity for you to 'apologize;' the matter was entirely my own fault—I should have had someone check on the time of the service before I started out."[22]

On September 28, 1960, Ike sent a thank-you letter to Rev. MacAskill for a note he had sent to Ike about his talk to the United Nations General Assembly six days before on assisting the developing nations of Africa.[23] Ike wrote, "I am gratified that you felt [the speech] restated the moral obligation that I know all the people of this country feel toward those individuals of the less developed nations."[24]

Rev. MacAskill remembered that Ike's favorite hymns were "Oh God Our Help in Ages Past, Our Hope for Years to Come," "What a Friend We Have in Jesus," and "I Love to Tell the Story."[25] "His background was not that of a churchman . . . when he went to West Point, beginning his military career from then on it was usually in post chapels, that type of thing, so he did not anchor into a church," Rev. MacAskill recollected.[26]

As Rev. MacAskill would find out, this was because of the nomadic military life that Ike and Mamie lived for much of their marriage. In some ways, the realities of that lifestyle provide a response to the accusations that Ike did not take church seriously until he ran for office; for decades it was logistically impossible for the Eisenhowers to build long-term commitments to churches because of the demands of military life. Once Ike acknowledged the importance of church, it stuck, both through his presidency and beyond. Just as Dr. Elson and National Presbyterian served as a spiritual anchor for Ike during his presidency, Gettysburg Presbyterian and Rev. MacAskill were the Eisenhowers' spiritual anchors in Ike's postpresidency years.

Rev. MacAskill recalled his conversations with Ike.

He was very careful not to try to suggest to me what I should be preaching about or anything like that. And in my preaching, I was careful not to [say], so to speak, "Now I have the President here, I'm going to tell him what he should be doing or shouldn't be doing.". . . I remember once in speaking with him, he said, "I come to church to get something out of the service."[27]

Ike's statement about wanting "to get something out of the service" is further evidence of how seriously he took his faith. He did not just want to "do church." He wanted to learn and to grow spiritually, even as he was entering his last days.

Ike and Rev. MacAskill would frequently meet to discuss questions or thoughts Ike had about a sermon or a passage of Scripture. Sometimes the two men met at the reverend's favorite place, the Lamp Post Tea Room, which was across the street from Ike's Gettysburg office. The Lamp Post was a typical small town café: enormous steaks sizzled on the grill while patrons enjoyed generous servings of country ham dinners and homemade pies. The restaurant was not shy about using Ike as a marketing tool. They made it a point to inform people that his office was across the street and that the Lamp Post was a good place to catch a glimpse of Gettysburg's most famous resident.

In another interview, Rev. MacAskill recalled,

> Often when I would talk with him, about a sermon or a service, it was interesting what he would pick up and you wouldn't think that he would be listening or quite observant, but he was a very intense listener and had the ability to assimilate, to evaluate, and he came to service for a purpose, it was not just a social thing. But he felt a strong need of affirming his faith, of, I think, recognizing the sovereign power of God in the affairs of men. And I think [he] saw himself as an instrumentality of that purpose and will, and that's quite evident, I think, throughout his life. And he was always growing and maturing in that respect.[28]

Rev. MacAskill later said his relationship with Ike was "a privileged one which you try to respect and yet, try not to neglect, in a way."[29]

David Eisenhower also noted that Rev. MacAskill was diligent about respecting Ike's privacy. He did not try to cultivate a deeper relationship with Ike than Ike wanted. David observed that Ike's relationship rules with most people was for them to tend to business. David added, "[Rev. MacAskill] was available when Granddad desired to discuss sermons and current events. He was also unavailable from time to time, which doubtlessly contributed to Granddad's respect for him."[30]

Ike's loyalties were to more than simply his home church; he gradually became more involved in nationwide Presbyterian culture. In the early 1960s, Ike lent his support to a fund-raising drive for the United Presbyterian Church's "Fifty Million Dollar Fund." According to Rev. MacAskill, the purpose of the drive was to "raise funds to undergird existing mission work, colleges, hospitals, schools, churches, [and] mission endeavor[s] around the world."[31] He added,

> If [Ike] would give his endorsement, or willingness to serve, as the chairman, what we call the honorary chairman, not having to work at the mechanics of the organization, that it would be a very fine identification and endorsement of the program. And he was quite willing to do that. And one occasion when he was in New York, arrangement was made to have an interview with him and so a motion picture film was made with his endorsement attached to the film and it was circulated throughout our denomination. And interestingly enough, that fund realized not only fifty million but ultimately nearly seventy million dollars, in its total receipts. So he identified himself in this way, and as they say, it helped to give support, endorsement, and encouragement to others to contribute.[32]

Ike and Mamie also donated a four-panel nativity scene to Gettysburg Presbyterian, which was crafted by an artist named Winfred Hyatt and had been displayed in the East Room of the White House during Ike's presidency. The church proudly exhibited the piece during the Advent season. (This nativity scene, which had deteriorated with age and use, was donated to the Eisenhower National Historic Site in 1998 and subsequently restored to its original condition.)[33]

Though the Eisenhowers became dedicated members of their new home church in Gettysburg, they did not forget their old congregation at National Presbyterian. Even before his presidency concluded, Ike worked with Henry Luce and J. Howard Pew, the president of Sunoco, to raise funds for the construction of a new home for the church, which had outgrown its building on Connecticut Avenue. In 1966, the church acquired a plot of land on Nebraska Avenue previously occupied by the Hillcrest Children's Center. Ike not only helped find financing for the $20 million construction but also reviewed the architectural proposals for the neo-Gothic building.

Ike took his membership at Gettysburg Presbyterian seriously, and it was clear that he viewed participation in a church as far more than just a Sunday morning activity. He was an actively engaged member who had regular interactions with his pastor and tried to use his influence judiciously to advance the mission of the church and his denomination. He made numerous small, personal gifts to the church. These gifts included a number of his original paintings and the first American flag featuring fifty stars after Hawaii's entrance into the United States in 1959.[34] Ike's personal administrative assistant, Ann C. Whitman, wrote to Rev. MacAskill, "The President requests that no one be told that the flag comes from him and that the entire matter be kept confidential."[35]

Beside these gifts of time and talent, the Eisenhowers were consistent financial supporters of the church. "[The Eisenhowers] supported the church very generously and did not want that to be known," said Rev. MacAskill.[36]

Visitors to the Eisenhower home in Gettysburg are often taken aback by the number of Bibles in Ike's library. While some have surmised that some of the Bibles were gifts, those who knew Ike said that their presence was not just a coincidence. Rev. MacAskill said, "I don't think a person buys Bibles just to be having Bibles, but he was a good student of the Scriptures and, I think, tried to increase his library and thus his knowledge in the whole area. So that would account for the various editions and versions of the Bible that he would have."[37]

After Ike ended his decades of public service and became a private citizen, he and Mamie settled easily into the quietness of life in Gettysburg. Ike continued to hone the craft of painting, while also tending the Eisenhowers' working farm with its small, prize-winning herd of Black Angus cattle.

Ike, like other former presidents, found that even after leaving office the spotlight followed him. Ike continued to make his political opinions known, occasionally endorsing Republican candidates for office and delivering speeches and lectures across the nation. Though no longer president, he continued to advocate strongly for the role of faith in the public square.

As seen in his conversations with Rev. MacAskill, Ike viewed church as far more than simply a social club. To him, the church had great influence in national and international affairs. He did not make the distinction so popular today between the faith of an individual and the faith of organized religious groups like churches; he believed that both were vital to American society and often spoke of the necessity of encouraging strong faith communities and churches across the country.

According to David Eisenhower, Ike once told Rev. MacAskill that the "church is the conscience of the nation."[38] David wrote that his grandfather approved of churches being involved in politics. Ike's approval stemmed from his experiences in the 1930s, when the European churches accommodated fascism with tragic results. David recalled that Ike's experience made him question whether religious, moral, and political questions could be divorced from one another without sacrificing all morality in politics.[39]

Ike's experience facing not one but two godless societies (Nazi Germany and the Soviet Union) also led him to believe it was impossible to have a strong, ethical society without retaining organized religious communities whose creed upheld the dignity of all humans. He believed that removing or repressing those communities created a moral vacuum at the heart of a society, with the vacuum filled by some malignant form of atheistic humanism that denied human dignity and degraded individual lives for the sake of some "greater good."

Ike's presidency ended in January 1961, the beginning of a tumultuous decade in which America's young people rejected organized religion in unprecedented numbers. The Sexual Revolution and the ideal of "free love" captured the imagination of generations with devastating consequences. Advocates of anti-Christian mores began laying the legal and social groundwork for the colossal social upheaval to come, manifest in skyrocketing divorce rates, broken marriages and families, legalized taking of innocent human life, and disregard for religious freedom.

Though Ike passed away before the bitter fruit of the 1960s' rejection of Judeo-Christian morality was fully evident, he was not blind to the direction the country was moving. As early as 1963, Ike recognized that religion's place as the moral core of American society was in jeopardy. Of special concern to Ike was the Supreme Court's decision in *School District of Abington Township v. Schempp*, striking down the recitation of the Lord's Prayer and Scripture reading in public schools.

Edward Schempp, a Unitarian Universalist, filed suit against the Abington Township, Pennsylvania, school district, claiming that the public school was violating the separation of church and state by requiring students to read or listen to passages from the Bible. The lawsuit, he claimed, was an effort to "shield" his children from being exposed to Christian teachings that he did not share.[40] The Supreme Court ruled in Schempp's favor, initiating a gradual but definite purge of all religious—and by extension, moral—language from American public education.

Not long after the ruling, Rev. MacAskill asked Ike to speak to the Carlisle Presbytery, a meeting of local church leaders at Gettysburg Presbyterian about how Christians and Christian churches should be involved in contemporary affairs. In the recorded talk, Ike exhorted the church leadership to embrace the importance of devout, moral religious individuals being active in society.

During his talk, Ike reiterated his deeply held belief that the source of America's strength in the world was her founding on the principle that human rights are a gift from God. Here are some excerpts taken from the original recording, which, given Ike's famous tortured syntax, has been edited for readability:

> It would be a very wise man, I think, [who] would avoid religious questions in facing [an] audience made up mostly of theologians. But I . . . have some [questions] that bother me from time to time. One of them relates to this matter of giving our children any education of a religious character in our public schools. . . .
>
> Is it possible to give to our children the kind of basic religious education or feeling that . . . we believe they should have without bringing religion directly into the curriculum? For example, certainly we don't object to reading the Declaration of Independence; yet in the very first paragraph, in the very preamble of this document . . . we find first nature and nature's God called upon to confirm . . . the rectitude of the decisions that our forbearers took. And immediately thereafter, they point out the very theory [that] our whole political system is based upon . . . men are endowed by their equal rights by their Creator, spelled with a capital "C." . . .
>
> And I think even when you go to the Constitution, while I believe there is no direct mention made to the deity, in the document itself when you get to section 7, when they were affixing their signatures and they said "and in the year . . . this year of our Lord, 1787." . . .
>
> When we just take these two documents . . . we have to say this: our civilization, our form of government is the political expression of some deeply felt religious faith. And I believe if we can accept . . . what they themselves told us, we can find a very fine textbook for bringing a lot of moral instruction into our schools.
>
> But suppose for a moment we just dropped the whole thought of a deity and Jesus Christ, but studied him. Studied the secular

history about him, and more than that, the things that have come about in our civilization because of his life. I do not mean anything . . . that takes theology into account. . . . We date our time in this era because he was born. Our whole . . . code of morals, ethics, [and] the things we teach our children [all] came about because of his life. The theory of the equality of men came about through the Judeo-Christian ethic. . . .

If we suggest [these things] as a basis for keeping [in] our schools the . . . kind of instruction that will bring our young ones up in a moral atmosphere and in which they [can] recognize the appearance, the existence of an overlord, a God. I think that there is no supreme court in the world [that] by taking those documents and the secular history of this whole civilization that has been so influenced so greatly by the light of Christ . . . could say "this is illegal."

Now if I'm wrong, some of you people are going to have to get out your books and write me long letters because I don't think I am. . . . At any rate, I just simply say that I think there is no need for us to limit Americans to raise our children like we were in a communist school denying the existence of any God.[41]

Ike's comment, "Bring our young ones up in a moral atmosphere and in which they [can] recognize the appearance, the existence of an overlord," was a pointed reference to Operation Overlord, the military name for the D-Day invasion. As David Eisenhower would put it, he "implied a clear connection between the mission of his forces and America's moral leadership in the world."[42]

According to David Eisenhower, comments such as these revealed a good deal about his grandfather's philosophy of life. David wrote that Ike believed that religious beliefs provided individuals with the ability to accomplish what was necessary and good, and that only through subordination in a transcendent order could an individual work toward something good. David concluded: "Like all those he respected, [he] saw himself as a subordinate in a larger scheme, and had believed so all his life."[43]

David's reflections echo Rev. MacAskill's belief that Ike saw himself as an instrument in the hands of a greater being. This philosophy was not singular to Ike among presidents. Abraham Lincoln, in the midst of the Civil War, came to see himself in much the same way.[44] Both David Eisenhower and Rev. MacAskill assert in their recollections that, despite what some critics say, Ike saw himself this way, long before he ever joined a church, was baptized, or confronted the challenges of the presidency with strongly faith-based language.

14

"God Take Me"

n 1967, National Presbyterian invited Ike to be present at a ceremony to lay the cornerstone for their new building, but due to his failing health, Ike responded with uncertainty about whether he would be able to attend. He wrote to Dr. Elson on June 22, 1967:

Quite naturally I am complimented by your invitation for my wife and me to be present at the cornerstone laying for the National Presbyterian Church on October 14. Certainly I would deem it a privilege to be present but my difficulty is that I'm getting to the point where I can no longer commit to fixed dates so far in advance. However, should circumstances be such that I am in this part of the country in mid-October and should other circumstances, such as my health, all be favorable than [sic] I certainly plan to be with you for the ceremonies that you are scheduling for that day.

However, I suggest that you plan for me no formal address. While I would not object to participating in the activities of the cornerstone laying or to address a few informal words to the gathering, I do not want to undertake the chore of preparing a formal talk. It is a great satisfaction to know that the building project is going well. Thank you again for the invitation.[1]

Though Ike's health continued to decline, he was able to attend the gathering. On October 14, 1967—which happened to be Ike's seventy-seventh birthday—at an official ceremony, the former president laid the cornerstone for the church's new building. Afterward, several of his old colleagues and friends, such as senators Frank Carlson, Everett Dirksen, and Henry Jackson; the actor Jimmy Stewart and his wife, Gloria; and Rev. and Mrs. Robert MacAskill, among others, sponsored a luncheon in honor of Ike at the Mayflower Hotel. The event was truly ecumenical as the Roman Catholic Archbishop of Washington, Patrick Cardinal O'Toole, delivered a special prayer of thanksgiving; Dr. Arthur S. Flemming, president of the National Council of Churches, gave an address; and Ike's old friend and pastor, Dr. Elson, gave a tribute.[2]

The luncheon started with those in attendance singing,

> Our fathers' God, to Thee,
> Author of liberty.
> To Thee we sing;
> Long may our land be bright
> With freedom's holy light;
> Protect us by Thy might,
> Great God, our King.[3]

This honorary luncheon was one of Ike's final public appearances. Throughout the sixties, his health had become increasingly precarious, and after a second heart attack in November 1965 while at Augusta National (he lived through seven such attacks throughout his life), he struggled to recover. Clifford Roberts would recall that after the 1965 attack, his trips to the fabled golf course became increasingly infrequent.[4] Even his church attendance declined—a sure sign that all was not well. In May 1965, he wrote to Rev. MacAskill that he and Mamie regretted missing church, but the remnants of a cold kept him away. He then added a personal PS of regret: "As of now it appears that both of us will be out of town this coming Sunday, she in Washington, I in New York."[5]

In February 1966, he wrote to Rev. MacAskill that he regretted not being able to go to church when he and Mamie were in Palm Desert, California, explaining,

> Mrs. Eisenhower and I have been enjoying the fine weather of this area but it was only last Sunday that we finally attended church. My doctors have been very urgent in their advice that I stay out of crowds because of the prevalence of influenza in the region. They seem to be fearful, in my case, of a congestion in the chest than they are of the past damage to my heart.[6]

In the spring of 1968, Ike suffered another heart attack. This latest attack placed him in such poor health that he had to move to the Walter Reed National Military Center for treatment, where he spent the remaining year of his life. Nevertheless, he still maintained a relationship with Rev. MacAskill, as this letter from May 21, 1968, attests:

> Thank you for your letter. I deeply appreciate your thoughtfulness and your concern for my well-being and am pleased to report that my doctors are allowing me to be up and around a couple of hours each day.
> It was kind of you to stop by my office to inquire about my progress and as soon as I am allowed visitors I would enjoy seeing you. However, I would not want you to make a trip to Washington, DC for that purpose only.[7]

In July, Mamie wrote Rev. MacAskill on Ike's behalf to update him on his health. She wrote,

> Thank you for your interesting letter and thoughtful phone calls. . . . This last attack was a great shock and setback. It doesn't look like we will be going home for quite some time, but the General is improving slowly and his spirits and appetite are good. Please convey our deep appreciation to the congregation for their prayers and good wishes for us.
> I have been so busy that I haven't been out of the hospital for three weeks, except to go to church.[8]

197

On December 4, 1968, Ike would send his final letter to Rev. Mac-Askill, who had sent him a note wishing him a happy birthday. Ike wrote,

> Some weeks ago the doctors allowed me to dictate a few letters. Soon thereafter they decided that they should not have been so impetuous, so yesterday morning was the first time that they renewed the privilege, to be exercised very cautiously. This accounts for the long delay in thanking you personally for your kind birthday greetings.
>
> I am more than delighted that you are taking a study leave to attend the Divinity School at Harvard University. I shall be looking forward to seeing you when the doctors have decided I should be released from the hospital.[9]

In these final, painful days, Ike continued to display a stoic serenity. In the last picture of him, taken a month before his death, a very thin and obviously ailing Ike is in his bathrobe, sitting in a chair, propped up by a pillow, and smiling for the camera. Another picture taken earlier that same day shows Ike grinning widely as he talks with his former vice president, now the newly elected President of the United States, Richard M. Nixon.

On March 4, 1969, Mamie would write Rev. MacAskill again.

> From friends in Gettysburg, General Eisenhower and I learned of the special prayer you offered last Sunday. We are deeply grateful for this personal remembrance during the regular worship service.
>
> We are aware of your many visits and phone calls to the General's office concerning our welfare, and we sincerely thank you for your constant support. It is comforting and heartening to know that you are thinking of us during the many anxious hours we have experienced over the past months.[10]

Ike's longtime friend Dr. Billy Graham frequently visited him in the hospital, and in his remarks for the one hundredth anniversary of Ike's birth, recalled those final days together,

President Eisenhower was in Walter Reed Hospital—the doctors did not give him much of a chance to survive—when I visited him for the last time. I was to stay twenty minutes, but it extended to thirty. And he asked the doctors and nurses to leave the room. . . . Then [he said], "You've told me several times how to be sure of my salvation. Would you tell me again?" I took out my New Testament, read him several passages of Scripture, and I could sense he had the assurance that he was going to go to heaven.

I know that one day we're going to meet General Eisenhower in heaven. Perhaps he can even see us here today and knows what we're doing. Hebrews 12:1 says that we're surrounded by a great crowd of witnesses that have gone on before. His eternal destiny and his place in heaven were not determined by being a great president or a great general. His achievements as a man had nothing to do with his standing before God. . . . President Eisenhower is in heaven today because he accepted Jesus Christ as his personal Savior and came to know Jesus as the one Friend who could bear his sins and sorrows.[11]

In his autobiography, *Just As I Am*, Graham added that he and Ike clasped hands in prayer, and afterward Ike told him, "Thank you. I'm ready."[12]

On March 28, 1969, Ike ordered the blinds in his room shut and then said, with his family surrounding him, "I want to go. God take me," and closed his eyes for the final time.[13] Before he died, he said to Mamie, "I have always loved my wife. I have always loved my children. I have always loved my grandchildren. And I have always loved my country."[14]

On March 29, an honor escort of generals and admirals accompanied the body of Dwight David Eisenhower to Bethlehem Chapel in the Washington National Cathedral. After the brief, private ceremony for family, honor guard, and honorary civilian pallbearers, Ike's body laid in repose for twenty-eight hours.

The next day, March 30, would find Ike's casket transported to the Capitol rotunda. There, Dr. Elson would offer a benediction and President Nixon would deliver a eulogy.[15] Nixon said,

We mourn Dwight Eisenhower's death, but we are grateful for his life. We gather, also, conscious of the fact that in paying tribute to Dwight Eisenhower, we celebrate greatness. When we think of his place in history, we think, inevitably, of the other giants of those days of World War II; and we think of the qualities of greatness and what his were that made his unique among all.

Once, perhaps without intending to do so, he, himself, put a finger on it. It was 1945, shortly after V-E Day, at a ceremony in London's historic Guildhall. The triumphant Supreme Commander of the Allied Forces in Europe was officially given the Freedom of the City of London. In an eloquent address that day, Dwight Eisenhower said, "I come from the heart of America."

Perhaps no one sentence could better sum up what Dwight Eisenhower meant to a whole generation of Americans. He did come from the heart of America, not only from its geographical heart, but from its spiritual heart. . . .

Dwight Eisenhower touched something fundamental in America which only a man of intense force of mind and spirit could have brought so vibrantly alive. He was a product of America's soil and of its ideals, driven by a compulsion to do right and to do well; a man of deep faith who believed in God and trusted in His will. . . .

His great love of people was rooted in his faith. He had a deep faith in the goodness of God and in the essential goodness of man as a creature of God. . . .

Dwight Eisenhower was that rarest of men—an authentic hero. . . . And, yet, he always retained a saving humility. His was the humility not of fear but of confidence. He walked with the great of the world, and he knew that the great were human. His was the humility of man before God and before the truth. . . . The principles he believed in, the ideals he stood for, these were bigger than his own country. . . .

His life reminds us that there is a moral force in this world more powerful than the might of arms or the wealth of nations. This man led the most powerful armies that the world has ever seen, this man who led the most powerful nation in the world, this essentially good and gentle and kind man—that moral force was his greatness. For a quarter of a century to the very end of his life Dwight Eisenhower exercised a moral authority without parallel in America and in the world. And America and the world are better for it.[16]

On March 31, the casket returned to the National Cathedral for the main service. Dr. Elson, now serving as Chaplain of the Senate, conducted the service based on Psalms 46 and 121, two of Ike's favorites.[17] At 5:00 p.m., a train bearing Ike's body wound out of Washington, DC, toward Abilene, Kansas.

Once the train arrived in Abilene, a procession took the casket through Abilene to the Dwight D. Eisenhower Library. Rev. Mac-Askill conducted the funeral service. He read from John 14:1–3.

Let not your hearts be troubled. Believe in God; believe also in me. In my Father's house are many rooms. If it were not so, would I have told you that I go to prepare a place for you? And if I go and prepare a place for you, I will come again and will take you to myself, that where I am you may be also.

He then went on to read the words of the apostle Paul from 2 Timothy 4:6–8.

For I am already being poured out as a drink offering, and the time of my departure has come. I have fought the good fight, I have finished the race, I have kept the faith. Henceforth there is laid up for me the crown of righteousness, which the Lord, the righteous judge, will award to me on that day, and not only to me but also to all who have loved his appearing.

Rev. MacAskill then said about Ike,

"I have kept the faith." This was an expression of his life that impressed those who knew him. He had a vibrant faith in God, his fellowmen, and his country. He said, "We have to proclaim our faith. It was our faith in the deathless dignity of man.". . .

He spoke of a faith in the beneficence of the Almighty. To him, "faith was the substance of things hoped for, the evidence of things not seen." . . .

Here then, was the simple, straightforward, uncomplicated faith of a world leader. He not so much articulated a faith as he acted upon it. His faith in God gave him a humility and a high regard for human life. It caused him to be dedicated to the preservation and perpetuation of such a way of life.

Because of this faith he was liberated from provincialism and little things and given a world vision and concern for all men. He believed in the words of a favorite hymn: "Faith of our Fathers living still, in spite of fire, dungeon, and sword." . . .

His example of character, integrity, humility, and dedication is indeed a rich legacy and will give us inspiration to resist the forces of tyranny and help us to usher in a new day of brotherhood and good will to the glory of God and the welfare of mankind.[18]

Following MacAskill's remarks was a memorial service led by the Rev. Dean W. Miller of Palm Desert Community Presbyterian, where Ike and Mamie worshiped when vacationing and golfing there. Miller said,

Someday, he firmly believed, he would stand before his God; for his personal faith told him there is a life ahead. And of this, too, he was convinced; that the same Lord who was with him on Malta, and during those anxious early hours of D-Day, when he headed the mightiest invasion in history, will stand with him at the beginning of the greatest adventure of his career . . . entrance into eternal life. "Well done, good and faithful servant, enter into the joy of your Master."[19]

Finally, a burial service held in the Place of Meditation was officiated by Major General Luther D. Miller, the former Chief of Army Chaplains.[20] The service featured Ike's favorite hymns, such as "God of Our Fathers," "Onward Christian Soldiers," "A Mighty Fortress Is Our God," "The Old Rugged Cross," and "Lead, Kindly Light."[21]

One of Ike's last requests was that his final resting place be in an eighty-dollar government-issue casket, the same resting place as that of countless men and boys he had coached, trained, prayed for, and led into battle decades before. The only enhancement to the casket that held the Supreme Commander of the Allied Forces in World War II and the former president of the United States was an inner glass seal that cost $115.[22] Even though he could have been buried at Arlington National Cemetery, Ike chose to be laid to rest alongside his beloved little son Icky, back in Abilene, his humble roots where his journey started. Ten years later, in 1979, Mamie would be laid to rest next to Ike and their little boy.

Today, the Eisenhower Presidential Library stands around the site, and the Eisenhower family lies in the Place of Meditation. On a large tapestry, the words of Ike's inaugural prayer in 1953 hang on the wall. A plaque from the Eisenhower Library says that, "according to General Eisenhower's wishes, it was hoped that visitors would reflect upon the ideals that made this a great nation and pledge themselves again to continued loyalty to those ideals."[23] For Ike, those ideals were based on faith in God and the belief in the human dignity of all persons.

With that, the spiritual journey of the simple soldier from the dusty streets of Abilene to the battlefields of World War II to Washington, DC, as the leader of the free world came to a close.

Epilogue

Alan Sears

Several years before this book was even an idea, I had the good fortune to have breakfast at the Hay-Adams Hotel in Washington, DC, with a table of Eisenhower experts and aficionados. One had recently published a groundbreaking and bestselling volume on the thirty-fourth president. Another had been a key official at the United States Archives who handled Ike's official papers and memorabilia for many years. Another had recently concluded years of service to another president on his White House staff. The conversation, needless to say, was lively and full of fascinating insights into this great man's life and service. However, I could not help but notice that one subject went strangely unmentioned.

At the time, the story of Ike's faith had been on my mind, though I knew only the bare outline: he had come from a Bible-centered background and moved away from regular church attendance during his years in the US Army but renewed his faith during his presidency.

When I voiced my interest in understanding Eisenhower's religious beliefs, the conversation at that breakfast ground to a halt. My companions, so well versed in Ike minutiae, had never seriously considered the man's religious background or beliefs. A few of them expressed surprise at the thought that there was any story there at all.

My companions were not alone in overlooking this aspect of Ike's character. From his time to ours, there have been hundreds of books published about Eisenhower. Naturally, many of these books focused on his wartime leadership and presidency. Others dealt with his warnings about the military-industrial complex; his policies in the Middle East and North Korea; his relationship with his vice president, Richard Nixon; or with the transition to power of his successor in office, John F. Kennedy. One even focuses on his love for golf after World War II. The list of Ike-related subjects is seemingly endless.

Conspicuously absent, however, was a book about Eisenhower's religion. Very few of those dozens of scholarly works even make mention of his faith. Among those that do, many take a cynical view that accuses Ike of using religious faith as a means to stir up patriotic fervor during the Cold War. Some entirely dismiss the idea that Ike's faith was legitimate, such as Kevin Kruse's book *One Nation Under God: How Corporate America Invented Christian America* or Jean Edward Smith's scholarly *Eisenhower in War and Peace*. Smith wrote that Ike was merely heeding "political advice" when he joined National Presbyterian in 1953, but in the same paragraph detailed the president's fury at the notion that Dr. Elson had publicized his attendance at the church.[1]

This is a major scholarly problem, for the latter situation (Ike's frustration with Elson) is simply incompatible with the narrative that Ike had no interest in religion beside political utility. If Ike had come to religion from purely political motives, why would he even care, let alone be angry, if Dr. Elson had tipped reporters to his attendance at National Presbyterian? Would not the national attention have been a boon if he saw his personal religion as a political asset?

All this makes one wonder: Did Smith never read Ann C. Whitman's comments about Ike talking religion with her all the time? What about the stories about Ike's close friendships with Billy Graham, Dr.

Elson, and Rev. MacAskill? Why was he only the second president to make his way to the Vatican to visit the Pope? When one considers the full story of Ike's life, it seems as though scholars have to do some rather serious mental gymnastics to present Ike's faith as merely political or as secondary to his life! I found myself thinking that it would have been simpler for Smith, who is consistently antireligious in his books, to take the path he chose in the biography *Bush*, where he portrayed the forty-third president as a religious zealot.

It is not hard to imagine atheistic scholars portraying Ike—the man who put "In God We Trust" on America's money, inserted "One Nation Under God" into the Pledge of Allegiance, and publicly prayed and encouraged the American people to pray—as a zealot as well.

However, they do not. Instead, contemporary scholars often act as if Ike's faith and his constant faith references in speech after speech do not exist. The modern image of Ike is of an ideal politician and president: a conservative on fiscal matters, a moderate or liberal on most other issues, a hero of World War II, and a cold warrior who cast a skeptical eye on the unchecked growth of the American military. In 2016, while running for the Democratic nomination for president, Bernie Sanders, a self-avowed socialist whose economic policies and attitude toward Christian morality are totally unlike anything Ike proclaimed, told an audience that he was not "that much of a socialist compared to Eisenhower."[2]

Evidently, for every political persuasion, there is something to like about Ike.

Apart from the work of academic historians such as Jerry Bergman, who examined Ida Eisenhower's dalliance with the Bible Student movement, which eventually became the Jehovah's Witnesses, this aspect of Ike's life and character has gone largely unexamined. That is why we wrote this book. However, it is important to note that our intention was to conduct an honest inquiry based on the fullest possible examination of the facts. History shows that Ike joined a church, attended regularly, and urged Americans to do the same. The question is, Were these actions genuine? Or, on the other hand, were they, as historians such as Smith and Kruse state, a ploy?

After several years of writing and researching, traveling to Abilene, Augusta, Denver, and Gettysburg, and reading countless interviews of people who knew Ike and Mamie, we felt the facts and the historical record were clear: the life of Dwight D. Eisenhower has all the signs of that of a man of firm, personal faith. His character and his conduct, both in and out of office, show unmistakable signs of the influence of his religious beliefs. The available resources on Ike's life—archival documents, contemporary records, and the recollections of his contemporaries—show that from his childhood Ike was surrounded by religion and leaned on it only more heavily throughout his life.

Historians who deny this either are missing many of the facts or have deliberately stuck their heads in the sand. By ignoring and missing this part of the story, they have written incomplete biographies about him. These biographies show only one side—the leadership side—of a deeply complex man who struggled greatly to understand the many tragedies he witnessed, and who found the strength to leave such a notable impact on this world because his eyes and heart were fixed on another.

It is interesting, for example, that as the election of 1952 approached, those around Ike encouraged him to join a church because voters in the 1950s would not tolerate a president who did not do so. Ike responded with frustration, rejecting the idea of using faith for political gain. In the end, after the election he did join a church, but he did it out of not political but personal need.

Yes, Ike's presidency corresponded with a resurgence of religion in America, and he no doubt saw great value in this. His faith grew for the same reasons his countrymen flocked to churches and synagogues in the 1950s: World War II had exposed unimagined depths of evil. The war only ended with technology that could destroy the world. To this day, the possibility of another world war and a nuclear holocaust haunts us.

Ike had firsthand experience with these realities. In North Africa and Europe, he sent men and boys to their deaths. At the Ohrdruf camp at Buchenwald, he saw piles of human bodies covered in lime and left to decay. Days before he was elected, the United States detonated the first thermonuclear weapon, and the Soviet Union first tested a hydrogen bomb just months later.[3] It is no exaggeration to say that Ike's task in life, more than once, was literally preventing the end of the world as we know it. Considered this way, his increasing reliance on God throughout his life comes as no surprise.

He was not the only president to have this experience. Abraham Lincoln never formally belonged to or regularly attended church, but in 1863, during the dark days of the Civil War and just a year after the loss of his son, Willie, something changed for him. Lincoln reportedly told Union General Dan Sickles,

> [I] went to my room one day and got down on my knees. Never before had I prayed with so much earnestness. . . . I felt I must put all my trust in Almighty God. He gave our people the best country ever given to man. He alone could save it from destruction. I had tried my best to do my duty and had found myself unequal to the task. The burden was more than I could bear. I asked Him to help us achieve victory now. I was sure my prayer was answered. I had no misgivings about the result at Gettysburg.[4]

One of the great challenges of a project such as this—seeking to document a very private part of a public life—is that half a century after the fact, firsthand perspectives are difficult to find.

As our writing reached its end, though, a living link to the past and to this project materialized. We were able to make contact with Rev. Clyde Raynor Brown, the former pastor at Gettysburg Presbyterian Church who had given Ike and Mamie Communion in the church in the summer of 1955 and participated in the house blessing at the Eisenhower farm. Well into his nineties, Rev. Brown was generous enough to share his memories of Ike.

"Ike was a man of character who definitely believed," Rev. Brown recalled. "I felt very much that he was a man of faith."[5] Rev. Brown, like Dr. Elson, commented that Ike "never missed church" in Gettysburg and suggested that his faith was a response to his time and the challenges he faced. Rev. Brown said,

> What he had gone through, after all—the war had just ended with a very literal kind of bang, and that was a sobering and shattering kind of reminder . . . we could destroy the earth with this bomb and that's a very humbling kind of thing to realize.[6]

That humility allowed Ike to see, in an atomic era with often-dangerous technological advancements, that faith provided the way forward.

I will always remember the day of Ike's death. It occurred on Friday, March 28, 1969, at 12:25 p.m. EST. I was in my junior year of high school, and my family was in a restaurant in Kentucky when we heard the news. Everyone stopped their conversations and started talking about Ike's death. The next week, as a high school photographer, I rode my bike around town, taking pictures of the flags, now at half-mast in tribute to the fallen soldier. There was a real sense of loss. Our community and our nation knew that we had lost a great man, and on that day there were no Democrats or Republicans; we were all mourning the loss of Ike.

For Craig, Ike died on his ninth birthday, when he was in fourth grade. Like me, Craig loved history from a very early age and vividly remembers watching the news coverage in the days before Ike's death, when he seemingly was having heart attack after heart attack, and the nation stood on edge waiting for the word that we all knew was inevitable. Craig could also feel the immense sense of sadness and national loss as this great warrior's journey concluded. Watching the news coverage of Ike's body lying in state in the Capitol rotunda left a lasting impression on him.

Dwight David Eisenhower, "Ike," lived one of the most singular lives of the twentieth century. From his inauspicious birth in Denison, Texas, to his death mourned by millions around the world, his story is one of historical events and happenings but also of deep personal wrestling with God and the strong faith that resulted from this wrestling.

Ike's story is indicative of the story of the seed that fell upon good soil found in Matthew 13:23. "As for what was sown on good soil, this is the one who hears the word and understands it. He indeed bears fruit and yields, in one case a hundredfold, in another sixty, and in another thirty."

The seed of faith sown in his childhood withstood several storms. From his parents forsaking their River Brethren faith and embracing the Bible Student movement (Jehovah's Witnesses) to his apparently endless number of seemingly dead-end assignments to the tragic death of his beloved son Icky to the years of serving under the autocratic General MacArthur to witnessing humanity's incredible inhumanity at the Nazi concentration camps—through it all, Ike persevered. His faith, while seemingly dormant for a while, grew and eventually emerged as a shining light to the world in a very dangerous time.

Without a basic understanding of how his faith shaped Ike, students of American history will fail to fully understand Ike's soul, the nature of his times, or his leadership.

At the Eisenhower Presidential Library, above Ike's final resting place, is a quote from his 1952 Abilene homecoming speech: "The real fire within the builders of America was faith—faith in a provident God who had supported and guided them."[7] A small wooden cross stands behind these words, dark against the colored light from the stained glass windows behind. If there is any fitting image to sum up a life as varied as Ike's, it is this background of mingling colors—historical moments, activity, choices, words, deeds—all of which serve to make clearer the outline of the old rugged cross, which was, as Ike knew, the one and only certain thing of it all.

Alan Sears
January 2019

Notes

Introduction

1. Gaston Espinosa, ed., *Religion and the American Presidency: George Washington to George W. Bush* (New York: Columbia University Press, 2009), 264.

2. *The Farmer's Almanac*, Sunday, January 25, 1953, http://www.farmersalmanac.com /weather-history/20071/1953/01/25/.

3. Kenneth Dole, "Eisenhower Goes Alone to Church," *Washington Post*, January 26, 1953.

4. "History of the National Presbyterian Church," accessed May 3, 2017, http://www .natpresch.org/sites/default/files/HistoryofTheNationalPresbyterianChurch.pdf.

5. Ibid.

6. Ibid.

7. Dole, "Eisenhower Goes Alone to Church."

8. Carlo D'Este, *Eisenhower: A Soldier's Life* (New York: Harry Holt and Company, 2002), 646.

9. Arthur Schlesinger Jr., "Rating the Presidents: Washington to Clinton," *Political Science Quarterly*, Summer 1997.

10. Ibid.

11. "President Historians Survey 2017," *C-Span.org*, accessed March 24, 2017, https:// www.c-span.org/presidentsurvey2017/?personid=3465.

12. Frank Newport, "Near-Record High See Religion Losing Influence in America," Gallup .com, December 29, 2010, http://www.gallup.com/poll/145409/Near-Record-High-Religion -Losing-Influence-America.aspx?g_source=position2&g_medium=related&g_campaign=tiles.

13. "Religion," Gallup.com, accessed February 1, 2017, http://www.gallup.com/poll/1690 /Religion.aspx.

14. Frank Newport, "In US, Four in 10 Report Attending Church in Last Week," Gallup .com, December 24, 2013, http://www.gallup.com/poll/166613/four-report-attending-church -last-week.aspx.

15. "Attendance at Religious Services," *Pew Research Center*, accessed May 2, 2017, http:// www.pewforum.org/religious-landscape-study/attendance-at-religious-services/.

16. Stephen J. Whitfield, *The Culture of the Cold War* (Baltimore: Johns Hopkins University Press, 1991), 83.

17. "Jesus: Man, Myth, or God?" Barna.com, April 13, 2017, https://www.barna.com/research/jesus-man-myth-god/.

18. Mark Tooley, "Eisenhower's Religion," *The American Spectator*, February 24, 2011, https://spectator.org/38107_eisenhowers-religion/.

19. "The History of the National Prayer Breakfast," *Smithsonian Magazine*, February 2, 2017, https://www.smithsonianmag.com/history/national-prayer-breakfast-what-does-its-history-reveal-180962017/.

20. Gerald Bergman, "The Influence of Religion on President Eisenhower's Upbringing," *Journal of American and Comparative Cultures* 23, no. 4 (2000): 97.

21. Dwight D. Eisenhower, "Statement by the President Upon Signing Bill to Include the Words 'Under God' in the Pledge to the Flag (June 14, 1954)," *The American Presidency Project*, accessed February 1, 2017, http://www.presidency.ucsb.edu/ws/?pid=9920.

22. Dwight D. Eisenhower, "Farewell Speech," McMillan Theatre, Columbia University, January 16, 1953.

23. Dwight D. Eisenhower, "Radio and Television Address to the American People on the Situation in Little Rock (September 24, 1957)," accessed February 1, 2017, http://www.presidency.ucsb.edu/ws/index.php?pid=10909.

24. "Clovis I Converts to Roman Catholicism," *History of Information*, accessed February 1, 2017, http://www.historyofinformation.com/expanded.php?id=1962.

25. Nancy Gibbs and Michael Duffy, *The Preacher and the Presidents: Billy Graham in the White House* (New York: Center Street, 2007), 31–76; Douglas Dales, "Eisenhower Visits Cardinal's Home," *New York Times*, September 1, 1952, http://www.nytimes.com/1952/09/01/archives/eisenhower-visits-cardinals-home-will-speak-today-general-and-wife.html.

26. Gary Scott Smith, *Faith and the Presidency: From George Washington to George W. Bush* (New York: Oxford University Press, 2009), 226.

27. William Lee Miller, *Piety Along the Potomac: Notes on Politics and Morals in the 50s* (Boston: Houghton-Mifflin, 1964).

28. Jean Edward Smith, *Eisenhower in War and Peace* (New York: Random House, 2012), 11.

29. In his book, *Five Presidents*, former Secret Service agent Clint Hill mentions a particularly salty exchange he witnessed when Ike heard about the U2 spy plane fiasco while on the golf course. See Clint Hill with Lisa McCubbin, *Five Presidents: My Extraordinary Journey with Eisenhower, Kennedy, Johnson, Nixon, and Ford* (New York: Gallery Books, 2016), 67.

30. "The Man Who Beat Hitler," *Time*, June 6, 1994.

Chapter 1 The Plain People

1. "1525: The Anabaptist Movement Begins," *Christian History*, accessed December 12, 2016, http://www.christianitytoday.com/history/issues/issue-28/1525-anabaptist-movement-begins.html.

2. As quoted in D. Patrick Ramsey, "Sola Fide Compromised? Martin Luther and the Doctrine of Baptism," *The Melios* 34, no. 2 (July 2009), http://themelios.thegospelcoalition.org/article/sola-fide-compromised-martin-luther-and-the-doctrine-of-baptism; John Calvin, "Institutes of the Christian Religion," chapter 16, *Christian Classics Ethereal Library*, accessed December 12, 2016, http://www.ccel.org/ccel/calvin/institutes.html.

3. Simons would go on to write *Christian Baptism* in 1539.

4. "Menno Simons: Anabaptist Peacemaker," *Christian History*, accessed September 10, 2018, https://www.christianitytoday.com/history/people/denominationalfounders/menno-simons.html.

5. Ibid.

6. Carlo D'Este, *Eisenhower: A Soldier's Life* (New York: Harry Holt and Company, 2002), 9–10.

7. Thomas Gerhart, "The Eisenhower Family of Pennsylvania: The Pennsylvania German Legacy of President Dwight D. Eisenhower," *Journal of the Pennsylvania German Society* 50, no. 1 (2016): 15–16.

8. Dwight D. Eisenhower, *At Ease: Stories I Tell to Friends* (New York: Doubleday & Co., 1967), 58.

9. Lawrence Knorr, *The Relations of Dwight D. Eisenhower: His Pennsylvania German Roots* (Mechanicsburg, PA: Sunbury Press, 2016).

10. "Oral History Interview: Rev. Ray I. Witter, August 28, 1964," accessed December 12, 2016, https://www.eisenhower.archives.gov/all_about_ike/abilene_years/ikes_abilene /city_life_1900/reminiscences/founding.pdf.

11. "Plain People," Dictionary.com, accessed June 16, 2017, http://www.dictionary.com /browse/plain-people.

12. Eisenhower, *At Ease*, 61.

13. Ibid., 62.

14. Ibid., 63.

15. D'Este, *Eisenhower*, 11; Michael Korda, *Ike: An American Hero* (New York: Harper Collins, 2007), 60.

16. Gerhart, "The Eisenhower Family of Pennsylvania," 16.

17. "Eisenhower / Stover Family Genealogy," Dwight D. Eisenhower Presidential Library, Museum and Boyhood Home, accessed May 2, 2017, https://www.eisenhower.archives.gov /all_about_ike/family_tree.html.

18. "Genealogy of Ida Stover Eisenhower," Geni.com, accessed May 2, 2017, https://www .geni.com/people/Ida-Elizabeth-Eisenhower/6000000003977760012; D'Este, *Eisenhower*, 15.

19. D'Este, *Eisenhower*, 16.

20. Ibid., 15.

21. Gerhart, "The Eisenhower Family of Pennsylvania," 17.

22. Ibid.

23. Ibid.

24. Eisenhower, *At Ease*, 61.

25. Ibid., 62.

26. Gerhart, "The Eisenhower Family of Pennsylvania," 17.

27. D'Este, *Eisenhower*, 16.

28. Robert R. Dykstra, *The Cattle Towns* (Lincoln: University of Nebraska Press, 1968), 38.

29. D'Este, *Eisenhower*, 17.

30. Ibid.

31. Thomas Branigar, "No Villains–No Heroes: The David Eisenhower–Milton Good Controversy," *Kansas History* (Autumn 1990): 170.

32. Ibid., 174.

33. Ibid.

34. Eisenhower, *At Ease*, 72.

35. Ibid., 86.

36. Ibid., 86–87.

37. D'Este, *Eisenhower*, 20.

38. Ibid., 21.

39. Ibid., 22; "Dwight L. Moody Is Ill: Heart Trouble Overcomes Him While at Kansas City—Coming Home in a Serious Condition," *New York Times*, November 18, 1899, https://

www.nytimes.com/1899/11/18/archives/dwight-l-moody-is-ill-heart-trouble-overcomes-him
-while-at-kansas.html.

40. D'Este, *Eisenhower*, 22.

41. Kenneth S. Davis, *Soldier of Democracy* (Garden City, NY: Doubleday, Doran & Co., 1945), 49.

42. D'Este, *Eisenhower*, 33.

43. Ibid.

44. Several examples are shared in D'Este, *Eisenhower*, 29–30.

45. Bela Kornitzer, *The Great American Heritage—The Story of the Five Eisenhower Brothers* (New York: Farrar, Straus and Cudahy, 1955), 55.

Chapter 2 The Watch Tower

1. Watchtower Bible and Tract Society, "2016 Yearbook of Jehovah's Witnesses," (2016), 176.

2. M. James Penton, *Apocalypse Delayed: The Story of Jehovah's Witnesses* (Toronto: University of Toronto Press, 1997), 3.

3. Gerald Bergman, "The Influence of Religion on Eisenhower's Upbringing," *Journal of American and Comparative Culture* 23, no. 4 (Winter 2000): 92.

4. Ibid.

5. Ibid., 91, 98–101.

6. Dwight D. Eisenhower, *At Ease: Stories I Tell to Friends* (New York: Doubleday & Co., 1967), 305.

7. Ibid., 106.

8. Ibid., 108.

9. Bergman, "Influence of Religion on Eisenhower's Upbringing," 97.

10. Ibid., 99.

11. Joint Congregational Committee on Inaugural Ceremonies, "The 42nd Presidential Inauguration: Dwight D. Eisenhower," accessed March 19, 2018, https://www.inaugural.senate
.gov/about/past-inaugural-ceremonies/42nd-inaugural-ceremonies/index.html#facts.

12. Bergman, "Influence of Religion on President Eisenhower's Upbringing," 97.

13. Dean Curry, "The Roots of Greatness: A Profile of Dwight David Eisenhower," Messiah College, accessed March 18, 2018, https://www.messiah.edu/centennial/history/People
%20and%20Stories/eisenhower.html.

14. Ibid.

Chapter 3 The Road from Abilene

1. Lowell Limpus, "West Point Ike's First Step Up: Was Boy from the Wrong Side of the Tracks," *Abilene Daily News* (April 7, 1952): 26.

2. Ibid.

3. Carlo D'Este, *Eisenhower: A Soldier's Life* (New York: Harry Holt and Company, 2002), 51.

4. "Abilene Years 1892 to 1911; 1913; 1915; 1969," Dwight D. Eisenhower Presidential Library, Museum and Boyhood Home, accessed March 19, 2018, https://www.eisenhower
.archives.gov/all_about_ike/abilene_years.html.

5. Dwight D. Eisenhower, *At Ease: Stories I Tell to Friends* (New York: Doubleday & Co., 1967), 104.

6. Ibid., 53.

7. Ibid.

8. Ibid., 54.

9. Ibid., 104.

10. Ibid.

11. Ibid., 105.

12. Ibid.

13. Ibid., 106.

14. Ibid.

15. Ibid.

16. Ibid.

17. Ibid., 107.

18. Ibid., 108.

19. "The Class the Stars Fell On," *West Point in the Making of America*, accessed May 5, 2017, http://americanhistory.si.edu/westpoint/history_6b.html.

20. Eisenhower, *At Ease*, 12.

21. Ibid., 7.

22. Ibid., 14–15.

23. Ibid., 11.

24. David L. Holmes, *Faiths of the Postwar Presidents: From Truman to Obama* (Athens, GA: University of Georgia Press, 2012), 31.

25. Eisenhower, *At Ease*, 26.

26. Harry Reasoner, "Young Mr. Eisenhower," *CBS News*, September 13, 1966.

27. Eisenhower, *At Ease*, 112.

28. Ibid., 111–12.

29. D'Este, *Eisenhower*, 93.

30. Eisenhower, *At Ease*, 113.

31. "About Us," Corona Presbyterian Church, accessed May 5, 2017, http://www.corona church.com/#/about-us/history.

32. "Oral History Interviews with Mamie Doud Eisenhower," August 16, 1972, National Archives and Records Administration, Office of Presidential Libraries, Dwight D. Eisenhower Library.

33. Susan Eisenhower, *Mrs. Ike* (New York: Farrar, Straus & Giroux, 1996), 21.

34. D'Este, *Eisenhower*, 109.

35. Michael Korda, *Ike: An American Hero* (New York: Harper Collins, 2007), 121.

Chapter 4 Little "Icky"

1. There is some debate as to whether the nickname was "Icky" or "Ikky." Doud Dwight Eisenhower's nickname was originally "Little Ike," but it was changed within a few days of his birth to "Ikey," then changed again to "Ikky" and was spelled that way throughout his life. Years later, "Icky" became the preferred spelling, and even Ike offered that spelling in his 1967 memoir, *At Ease*. However, family correspondence at the time refers to him as "Ikky." While, ultimately, "Ikky" or "Ikey" may have been originally correct, for continuity's sake we have chosen to go with "Icky."

2. Michael Beschloss, "D-Day Wasn't the First Time Eisenhower Felt as if He Had Lost a Son," *New York Times*, June 11, 2014, https://www.nytimes.com/2014/06/12/upshot/ike-and -his-sons-the-grief-of-a-supreme-commander-and-a-father.html.

3. Michael Korda, *Ike: An American Hero* (New York: Harper Collins, 2007), 132.

4. Ibid., 122.

5. Carlo D'Este, *Eisenhower: A Soldier's Life* (New York: Harry Holt and Company, 2002), 122.

6. Dwight D. Eisenhower, *At Ease: Stories I Tell to Friends* (New York: Doubleday & Co., 1967), 133.

7. Ibid., 136; D'Este, *Eisenhower*, 125.

8. Eisenhower, *At Ease*, 137.

9. Dale E. Wilson, *Treat 'Em Rough: The Birth of American Armor* (New York: Presidio Press, 1990), 60.

10. D'Este, *Eisenhower*, 133.

11. Jeffery K. Taubenberger and David M. Morens, "1918 Influenza: The Mother of All Pandemics," *Emerging Infectious Diseases* vol. 12, no. 1 (January 2006): 15–22, https://www.ncbi.nlm.nih.gov/pmc/articles/PMC3291398/.

12. Eisenhower, *At Ease*, 150.

13. Ibid.

14. Ibid.

15. Ibid., 155.

16. Ibid., 156.

17. Ibid., 157.

18. D'Este, *Eisenhower*, 142.

19. "Principal Facts Concerning the First Transcontinental Army Motor Transport Expedition, Washington to San Francisco, July 7 to September 6, 1919," accessed March 19, 2018, https://www.eisenhower.archives.gov/research/online_documents/1919_convoy/principal_facts.pdf.

20. D'Este, *Eisenhower*, 157.

21. Ibid., 142–43.

22. Eisenhower, *At Ease*, 151.

23. D'Este, *Eisenhower*, 143.

24. Eisenhower, *At Ease*, 180.

25. D'Este, *Eisenhower*, 155.

26. Susan Eisenhower, *Mrs. Ike* (New York: Farrar, Straus & Giroux, 1996), 66–69.

27. "Scarlet Fever," Mayo Clinic, accessed February 8, 2017, http://www.mayoclinic.org/diseases-conditions/scarlet-fever/basics/definition/con-20030976.

28. Eisenhower, *At Ease*, 90.

29. D'Este, *Eisenhower*, 155.

30. Eisenhower, *At Ease*, 181.

31. Ibid., 181–82.

32. D'Este, *Eisenhower*, 156.

33. Ibid., 157.

34. Eisenhower, *Mrs. Ike*, 74.

35. Dorothy Brandon, *Mamie Doud Eisenhower: A Portrait of a First Lady* (New York: Scribner & Sons, 1954), 122.

36. Beschloss, "D-Day Wasn't the First Time Eisenhower Felt as if He Had Lost a Son."

37. Julie Nixon Eisenhower, *Special People* (New York: Simon & Schuster, 1977), 198–99.

38. Beschloss, "D-Day Wasn't the First Time Eisenhower Felt as if He Had Lost a Son."

39. D'Este, *Eisenhower*, 171.

40. Ibid., 171–72.

Chapter 5 Perseverance

1. Rick Atkinson, *An Army at Dawn: The War in North Africa, 1942–1943*, Liberation Trilogy, vol. 1 (New York: Henry Holt and Co., 2002), 9.

2. Russell F. Weigley, *History of the United States Army* (New York: Macmillan, 1967), 402.

3. Carlo D'Este, *Eisenhower: A Soldier's Life* (New York: Harry Holt and Company, 2002), 138.

4. Edward Cox, *Grey Eminence: Fox Conner and the Art of Mentorship* (Stillwater, OK: New Forums, 2011), 11; Michael Korda, *Ike: An American Hero* (New York: Harper Collins, 2007), 155.

5. Cox, *Grey Eminence*, 11.

6. Korda, *Ike: An American Hero*, 155.

7. D'Este, *Eisenhower*, 164.

8. Ibid.

9. Dwight D. Eisenhower, *At Ease: Stories I Tell to Friends* (New York: Doubleday & Co., 1967), 184.

10. D'Este, *Eisenhower*, 165.

11. Dorothy Brandon, *Mamie Dowd Eisenhower: A Portrait of a First Lady* (New York: Scribner & Sons, 1954), 126.

12. Susan Eisenhower, *Mrs. Ike* (New York: Farrar, Straus & Giroux, 1996), 77.

13. Eisenhower, *At Ease*, 184.

14. Lester David, *Ike & Mamie: The Story of a General and His Lady* (New York: Putnam Group, 1983), 90; D'Este, *Eisenhower*, 166.

15. D'Este, *Eisenhower*, 166.

16. Ibid., 167.

17. Cox, *Grey Eminence*, 15.

18. D'Este, *Eisenhower*, 167.

19. F. Douglas Mehle, "Sponsorship," *Army* vol. 28 (March 1978): 41–44.

20. Stephen E. Ambrose, *Eisenhower: Soldier and President*, vol. 1 (New York: Simon and Schuster, 1983), 40.

21. Cox, *Grey Eminence*, 15.

22. D'Este, *Eisenhower*, 169.

23. Eisenhower, *At Ease*, 194.

24. Susan Eisenhower, *Mrs. Ike*, 83.

25. Korda, *Ike: An American Hero*, 166.

26. D'Este, *Eisenhower*, 171.

27. Carlo D'Este, "John S. D. Eisenhower: August 3, 1922–December 21, 2013," *Armchair General*, accessed May 31, 2017, http://www.armchairgeneral.com/john-s-d-eisenhower.htm.

28. Eisenhower, *At Ease*, 195–96.

29. Ibid.

30. D'Este, *Eisenhower*, 175.

31. Eisenhower, *At Ease*, 196.

32. Ibid., 198.

33. Ibid.

34. D'Este, *Eisenhower*, 177.

35. Ibid.

36. Eisenhower, *At Ease*, 200.

37. Ibid., 203.

38. D'Este, *Eisenhower*, 183.

39. Ibid., 192.

40. Eisenhower, *At Ease*, 205.

41. D'Este, *Eisenhower*, 194.

42. Ibid., 193.

43. Ibid., 195.

44. Eisenhower, *At Ease*, 206–7.
45. Korda, *Ike: An American Hero*, 184.
46. Eisenhower, *At Ease*, 208.
47. D'Este, *Eisenhower*, 199.
48. Eisenhower, *At Ease*, 209.
49. D'Este, *Eisenhower*, 201.
50. Korda, *Ike: An American Hero*, 184.
51. Ibid.,194; D'Este, *Eisenhower*, 229.
52. "The Bonus March," *U.S. History*, accessed May 9, 2017, http://www.ushistory.org /us/48c.asp; D'Este, *Eisenhower*, 231.
53. Eisenhower, *At Ease*, 217.
54. Ibid.
55. D'Este, *Eisenhower*, 232.
56. Robert L. Eichelberger, "Unpublished Memoir of Lt. General Robert L. Eichelberger," Eichelberger Papers, USAMHI.

Chapter 6 From MacArthur to Major General

1. Carlo D'Este, *Eisenhower: A Soldier's Life* (New York: Harry Holt and Company, 2002), 236.
2. Ibid., 234–35; Dwight D. Eisenhower, *At Ease: Stories I Tell to Friends* (New York: Doubleday & Co., 1967), 228–29.
3. D'Este, *Eisenhower*, 238.
4. Michael Korda, *Ike: An American Hero* (New York: Harper Collins, 2007), 211.
5. Dwight Eisenhower, "Oral History Interview with D. Clayton James," August 29, 1967, Eisenhower Presidential Library, Abilene, Kansas.
6. D'Este, *Eisenhower*, 238–39.
7. Korda, *Ike: An American Hero*, 212; D'Este, *Eisenhower*, 242.
8. Korda, *Ike: An American Hero*, 215; D'Este, *Eisenhower*, 240; Eisenhower, *At Ease*, 228.
9. D'Este, *Eisenhower*, 241.
10. Ibid.
11. Korda, *Ike: An American Hero*, 218.
12. D'Este, *Eisenhower*, 242.
13. Ibid., 243.
14. Ibid.
15. Susan Eisenhower, *Mrs. Ike* (New York: Farrar, Straus & Giroux, 1996), 147.
16. D'Este, *Eisenhower*, 245.
17. Ibid.
18. Ibid., citing "Letter from Mamie Doud Eisenhower to the Douds, Easter, 1938," Box 2, Barbara Thompson Eisenhower Papers, Eisenhower Presidential Library.
19. See, for instance, Mark Perry, *Partners in Command: George Marshall and Dwight Eisenhower in War and Peace* (New York: Penguin Books, 2007), 363; Stanley Weintraub, *15 Stars: Eisenhower, MacArthur, Marshall: Three Generals Who Saved the American Century* (New York: Simon and Schuster, 2007), 341; Robert H. Ferrell and Francis H. Heller, "Plain Faking?" *American Heritage Magazine* 46, no. 3 (May–June 1995).
20. "Lot #240: Dwight Eisenhower WWII Autograph Letter Signed—'...we thought we were cute as the devil...We are having a hard time lately with flying...'—with Original Envelope Also Signed by Eisenhower," *Nate D. Sanders Auctions*, accessed May 5, 2017, https://natedsanders.com/mobile/lotdetail.aspx?inventoryid=10678&seo=dwight-eisenhower -wwii-autograph-letter-signed----.

21. Eisenhower, *At Ease*, 227–28.

22. Ibid.

23. Ibid., 228.

24. Ibid.

25. Geoffrey Perret, *Old Soldiers Never Die: The Life of Douglas MacArthur* (New York: Random House, 1996), 288.

26. "Dwight David Eisenhower War Department Diary," January 23, 1942, Box 26, Pre-Pres Papers, Eisenhower Presidential Library.

27. Waldo Henrichs and Marc Gallicchio, *Implacable Foes: War in the Pacific, 1944–1945* (New York: Oxford University Press, 2017), 46–47.

28. D'Este, *Eisenhower*, 247.

29. Ibid., 247–48.

30. Robert L. Eichelberger, "Unpublished Memoir of Lt. General Robert L. Eichelberger," Eichelberger Papers, US Army Military History Institute.

31. Neville Chamberlain, "'Peace for Our Time,' September 30, 1938," *Brittania Historical Documents*, accessed September 11, 2018, http://www.britannia.com/history/docs/peacetime.html.

32. Eisenhower, *At Ease*, 231.

33. Ibid.

34. According to Carlo D'Este, writing in reference to a picture of Ike from 1929 in civilian clothes, "During the interwar years there was a backlash against military personnel. Those, like Eisenhower, who were stationed in Washington, DC, rarely wore their uniforms" (D'Este, *Eisenhower*, caption in photo insert).

35. Thomas Parrish, *Roosevelt and Marshall: Partners in Politics and War* (New York: William Morrow & Co., 1989), 114.

36. Rick Atkinson, *An Army at Dawn: The War in North Africa, 1942–1943*, Liberation Trilogy, vol. 1 (New York: Henry Holt and Co., 2002), 9.

37. D'Este, *Eisenhower*, 277.

38. "Letter from Dwight D. Eisenhower to Lt. Col. Omar Bradley," July 1, 1940; D'Este, *Eisenhower*, 262.

39. D'Este, *Eisenhower*, 262.

40. Ibid., 266.

41. Ibid., 263.

42. Eisenhower, *At Ease*, 238.

43. D'Este, *Eisenhower*, 268.

44. Eisenhower, *At Ease*, 241.

45. Ibid., 242; "Letter from Dwight D. Eisenhower to Hugh A. Parker, Addendum to Letter of February 8, 1941," Misc. Manuscripts, Eisenhower Presidential Library.

46. John Sheldon David Eisenhower, *Strictly Personal* (New York: Doubleday & Co., 1974), 32.

47. D'Este, *Eisenhower*, 269.

48. Ibid., 271.

49. D'Este, *Eisenhower*, 275.

50. "Walter Krueger," *World War II Database*, accessed May 12, 2017, http://ww2db.com/person_bio.php?person_id=285.

51. D'Este, *Eisenhower*, 277.

52. "Letter from Dwight Eisenhower to General Gerow," September 25, 1941.

53. D'Este, *Eisenhower*, 280.

54. Ibid.

55. Mark Perry, "Louisiana Maneuvers 1940–41," *HistoryNet*, November 25, 2008, http://www.historynet.com/louisiana-maneuvers-1940-41.htm.

56. D'Este, *Eisenhower*, 280.

57. Ibid., 281.

58. Ibid., 276.

59. Korda, *Ike: An American Hero*, 243.

60. D'Este, *Eisenhower*, 282–83.

61. Ibid., 283.

62. Ibid.; Craig Nelson, *Pearl Harbor: From Infamy to Greatness* (New York: Scribner, 2016), 354.

63. Eisenhower, *At Ease*, 248.

64. Ibid., 249.

65. Ibid., 250.

66. Ibid.

Chapter 7 Nothing We Can Do but Pray

1. Gerald Mygatt and Henry Darlington, eds., *The Soldiers' and Sailors' Prayer Book* (New York: Alfred A. Knopf, 1944).

2. "Defending Principles Expounded by Jesus—Dwight D. Eisenhower," BibleMesh .com, June 30, 2011, https://biblemesh.com/blog/defending-principles-expounded-by-jesus -dwight-d-eisenhower-1890-1969/.

3. Remarkably, the Second Vatican Council's 1965 *Declaration on Religious Freedom* (Dignitatis Humanae), in spelling out the Church's support for religious freedom, declared as its foundation the essential dignity of each human being, exactly what this "simple soldier's" prayer embraces.

4. Kay Summersby, *Eisenhower Was My Boss* (New York: Dell Publishing, 1948), 102–3.

5. "Letter from Dwight Eisenhower to Mamie Eisenhower," December 2, 1943, Dwight D. Eisenhower Presidential Library, Abilene, Kansas.

6. This promotion would be the beginning of an intense several years for Ike. In December 1943, he was appointed Supreme Commander. In January 1944, he set up the Allied headquarters in London. In December 1944, he received his fifth star during the Battle of the Bulge. On May 7, 1945, he accepted Germany's unconditional surrender and then became the military governor of the United States zones of occupation. In 1948, he retired from the Army and assumed the presidency of Columbia University, where he would remain—with long-term absences for other duties—until he was elected president. These absences included serving as the Supreme Commander of NATO.

7. "Map: German Conquests in Europe 1939–1942," *Holocaust Encyclopedia*, accessed March 20, 2018, https://www.ushmm.org/wlc/en/media_nm.php?ModuleId=0&MediaId=363.

8. "Gen. Dwight D. Eisenhower's D-Day Message," *Department of Defense Videos*, accessed May 12, 2017, http://www.defense.gov/News/SpecialReports/D-Day-and-the-Invasion-of -Normandy/Gen-Dwight-D-Eisenhowers-D-Day-Message.

9. Franklin Roosevelt, "Prayer on D-Day, June 6, 1944," *The American Presidency Project*, accessed June 13, 2017, http://www.presidency.ucsb.edu/ws/?pid=16515.

10. "D-Day Casualties: Total Axis and Allied Numbers," *History on the Net*, November 11, 2016, http://www.historyonthenet.com/d-day-casualties/.

11. "Eisenhower's Trip to a Concentration Camp: 'I Never Dreamed . . . It Was Horrible,' letter from Dwight Eisenhower to Mamie Eisenhower, April 15, 1945, *Shapell*, accessed May 12, 2017,

http://www.shapell.org/manuscript/General%20Eisenhower%20Ohrdruf%20Concentration
%20Camp.

12. Omar Bradley, *A Soldier's Story* (New York: Henry Holt and Company, 1951), 555.

13. "Ohrdruf," Georgia Tech Library, accessed October 31, 2017, http://www.library.gatech
.edu/holocaust/ohrdrufdes.htm. Also see "National Days of Remembrance: Liberation 1945,"
United States Holocaust Memorial Museum, accessed October 31, 2017, https://www.ushmm
.org/m/pdfs/20141010-dor-essay-liberation.pdf.

14. Ibid.

15. Dwight D. Eisenhower, *Crusade in Europe* (New York: Doubleday, 1949), 409.

16. Dwight D. Eisenhower, "No Country Fears a Strong America," speech delivered at
dinner of the American Legion National Commanders, Chicago, IL, November 20, 1945,
Ibiblio, accessed May 12, 2017, http://www.ibiblio.org/pha/policy/post-war/1945-11-20a.html.

17. Dwight D. Eisenhower, "Message from the Army Chief of Staff to the Annual Convention of the Chaplains Association, October 1946," Dwight D. Eisenhower Presidential
Library, Abilene, Kansas.

18. Dwight D. Eisenhower, "Notes for Address at C.I.O. Convention, Atlantic City, New
Jersey, November 20, 1946," Eisenhower Presidential Library.

19. Dwight D. Eisenhower, "Talk at the Jewish Theological Seminary of America, September 27, 1948," Eisenhower Presidential Library.

20. Dwight D. Eisenhower, "World Peace: A Balance Sheet," address at Columbia University, New York City, March 23, 1950.

21. See Kevin Kruse, *One Nation Under God: How Corporate America Invented Christian
America* (New York: Basic Books, 2015); Jean Edward Smith, *Eisenhower in War and Peace*
(New York: Random House, 2012).

22. John Henry Newman, "Lead, Kindly Light, amid the Encircling Gloom" (1833),
Hymnary, public domain, accessed June 14, 2017, http://hymnary.org/text/lead_kindly_light
_amid_the_encircling_gl.

Chapter 8 The Approach to the Presidency

1. Merlo J. Pusey, *Eisenhower, the President* (New York: MacMillan, 1956), 2–3.

2. Ibid.

3. Harry S. Truman, "Diary: July 25, 1947," Truman Presidential Library, accessed May
16, 2017, https://www.trumanlibrary.org/diary/page23.htm.

4. Michael Korda, *Ike: An American Hero* (New York: Harper Collins, 2007), 616.

5. Ibid., 619.

6. Dwight D. Eisenhower, *At Ease: Stories I Tell to Friends* (New York: Doubleday & Co.,
1967), 371.

7. Ibid.

8. Ibid.

9. Ibid.

10. Ibid., 372.

11. "Senate Leaders: Robert A. Taft," *United States Senate*, accessed March 20, 2018,
https://www.senate.gov/artandhistory/history/common/generic/People_Leaders_Taft.htm.

12. Korda, *Ike: An American Hero*, 637.

13. Mark Tooley, "Eisenhower's Religion," *The American Spectator*, February 14, 2011,
https://spectator.org/38107_eisenhowers-religion.

14. "Jehovah's Witnesses Abilene Congregation, Records and Related Materials, 1912–
1943," Dwight D. Eisenhower Presidential Library, Abilene, Kansas.

15. "Letter from Dwight D. Eisenhower to Milton Eisenhower," May 16, 1943.

16. "*West Virginia Board of Education v. Barnette*, 319 U.S. 624, (1943)," *Justia*, accessed June 14, 2017, https://supreme.justia.com/cases/federal/us/319/624/.

17. Merle Miller, *Ike the Soldier: As They Knew Him* (New York: G.P. Putnam's Sons, 1987).

18. Robert Williams, *Williams Intelligence Summary* (1952), special Eisenhower edition.

19. Ibid.

20. Albin Krebs, "Gerald L. K. Smith Dead; Anti-Communist Crusader, *New York Times*, April 16, 1976, http://www.nytimes.com/1976/04/16/archives/gerald-lk-smith-dead-anti communist-crusader.html?_r=0.

21. "Anti-Semite Winrod Joins Eisenhower Smear Brigade," *The Sunday Herald* (May 18, 1952): 16.

22. Green Peyton, *San Antonio: City in the Sun* (New York: Whittlesey House-McGraw Hill, 1946).

23. Peter Edson, "Answer in Response to Query on Candidate's Faith," *Frederick News* (April 24, 1952): 16.

24. Clifford Roberts, *The Story of the Augusta National Golf Club* (New York: Doubleday, 1976), 124.

25. Ibid.

26. "Oral History with Clare Boothe Luce, OH #220," Columbia University Oral History Project, DDEPL, 8–14, 237, as cited in David L. Holmes, *Faiths of the Postwar Presidents: From Truman to Obama* (Athens, GA: University of Georgia Press, 2012), 37.

27. Ibid.

28. Ibid.

29. Ibid.

30. Ibid.

31. Ibid., 37–38.

Chapter 9 Spiritual Renewal

1. Nancy Gibbs and Michael Duffy, *The Preacher and the Presidents: Billy Graham in the White House* (New York: Center Street, 2007), 31.

2. Kevin Kruse, *One Nation Under God: How Corporate America Invented Christian America* (New York: Basic Books, 2015), 58.

3. Gibbs and Duffy, *Preacher and the Presidents*, 32.

4. Ibid.

5. Ibid.

6. Ibid.

7. Ibid., 33.

8. Ibid., 34.

9. Rev. Dr. Billy Graham, "Remarks at Eisenhower Centennial Church Service, Abilene, Kansas," *The Congressional Record*, October 14, 1990.

10. Ibid.

11. Gibbs and Duffy, *Preacher and the Presidents*, 34.

12. Ibid., 35.

13. Billy Graham, *Just As I Am: The Autobiography of Billy Graham* (New York: Harper Collins, 1997), 189–92.

14. Ibid.

15. Ibid.

16. Graham, "Remarks at Eisenhower Centennial Church Service."

17. Gibbs and Duffy, *Preacher and the Presidents*, 33.

18. Ibid.

19. Ibid., 39.

20. Ibid., 53.

21. Morton Smutz, "Interview of Mrs. Helen Elson," March 26, 1997 (final transcript completed June 23, 1998), The Oral History Program, Chapman Memorial Archives, The National Presbyterian Church & Center, http://nationalpres.org/library. Provided by Rev. John Boyles, former pastor of National Presbyterian Church.

22. "Oral history of Eleanor Elson Heginbotham," August 2006, The Oral History Program, Chapman Memorial Archives, The National Presbyterian Church & Center, http://nationalpres.org/library.

23. Smutz, "Interview of Mrs. Helen Elson."

24. Edward L. R. Elson, *Wide Was His Parish* (Downers Grove, IL: Tyndale, 1986), 15–33.

25. Smutz, "Interview of Mrs. Helen Elson."

26. B. C. Mossman and M. W. Stark, "Former Secretary of State John Foster Dulles, Official Funeral, 24–27 May 1959," *The Last Salute: Civil and Military Funerals 1921–1969*, accessed March 20, 2018, https://history.army.mil/books/Last_Salute/Ch16.htm.

27. "Letter from Edward L. R. Elson to Dwight D. Eisenhower," November 23, 1952. Provided by Rev. John Boyles, former pastor of National Presbyterian Church.

28. "Letter from Senator Edward Martin to Dwight D. Eisenhower," December 8, 1952. Provided by Rev. John Boyles, former pastor of National Presbyterian Church.

29. "Letter from Edward L. R. Elson to Dwight D. Eisenhower," November 28, 1952. Provided by Rev. John Boyles, former pastor of National Presbyterian Church.

30. "Letter from Arthur Vandenberg to Edward L. R. Elson," December 2, 1952. Provided by Rev. John Boyles, former pastor of National Presbyterian Church.

31. "Memo from Anne Wheaton to Mamie Eisenhower," December 2, 1952. Provided by Rev. John Boyles, former pastor of National Presbyterian Church.

32. "Letter from Edward L. R. Elson to Arthur Vandenberg," December 9, 1952. Provided by Rev. John Boyles, former pastor of National Presbyterian Church.

33. "Letter from Edward L. R. Elson to Dwight D. Eisenhower," December 21, 1952. Provided by Rev. John Boyles, former pastor of National Presbyterian Church.

34. "Memorandum from Arthur Vandenberg to Dwight D. Eisenhower," December 12, 1952. Provided by Rev. John Boyles, former pastor of National Presbyterian Church.

35. Elson, *Wide Was His Parish*, 115.

36. Ibid.

37. "Oral History of Eleanor Elson Heginbotham."

38. Robert H. Ferrell, ed., *The Eisenhower Diaries* (New York: W.W. Norton & Co., 1976), 225.

39. Graham, "Remarks at Eisenhower Centennial Church Service."

40. Gibbs and Duffy, *Preacher and the Presidents*, 43.

41. Elson, *Wide Was His Parish*, 115.

42. Edward L. R. Elson, "Memorable Years in a Washington Pulpit," *Christianity Today*, March 30, 1973.

43. Dwight D. Eisenhower, "Inaugural Address: January 20, 1953," *The American Presidency Project*, accessed April 18, 2017, http://www.presidency.ucsb.edu/ws/index.php?pid=9600.

44. Graham, "Remarks at Eisenhower Centennial Church Service."

45. Ibid.

46. Gibbs and Duffy, *Preacher and the Presidents*, 42.

47. Ibid., 44.

48. Virgil Pinkley, *Eisenhower Declassified* (Old Tappan, NJ: Fleming H. Revell, 1979), 270.

49. "Oral history of Eleanor Elson Heginbotham."

50. "Session Minutes: Special Meeting," February 1, 1953, National Presbyterian Church, Washington, DC.

51. "Faith Staked Down," *Time*, February 9, 1953, 20, http://content.time.com/time /magazine/article/0,9171,889614,00.html.

52. "Longines Chronoscope with Rev. Edward L. R. Elson," YouTube video, 14:47, uploaded by PublicResourceOrg, April 4, 2011, https://www.youtube.com/watch?v=gsVzMtM7nes.

53. "Oral history of Eleanor Elson Heginbotham."

54. Kenneth Dole, "Eisenhower Goes Alone to Church," *Washington Post*, January 26, 1953.

55. Kruse, *One Nation Under God*, 73.

56. Ibid.

57. Elson, *Wide Was His Parish*, 117.

58. Ibid., 118.

Chapter 10 The President and the Pastor

1. "Letter from Edward L. R. Elson to Dwight David Eisenhower," January 14, 1953. Provided by Rev. John Boyles, former pastor of National Presbyterian Church.

2. Lillian Ross and Brendan Gill, "To Start with a Prayer," *The New Yorker*, January 24, 1953 (22), http://www.newyorker.com/magazine/1953/01/24/to-start-with-a-prayer.

3. Paul Reeve and Ardis Parshall, *Mormonism: A Historical Encyclopedia* (Santa Barbara, CA: ABC-CLIO, 2010), 132.

4. Thomas E. Ricks, "Eisenhower on Prayer in His Cabinet," *Foreign Policy*, May 4, 2015, http://foreignpolicy.com/2012/05/04/eisenhower-on-prayer-in-his-cabinet/.

5. William Bole, "He Broke Ranks with His Powerful Family's Politics, Religion: Father Avery Dulles Remains Diplomatic Amid Catholic Debate," *Los Angeles Times* (September 17, 1988), http://articles.latimes.com/1988-09-17/local/me-1943_1_avery-dulles.

6. Geoffrey Perret, *Eisenhower* (New York: Random House, 1999), 437.

7. Robert Divine, *Since 1945: Politics and Diplomacy in Recent American History* (Hoboken, NJ: John A. Wiley & Sons, 1975), 55.

8. Diane Winston, "The History of the National Prayer Breakfast," *Smithsonian Magazine* (February 2, 2017), https://www.smithsonianmag.com/history/national-prayer-breakfast -what-does-its-history-reveal-180962017/.

9. Ibid.

10. Dwight D. Eisenhower, "Remarks at the Dedicatory Prayer Breakfast of the International Christian Leadership, February 5, 1953," *The American Presidency Project*, accessed April 19, 2017, http://www.presidency.ucsb.edu/ws/index.php?pid=9851.

11. Dwight D. Eisenhower, "Remarks Recorded for the American Legion 'Back to God' Program: February 1, 1953," *The American Presidency Project*, accessed April 19, 2017, http:// www.presidency.ucsb.edu/ws/?pid=9818.

12. Edward L. R. Elson, "Memorable Years in a Washington Pulpit," *Christianity Today*, March 30, 1973.

13. Nancy Gibbs and Michael Duffy, *The Preacher and the Presidents: Billy Graham in the White House* (New York: Center Street, 2007), 45.

14. "Korean War," *History*, accessed June 14, 2017, http://www.history.com/topics/korean -war.

15. Carol Tucker, "The 1950s—Powerful Years for Religion," *USC News*, June 16, 1997, https://news.usc.edu/25835/The-1950s-Powerful-Years-for-Religion/.

16. "The American Synagogue: Recent Issues and Trends," March 27, 2005, http://research .policyarchive.org/10414.pdf.

17. "National Affairs: Nothing Sacred," *Time*, April 11, 1955, http://content.time.com /time/magazine/article/0,9171,891417,00.html.

18. Gary Scott Smith, *Faith and the Presidency from George Washington to George W. Bush* (New York: Oxford University Press, 2009), 226.

19. Ibid.

20. Edward L. R. Elson, *Wide Was His Parish* (Downers Grove, IL: Tyndale House, 1986), 122.

21. Morton Smutz, "Interview of Mrs. Helen Elson," March 26, 1997 (final transcript completed June 23, 1998), The Oral History Program, Chapman Memorial Archives, The National Presbyterian Church & Center, http://nationalpres.org/library. Provided by Rev. John Boyles, former pastor of National Presbyterian Church.

22. Elson, *Wide Was His Parish*, 121.

23. "Letter from Dwight D. Eisenhower to Rev. Edward Elson," January 18, 1954; "Letter from Dwight D. Eisenhower to Rev. Edward Elson," February 6, 1954. Provided by Rev. John Boyles, former pastor of National Presbyterian Church.

24. "Letter from Dwight David Eisenhower to Rev. Edward Elson," February 4, 1954. Provided by Rev. John Boyles, former pastor of National Presbyterian Church.

25. "Oral History of Eleanor Elson Heginbotham," August 2006, The Oral History Program, Chapman Memorial Archives, The National Presbyterian Church & Center.

26. Ibid.

27. "Letter from Edward L. R. Elson to Dwight D. Eisenhower," November 5, 1954. Provided by Rev. John Boyles, former pastor of National Presbyterian Church.

28. "Letter from Edward L. R. Elson to Dwight D. Eisenhower," February 24, 1954. Provided by Rev. John Boyles, former pastor of National Presbyterian Church.

29. "Letter from Dwight D. Eisenhower to Edward L. R. Elson," March 23, 1956. Provided by Rev. John Boyles, former pastor of National Presbyterian Church.

30. "Letter from Dwight D. Eisenhower to Edward L. R. Elson," November 25, 1956. Provided by Rev. John Boyles, former pastor of National Presbyterian Church.

31. "Letter from Ann Whitman to E. S. Whitman," July 1953. Provided by Rev. John Boyles, former pastor of National Presbyterian Church.

32. William Inboden III, *Religion and American Foreign Policy, 1945–1960: The Soul of Containment* (Cambridge, UK: Cambridge University Press, 2008), 276.

Chapter 11 Spiritual Weapons for the Cold War

1. Dr. Edward L. R. Elson, *America's Spiritual Recovery* (Old Tappan, NJ: Fleming H. Revell, 1954), 9.

2. Ibid., "Introduction."

3. "Soviets Explode Atomic Bomb," *History*, accessed April 10, 2017, http://www.history .com/this-day-in-history/soviets-explode-atomic-bomb.

4. "Soviets Test 'Layer Cake' Bomb," *History*, accessed May 31, 2017, http://www.history .com/this-day-in-history/soviets-test-layer-cake-bomb.

5. Footage of the actual detonation of the bomb can be watched at "1954 Soviet Nuclear Test Footage Released—1993," *Efootage*, accessed April 11, 2017, http://www.efootage.com /stock-footage/45863/1954_Soviet_Nuclear_Test_Footage_Released_-_1993/.

6. Robert Schlesinger, *White House Ghosts: Presidents and Their Speechwriters* (New York: Simon & Schuster, 2008), 71.

7. Dwight D. Eisenhower, "Statement Upon Signing Public Law 83–396, June 14, 1954," *The American Presidency Project*, accessed May 2, 2017, http://www.presidency.ucsb.edu/ws /index.php?pid=9920.

8. Dwight D. Eisenhower, "Message to the National Co-Chairmen, Commission of Religious Organizations, National Conference on Christians and Jews, July 9, 1953," *The American Presidency Project*, accessed September 11, 2018, http://www.presidency.ucsb.edu/ws/index .php?pid=9637.

9. Paul Gabel, *And God Created Lenin: Marxism vs. Religion in Russia, 1917–1929* (Amherst, NY: Prometheus Books, 2005), 125.

10. Helen Rappaport, *Joseph Stalin: A Biographical Companion* (Santa Barbara, CA: ABC-CLIO, 1999), 95.

11. C. Peter Chen, "Joseph Stalin," *World War II Database*, accessed May 31, 2017, http:// ww2db.com/person_bio.php?person_id=64.

12. Dwight D. Eisenhower, "Campaign Speech, Fort Worth, Texas, October 15, 1952," Dwight D. Eisenhower Presidential Library, Abilene, Kansas. Ironically, Alliance Defending Freedom had to defend a Phoenix, Arizona, pastor who was sentenced to jail for ringing the bells of his church: *State of Arizona v. Painter* (2010).

13. Bill Keller, "Major Soviet Paper Says 20 Million Died as Victims of Stalin," *New York Times* (February 4, 1989): 1.

14. Dwight D. Eisenhower, "Statement by the President Concerning the Illness of Joseph Stalin, March 4, 1953," *The American Presidency Project*, accessed May 2, 2017, http://www .presidency.ucsb.edu/ws/index.php?pid=9712.

15. Rappaport, *Joseph Stalin*, 95.

16. Ralph A. Uttaro, "The Voices of America in International Radio Propaganda," *Law and Contemporary Problems* 45, no. 4 (Winter 1982): 104.

17. William Inboden III, *Religion and American Foreign Policy, 1945–1960: The Soul of Containment* (Cambridge, UK: Cambridge University Press, 2008), 303–9.

18. "Ike's Faith," *Time*, April 13, 1953, 91, http://content.time.com/time/magazine/article /0,9171,818247,00.html.

19. Andrew Preston, *Sword of the Spirit, Shield of Faith: Religion in American War and Diplomacy* (New York: Anchor Books, 2012), 442.

20. Thomas F. Farr, "Cold War Religion," *First Things*, June 2009, https://www.firstthings .com/article/2009/06/cold-war-religion.

21. Nancy Gibbs and Michael Duffy, *The Preacher and the Presidents: Billy Graham in the White House* (New York: Center Street, 2007), 44.

22. Inboden, *Religion and American Foreign Policy*, 278–80.

23. Dwight D. Eisenhower, "Remarks to the First National Conference on the Spiritual Foundations of American Democracy, November 9, 1954," *The American Presidency Project*, accessed May 2, 2017, http://www.presidency.ucsb.edu/ws/index.php?pid=10127.

24. "Letter from Dwight David Eisenhower to Edward L. R. Elson," April 17, 1954.

25. See "How the Words 'Under God' Came to Be Added to the Pledge of Allegiance to the Flag," The Knights of Columbus, accessed May 25, 2017, http://www.kofc.org/un/en /resources/communications/pledgeAllegiance.pdf.

26. Ibid.

27. Dwight D. Eisenhower, "Statement Upon Signing Public Law 83–396, June 14, 1954," *The American Presidency Project*, accessed May 2, 2017, http://www.presidency.ucsb.edu/ws /index.php?pid=9920.

28. William J. Federer, *The Ten Commandments and Their Influence on American Law: A Study in History* (Virginia Beach, VA: Amerisearch, 2002), 48; Tony Pettinato, "Flag Day:

'Under God' Added to Pledge of Allegiance," *Genealogy Bank*, June 14, 2016, https://blog
.genealogybank.com/flag-day-under-god-added-to-pledge-of-allegiance.html.

29. "How the Words 'Under God' Came to Be Added to the Pledge of Allegiance to
the Flag."

30. Schuyler Colfax, "Eulogy Upon the Life and Principles of Abraham Lincoln," in
Ambrose Yoemans More, *The Life of Schuyler Colfax* (Philadelphia: T.B. Peterson and Brothers, 1868), 273.

31. "A Legislative History of 'In God We Trust,'" *ACLJ*, accessed May 31, 2017, https://
aclj.org/in-god-we-trust/a-legislative-history-of-the-national-motto.

32. "History of 'In God We Trust,'" US Department of the Treasury, accessed April 7,
2017, https://www.treasury.gov/about/education/Pages/in-god-we-trust.aspx.

33. *Elk Grove Unified School District v. Newdow* 542 U.S. 1 (2004); "Lawsuit Demands US
Remove 'In God We Trust' from Money," *Fox News*, January 14, 2016, http://www.foxnews
.com/us/2016/01/14/lawsuit-demands-us-remove-in-god-trust-from-money.html.

34. Kimberly Amadeo, "The History of Recessions in the United States," *The Balance*,
October 18, 2017, https://www.thebalance.com/the-history-of-recessions-in-the-united-states
-3306011.

35. Mike DellaVecchia, "The Miss America Pageant Was First Televised in 1954," *Press of
Atlantic City*, April 26, 2013, http://www.pressofatlanticcity.com/missamerica/the-miss-america
-pageant-was-first-televised-in/article_3b37c7a2-ae77-11e2-8b9e-0019bb2963f4.html.

36. "TV Ratings—1950s" *Fifties Web*, accessed April 11, 2017, http://fiftiesweb.com/tv
/tv-ratings/#53-54.

37. Stewart Alsop, "Eisenhower Pushes Operation Candor," *Washington Post*, September
21, 1953.

38. "Project 'Candor,' Security Information Sheet, July 22, 1953," Dwight D. Eisenhower
Presidential Library, Museum and Boyhood Home, accessed April 11, 2017, https://eisen
hower.archives.gov/research/online_documents/atoms_for_peace/Binder17.pdf.

39. Ibid.

40. Dwight D. Eisenhower, "Address before the General Assembly of the United Nations on Peaceful Uses of Atomic Energy, New York City, December 8, 1953," *The American
Presidency Project*, accessed April 11, 2017, http://www.presidency.ucsb.edu/ws/index.php
?pid=9774.

41. Ibid.

42. "Atoms for Peace Draft (C. D. Jackson Papers, Box 30, "Atoms for Peace—Evolution
(5)"; NAID #120221574)," Dwight D. Eisenhower Presidential Library, Museum and Boyhood Home, accessed September 12, 2018, https://www.eisenhower.archives.gov/research
/online_documents/atoms_for_peace/Atoms_for_Peace_Draft.pdf.

43. "History," International Atomic Energy Agency, accessed May 30, 2017, https://www
.iaea.org/about/overview/history.

44. "History of the USS Nautilus," Submarine Force Museum, accessed April 11, 2017,
http://www.ussnautilus.org/nautilus/.

45. Ibid.

46. Dwight D. Eisenhower, "Address before the Canadian Club," Ottawa, Canada, January 10, 1946.

47. Dianne Kirby, ed., *Religion and the Cold War* (London: Palgrave MacMillan, 2003), 96.

48. Wolfgang Saxon, "Elton Trueblood, 94, Scholar Who Wrote Theological Works,"
New York Times, December 23, 1994, http://www.nytimes.com/1994/12/23/obituaries/elton
-trueblood-94-scholar-who-wrote-theological-works.html.

49. Elton Trueblood, "Personal Testimony of D. Elton Trueblood, Chapter 3," *While It Is Day: An Autobiography*, accessed May 30, 2017, http://www.ccel.us/whileitisday.ch3.html.

50. Ibid.

51. D. Elton Trueblood, "Basic Christianity," as quoted in G. Paul Butler, ed., *Best Sermons, 1955 Edition* (New York: McGraw Hill, 1955), 18–30, http://www.qhpress.org/quakerpages/qhoa/detbasic.htm.

52. Saxon, "Elton Trueblood."

53. Inboden, *Religion and American Foreign Policy*, 278–80.

54. Gibbs and Duffy, *Preacher and the Presidents*, 64.

55. "Letter from Dwight D. Eisenhower to Edward L. R. Elson," July 31, 1958. Provided by Rev. John Boyles, former pastor of National Presbyterian Church.

56. Gibbs and Duffy, *Preacher and the Presidents*, 64.

57. Preston, *Sword of the Spirit, Shield of Faith*, 448.

Chapter 12 Spiritual Weapons for Civil Rights

1. Nancy Gibbs and Michael Duffy, *The Preacher and the Presidents: Billy Graham in the White House* (New York: Center Street, 2007), 64.

2. Ibid., 66.

3. Michael Gardner, *Harry Truman and Civil Rights: Moral Courage and Political Risks* (Carbondale, IL: Southern Illinois University Press, 2002), 111.

4. Dwight D. Eisenhower, "Annual Message to the Congress on the State of the Union, February 2, 1953," *The American Presidency Project*, accessed September 12, 2018, http://www.presidency.ucsb.edu/ws/index.php?pid=9829.

5. Paul Hutchison, "The President's Religious Faith," *The Christian Century* (March 24, 1954).

6. See "President's Committee on Government Contracts," The King Center, accessed October 26, 2017, http://www.thekingcenter.org/archive/document/presidents-committee -government-contracts-0.

7. "*District of Columbia v. John R. Thompson Co., Inc.*, 346 U.S. 100 (1953)," *Justia*, accessed September 12, 2018, https://supreme.justia.com/cases/federal/us/346/100/; "*Brown v. Board of Education of Topeka, Kansas*, 347 U.S. 483 (1954)," *Justia*, accessed September 12, 2018, https://supreme.justia.com/cases/federal/us/347/483.

8. Gibbs and Duffy, *Preacher and the Presidents*, 67.

9. Michael G. Long, *Billy Graham and the Beloved Community: America's Evangelist and the Dream of Martin Luther King, Jr.* (London: Palgrave MacMillan, 2006), 86.

10. Gibbs and Duffy, *Preacher and the Presidents*, 66.

11. David Eisenhower with Julie Nixon Eisenhower, *Going Home to Glory: A Memoir of Life with Dwight D. Eisenhower* (New York: Simon & Schuster, 2010), 105.

12. Kasey S. Pipes, *Ike's Last Battle: The Road to Little Rock and the Challenge of Equality* (Torrance, CA: World Ahead Publishing), 164.

13. Gibbs and Duffy, *Preacher and the Presidents*, 66.

14. Ibid.

15. Ibid., 68.

16. Ibid.

17. Ibid., 69.

18. "Letter from Dwight D. Eisenhower to Rev. Billy Graham," March 22, 1956, DDE's Papers as President, Name Series, Box 16, Billy Graham; NAID #12175790, Dwight D. Eisenhower Presidential Library, Abilene, Kansas.

19. "Letter from Rev. Billy Graham to Dwight D. Eisenhower," March 26, 1956, DDE's Papers as President, Name Series, Box 16, Billy Graham; NAID #12175813, Dwight D. Eisenhower Presidential Library, Abilene, Kansas.

20. "Letter from Dwight D. Eisenhower to Rev. Billy Graham," March 30, 1956, DDE's Papers as President, Name Series, Box 16, Billy Graham; NAID #12175800, Dwight D. Eisenhower Presidential Library, Abilene, Kansas.

21. "Letter from Billy Graham to Dwight D. Eisenhower," March 27, 1956, *Learn NC*, accessed September 12, 2018, http://www.learnnc.org/lp/editions/nchist-postwar/6121.

22. Gibbs and Duffy, *Preacher and the Presidents*, 70.

23. "Telegram from Dwight D. Eisenhower to the Governor of Arkansas in Response to His Request for a Meeting, September 11, 1957," *The American Presidency Project*, accessed September 12, 2018, http://www.presidency.ucsb.edu/ws/index.php?pid=10898.

24. Anthony Lewis, "President Sends Troops to Little Rock, Federalizes Arkansas National Guard; Tells Nation He Acted to Avoid an Anarchy," *New York Times* (September 25, 1957), http://www.nytimes.com/learning/general/onthisday/big/0925.html.

25. Jean Edward Smith, *Eisenhower in War and Peace* (New York: Random House, 2012), 719–22.

26. Gibbs and Duffy, *Preacher and the Presidents*, 71.

27. Lewis, "President Sends Troops to Little Rock."

28. Dwight D. Eisenhower, "Radio and Television Address to the American People on the Situation in Little Rock, September 24, 1957," *The American Presidency Project*, accessed September 12, 2018, http://www.presidency.ucsb.edu/ws/index.php?pid=10909.

29. Gibbs and Duffy, *Preacher and the Presidents*, 71.

30. "Telegram from Rev. Martin Luther King Jr., to Dwight D. Eisenhower, September 25, 1957," *The Martin Luther King, Jr. Papers Project*, accessed October 26, 2017, http://okra.stanford.edu/transcription/document_images/Vol04Scans/278_25-Sept-1957_To%20Dwight%20D%20Eisenhower.pdf.

31. "Letter from Dwight D. Eisenhower to Rev. Martin Luther King, Jr., October 7, 1957," *The Martin Luther King, Jr. Papers Project*, accessed October 26, 2017, http://okra.stanford.edu/transcription/document_images/Vol04Scans/284_7-Oct-1957_From%20Dwight%20D%20Eisenhower.pdf.

32. "Letter from Martin Luther King on Behalf of the Southern Christian Leadership Conference to Dwight D. Eisenhower, November 5, 2017," *The Martin Luther King, Jr. Papers Project*, accessed October 26, 2017, http://okra.stanford.edu/transcription/document_images/Vol04Scans/308_5-Nov-1957_To%20Dwight%20D%20Eisenhower.pdf.

33. Pipes, *Ike's Last Battle*, 258.

34. Pat McNamara, "'Racism Is a God-Damned Thing': Father John Markoe S.J.," *Patheos*, February 22, 2011, http://www.patheos.com/Resources/Additional-Resources/Racism-Is-a-God-Damned-Thing-Pat-McNamara-02-22-2011.

35. "Letter from John D. Markoe to Dwight D. Eisenhower," October 12, 1954, Dwight D. Eisenhower Presidential Library, Abilene, Kansas.

36. "Letter from Dwight D. Eisenhower to Swede Hazlett, Captain USN," July 22, 1957, Swede Hazlett Papers, Box 2, 1957 July 22; NAID #12171154.

37. "Civil Rights Act of 1957," Dwight D. Eisenhower Presidential Library, Museum and Boyhood Home, accessed March 22, 2018, https://eisenhower.archives.gov/research/online_documents/civil_rights_act.html.

38. Andrew Cohen, *Two Days in June: John F. Kennedy and the 48 Hours That Made History* (New York: Random House, 2014), 119.

39. "Longines Chronoscope with Rev. Edward L. R. Nelson," YouTube video, 14:47, uploaded by PublicResourceOrg, April 4, 2011, https://www.youtube.com/watch?v=gsVzMtM7nes.

40. Alex Wheeler, "All the Queen's Presidents," *International Business Times*, April 22, 2016, http://www.ibtimes.co.uk/all-queens-us-presidents-eisenhower-obama-pictures-1556278.

41. David L. Holmes, *Faiths of the Postwar Presidents* (Athens, GA: University of Georgia Press, 2012), 39.

42. "Eisenhower Left His Mark on National," *The Augusta Chronicle*, February 16, 2012, http://www.augusta.com/masters/history/eisenhower-left-mark-on-augusta-national.

43. Clifford Roberts, *The Story of the Augusta National Golf Club* (New York: Doubleday, 1976), 166.

44. Ibid., 140.

45. John Boyette, "Eisenhower Loved Augusta National, and the City Loved Him Back," *The Augusta Chronicle*, March 24, 2012, http://www.augusta.com/masters/story/history/eisenhower-loved-augusta-national-and-city-loved-him-back.

46. John Boyette, "Memories of Eisenhower's Visits Live on at Augusta Church," *The Augusta Chronicle*, March 26, 2012, http://www.augusta.com/masters/story/history/memories-eisenhowers-visits-live-augusta-church.

47. Ibid.

48. Ibid.

49. Clint Hill with Lisa McCubbin, *Five Presidents: My Extraordinary Journey with Eisenhower, Kennedy, Johnson, Nixon, and Ford* (New York: Gallery Books, 2016), 38.

50. Ibid., 27.

51. Ibid.

52. Rachel Wellford, "A History of Papal Visits by US Presidents," *PBS*, March 27, 2014, https://www.pbs.org/newshour/nation/history-presidential-visits-pope.

53. Joseph McAuley, "When Pope John and Ike Laughed at the Vatican," *America Magazine*, September 16, 2015, https://www.americamagazine.org/content/all-things/pope-and-president-john-xxiii-and-dwight-d-eisenhower-era-di-belli-was-beaut.

54. Ibid.

55. Ibid.

56. Hill with McCubbin, *Five Presidents*, 26.

57. Ibid., 38.

58. Ibid., 39.

Chapter 13 A Continued Commitment

1. Sean Braswell, "President Eisenhower's $14 Billion Heart Attack," *Yahoo*, April 12, 2016, https://www.yahoo.com/news/president-eisenhower-14-billion-heart-000000730.html.

2. Dwight D. Eisenhower, *At Ease: Stories I Tell to Friends* (New York: Doubleday & Co., 1967), 358.

3. Ibid.

4. "Eisenhower Suite: The President's 1955 Heart Attack," UC School of Medicine, accessed May 25, 2017, http://www.ucdenver.edu/academics/colleges/medicalschool/administration/history/Pages/Eisenhower-Suite.aspx.

5. "Letter from Dwight D. Eisenhower to Edward L. R. Elson," November 14, 1955. Provided by Rev. John Boyles, former pastor of National Presbyterian Church.

6. Ibid.

7. "Letter from Dwight D. Eisenhower to Edward L. R. Elson," November 19, 1955. Provided by Rev. John Boyles, former pastor of National Presbyterian Church.

8. John Boyles, "Interview with Rev. Clyde R. Brown," February 2017, transcribed by Elise Gillson.

9. "Ike and Mamie Worship Where Lincoln Did," *Associated Press*, May 15, 1955. Provided by Rev. John Boyles, former pastor of National Presbyterian Church.

10. Ibid.

11. "Oral History Interview with Dr. Robert MacAskill, June 11, 1998," Dwight D. Eisenhower Presidential Library, Museum and Boyhood Home, accessed September 12, 2018, https://www.eisenhower.archives.gov/research/oral_histories/oral_history_transcripts/MacAskill_Robert.pdf

12. Ibid.

13. Carol Hegman, "Oral History Interview with Dr. Robert MacAskill," August 31, 1983, Gettysburg Presbyterian Church Archives. Provided by Rev. John Boyles, former pastor of National Presbyterian Church.

14. Ibid.

15. "Oral History Interview with Dr. Robert MacAskill, June 11, 1998."

16. David Eisenhower with Julie Nixon Eisenhower, *Going Home to Glory* (New York: Simon & Schuster, 2010), 21.

17. Ibid., 105.

18. Ibid., 106.

19. Ibid.

20. "Letter from Dwight D. Eisenhower to Rev. Robert MacAskill," June 27, 1958. Provided by Linda MacAskill, widow of Rev. Robert MacAskill.

21. "Letter from Dwight D. Eisenhower to Rev. Robert MacAskill," May 27, 1959. Provided by Linda MacAskill, widow of Rev. Robert MacAskill.

22. "Letter from Dwight D. Eisenhower to Dr. Robert MacAskill," September 2, 1960. Provided by Linda MacAskill, widow of Rev. Robert MacAskill.

23. Dwight D. Eisenhower, "Address Before the 15th General Assembly of the United Nations, New York City, September 22, 1960," *The American Presidency Project*, accessed May 25, 2017, http://www.presidency.ucsb.edu/ws/index.php?pid=11954.

24. "Letter from Dwight D. Eisenhower to Dr. Robert MacAskill," September 28, 1960. Provided by Linda MacAskill, widow of Rev. Robert MacAskill.

25. "Oral History Interview with Dr. Robert MacAskill, June 11, 1998."

26. Hegman, "Oral History Interview with Dr. Robert MacAskill."

27. Ibid.

28. Ibid.

29. Ibid.

30. Eisenhower with Eisenhower, *Going Home to Glory*, 106.

31. Hegman, "Oral History Interview with Dr. Robert MacAskill."

32. Ibid.

33. "From the White House to Gettysburg, Pitcairn-Eisenhower Nativity Scenes," *Glencairn Museum News* 12 (2014).

34. Alan Sears has a watercolor painting of an old German church in his home office that Eisenhower painted in 1960; Hegman, "Oral History Interview with Dr. Robert MacAskill."

35. "Letter from Ann C. Whitman to Dr. Robert MacAskill," December 10, 1960. Provided by Linda MacAskill, widow of Rev. Robert MacAskill.

36. Hegman, "Oral History Interview with Dr. Robert MacAskill."

37. Ibid.

38. Ibid.

39. Ibid.

40. Scott A. Merriman, *Religion and the Law in America: An Encyclopedia of Personal Belief and Public Policy*, vol. 1 (Santa Barbara, CA: ABC-CLIO, 2007), 458.

41. Dwight D. Eisenhower, "Remarks to the Presbytery of Carlisle, Pennsylvania, Fall 1963," recording, transcribed by Elise Gillson, Gettysburg Presbyterian Church Archives.

42. Eisenhower with Eisenhower, *Going Home to Glory*, 109.

43. Ibid.

44. "Remarks to a Delegation of Progressive Friends, June 20, 1862," *Collected Works of Abraham Lincoln*, vol. 5, accessed May 25, 2017, http://quod.lib.umich.edu/cgi/t/text/text-idx?c=lincoln;cc=lincoln;type=simple;rgn=div1;q1=June%2020%2C%201862;view=text;subview=detail;sort=occur;idno=lincoln5;node=lincoln5%3A628. The summary reads,

> The President responded very impressively, saying that he was deeply sensible of his need of Divine assistance. He had sometime thought that perhaps he might be an instrument in God's hands of accomplishing a great work and he certainly was not unwilling to be. Perhaps, however, God's way of accomplishing the end which the memorialists have in view may be different from theirs.

Chapter 14 "God Take Me"

1. "Letter from Dwight D. Eisenhower to Dr. Edward L. R. Elson," June 22, 1967. Provided by Rev. John Boyles, former pastor of National Presbyterian Church.

2. "Program—A Luncheon to Honor General of the Army Dwight David Eisenhower—The Thirty Fourth President of the United States—On the Occasion of His Seventy-Seventh Birthday," October 14, 1967. Provided by Rev. John Boyles, former pastor of National Presbyterian Church.

3. Ibid.

4. Clifford Roberts, *The Story of the Augusta National Golf Club* (New York: Doubleday, 1976), 200.

5. "Letter from Dwight D. Eisenhower to Dr. Robert MacAskill," May 4, 1965. Provided by Linda MacAskill, widow of Rev. Robert MacAskill.

6. "Letter from Dwight D. Eisenhower to Dr. Robert MacAskill," February 18, 1966. Provided by Linda MacAskill, widow of Rev. Robert MacAskill.

7. "Letter from Dwight D. Eisenhower to Dr. Robert MacAskill," May 21, 1968. Provided by Linda MacAskill, widow of Rev. Robert MacAskill.

8. "Letter from Mamie Eisenhower to Dr. Robert MacAskill," July 9, 1968. Provided by Linda MacAskill, widow of Rev. Robert MacAskill.

9. "Letter from Dwight D. Eisenhower to Dr. Robert MacAskill," December 4, 1968. Provided by Linda MacAskill, widow of Rev. Robert MacAskill.

10. "Letter from Mamie Eisenhower to Dr. Robert MacAskill," March 4, 1969. Provided by Linda MacAskill, widow of Rev. Robert MacAskill.

11. Rev. Dr. Billy Graham, "Remarks at Eisenhower Centennial Church Service, Abilene, Kansas," *The Congressional Record*, October 14, 1990.

12. Billy Graham, *Just As I Am: The Autobiography of Billy Graham* (New York: Harper Collins, 1997), 232–33.

13. Bret Baier, *Three Days in January: Dwight Eisenhower's Final Mission* (New York: William Morrow, 2017), 279.

14. Richard M. Nixon, "Eulogy Delivered at the Capitol During the State Funeral of Dwight Eisenhower, March 30, 1969," *The American Presidency Project*, accessed May 25, 2017, http://www.presidency.ucsb.edu/ws/index.php?pid=1987.

15. "Dwight D. Eisenhower—Final Post, October 14, 1890 to March 28, 1969," Dwight D. Eisenhower Presidential Library, Museum and Boyhood Home, accessed April 21, 2017, https://www.eisenhower.archives.gov/all_about_ike/final_post.html.

16. Nixon, "Eulogy Delivered at the Capitol During the State Funeral of Dwight Eisenhower."

17. "Former President Dwight D. Eisenhower State Funeral, March 28–April 2, 1969," *The Last Salute: Civil and Military Funerals 1921–1969*, accessed May 30, 2017, http://www.history.army.mil/books/Last_Salute/ch29.htm.

18. "Funeral Service for the General of the Army and 34th President of the United States of America Dwight David Eisenhower, Abilene, Kansas, Wednesday, April 2, 1969," Dwight D. Eisenhower Presidential Library, Museum and Boyhood Home, accessed October 1, 2018, https://www.dwightdeisenhower.com/DocumentCenter/View/78/Funeral-Service-Program-Abilene-Kansas---April-2-1969-PDF.

19. "Memorial Service for the Honorable Dwight David Eisenhower, Abilene, Kansas, April 2, 1969," Dwight D. Eisenhower Presidential Library, Museum and Boyhood Home, accessed October 1, 2018, https://www.eisenhower.archives.gov/all_about_ike/final_post/abilene_memorial_service.html.

20. "The State Funeral of General Dwight David Eisenhower (1890–1969)."

21. Ibid.

22. Ibid.

23. "Dwight D. Eisenhower—Final Post, October 14, 1890 to March 28, 1969."

Epilogue

1. Jean Edward Smith, *Eisenhower in War and Peace* (New York: Random House, 2012), 567.

2. "Was Eisenhower More of a Socialist than Bernie Sanders?" *Christian Science Monitor*, November 15, 2015, http://www.csmonitor.com/USA/Politics/2015/1115/Was-Eisenhower-more-of-a-socialist-than-Bernie-Sanders.

3. Merrill Fabry, "What the First H-Bomb Test Looked Like," *Time*, November 2, 2015, http://time.com/4096424/ivy-mike-history; "Soviets Test 'Layer Cake' Bomb," *History*, accessed May 31, 2017, http://www.history.com/this-day-in-history/soviets-test-layer-cake-bomb.

4. Rufus Rockwell Wilson, ed., *Intimate Memories of Lincoln* (Caldwell, ID: Caxton Printers, 1942), 574.

5. John Boyles, "Interview with Rev. Clyde R. Brown," February 2017, transcribed by Elise Gillson.

6. Ibid.

7. "Place of Meditation," Eisenhower Foundation, accessed April 24, 2017, http://www.dwightdeisenhower.com/265/Place-of-Meditation.

Alan Sears, KSG, is an ardent student of history and the founder of Alliance Defending Freedom (ADF), which he led as president, CEO, and general counsel for twenty-three years. Under his leadership, ADF and its allied attorneys—which now number more than three thousand in forty-four nations—played important roles in more than fifty victories at the US Supreme Court and seventeen victories at the European Court of Human Rights. ADF International has established offices at the United Nations in New York and Geneva, the Organization of American States in Washington, DC, Brussels, London, Mexico City, Strasbourg, and Vienna. Sears served in numerous positions within the Reagan and Bush administrations, including the Department of Justice under Attorneys General William French Smith and Edwin Meese III, and with the Department of Interior under Secretary Donald Hodel. He has been profiled by the *New York Times*, the *Washington Post*, the *National Catholic Register*, and more.

Craig Osten serves as senior director of research and grant writing for Alliance Defending Freedom. Like Alan, he has been an ardent student of history from an early age. He has more than thirty years of experience providing writing and research expertise on more than one dozen books for bestselling authors such as Alan Sears, Tim Goeglein, Dr. James Dobson, and Dr. Wayne Grudem, among others. Before coming to ADF, he worked as a political reporter in Sacramento, California, created and managed the public policy constituent response division at Focus on the Family, and served as research assistant to Dr. James Dobson, assisting him with his monthly newsletter, daily radio broadcast, books, and various other communications.

"THE FUTURE SHALL BELONG TO THE FREE."

— *Dwight "Ike" Eisenhower*

Eisenhower knew this; so do we. That's why ADF has been fighting to defend the right of people to freely live out their faith today and tomorrow—worldwide.

Learn more at www.ADFlegal.org

ALLIANCE DEFENDING
FREEDOM
FOR FAITH. FOR JUSTICE.

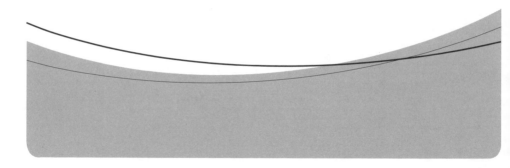